Behaviorism, Consciousness, and the Literary Mind

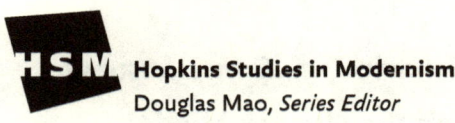

Hopkins Studies in Modernism

Douglas Mao, *Series Editor*

Behaviorism, Consciousness, and the Literary Mind

Joshua Gang

Johns Hopkins University Press
Baltimore

This book was brought to publication through the generous
assistance of the David L. Kalstone Memorial Fund, administered by
the Department of English at Rutgers University.

© 2021 Johns Hopkins University Press
All rights reserved. Published 2021
Printed in the United States of America on acid-free paper
9 8 7 6 5 4 3 2 1

Johns Hopkins University Press
2715 North Charles Street
Baltimore, Maryland 21218-4363
www.press.jhu.edu

Library of Congress Cataloging-in-Publication Data

Names: Gang, Joshua, 1981- author.
Title: Behaviorism, consciousness, and the literary mind / Joshua
   Gang.
Description: Baltimore : Johns Hopkins University Press, 2021. |
   Series: Hopkins studies in Modernism | Includes bibliographical
   references and index.
Identifiers: LCCN 2021003099 | ISBN 9781421440842 (hardcover) |
   ISBN 9781421440859 (paperback) | ISBN 9781421440866 (ebook)
Subjects: LCSH: Behaviorism (Psychology) | Literature, Modern—
   20th century—History and criticism. | Psychology and literature. |
   Modernism (Literature) | LCGFT: Literary criticism.
Classification: LCC PN56.B39 G36 2021 | DDC 809/.933530904—
   dc23
LC record available at https://lccn.loc.gov/2021003099

A catalog record for this book is available from the British Library.

Excerpts from Gilbert Ryle's *The Concept of Mind* are reproduced
with the permission of the Principal, Fellows and Scholars of
Hertford College, University of Oxford.

Excerpts from Samuel Beckett's "Psychology" notebook typescript
are reproduced with the permission of the Estate of Samuel Beckett,
Rosica Colin Ltd., and the Librarians of Trinity College, Dublin.

*Special discounts are available for bulk purchases of this book. For more
information, please contact Special Sales at specialsales@jh.edu.*

In honor of JHEJ

And for EAJJKAE

Contents

Acknowledgments ix

Introduction. Literary Experience and the Concept of Mind 1

1 **Behaviorism and the Beginnings of Close Reading** 32

2 **Inner Sights** 66

3 **Mental Acts** 102

4 **The Form of Thought** 139

Coda. Observations and/or Reflections 168

Notes 171
Works Cited 187
Index 203

Acknowledgments

Sometime in 2007 I started puzzling over the relation between mental states and linguistic representations of mental states. Four English departments, three time zones, and two countries later, those thoughts have become this book. My debts are therefore significant and widespread.

First, I want to thank my dissertation committee, as well as the Rutgers English department as a whole. I owe my dissertation director, Rebecca Walkowitz, far more than I can express either elegantly or concisely. Without her wisdom and kindness, I very much doubt my puzzling about mind and language would have been worth reading. I am also indebted to the other internal committee members, Jonathan Kramnick and Elin Diamond. Conversations about literature and philosophy with Jonathan and about aesthetics and performance with Elin are among this book's most important foundations. Additionally, I would like to thank Doug Mao, who, as my external reader in 2012, gave me nothing less than transformative feedback—and who, as a series editor, saw potential in my book manuscript in 2019. Thank you, Doug, for your guidance and for the critical conversations that your own work has made possible. Beyond my dissertation committee, my work benefited enormously from many faculty at Rutgers English and the Center for Cultural Analysis: Emily Bartels, Lynn Festa, Billy Galperin, Colin Jager, David Kurnick, Meredith McGill, Michael McKeon, Jonah Siegel, Henry Turner, and Carolyn Williams. My gratitude to the David L. Kalstone Memorial Fund at Rutgers English for subvention support. I also need to thank those friends I made at Rutgers English: Sarah Alexander, Jordan Aubry, Sean Barry, Manuel Betancourt, Mike Gavin, Octavio Gonzalez, Devin Griffiths, Alan Herring, Craig Iturbe, Devon McConaghy, Sarah Morgan, Elizabeth Oldfather, Brian Pietras, Emma Raub, Colleen Rosenfeld, John Savarese, Samantha Stern-Leaphart, Mark Vareschi, Meryl Winick, and Mary-Rush

Yelverton—with extra gratitude to Sarah Balkin, Daniel Crossen, Gregory Ellermann, Naomi Levine, Katherine Williams, and Emily Zubernis. And even though I left New Jersey years ago, Cheryl Robinson will always be my boss. Like most graduates of Rutgers English, I owe Cheryl and Courtney Borack so very much.

In the fall of 2012 I began a postdoctoral fellowship at Washington University-Saint Louis. It was there that I had the good fortune to become the employee, student, and friend of Vincent Sherry, whose faith in this book has meant the world. My thanks as well to Brendan Beirne, Dillon Brown, Jennifer Kronovet, Edward McPherson, Steven Meyer, Jessica Rosenfeld, and Rafia Zafar. Additionally, the Mellon Neuroscience and Humanities Seminar was an indispensable experience for me right when I needed it most. In 2013 I began a job at the University of Toronto, where new colleagues and friends helped me realize my project's aims. In particular, I would like to thank Liza Blake, Denise Cruz, Thom Dancer, Greig Henderson, Alexander Hernandez, Mark Knight, Deidre Lynch, Jeremy Lopez, Terry Robinson, Matthew Sergi, Simon Stern, David Taylor, and Morgan Vanek, as well as department chairs Alan Bewell and Paul Stevens. An extra note of thanks to Kara Gaston and Danny Wright. Conversations with Danny opened this project up in ways I never anticipated and made me a better critic. And every part of this book has benefited from Kara's brilliance and humor.

In fall 2015 I moved to Berkeley, where, in many ways, *Behaviorism, Consciousness, and the Literary Mind* became the book it is now. I am indebted to all my colleagues in Berkeley's English department for their investment in my research. Dan Blanton, Eric Falci, Catherine Flynn, Mark Goble, Donna Jones, and Steven Justice all read the manuscript in its entirety and offered incredibly helpful feedback. During the final year of manuscript revisions, most of which happened during the COVID-19 lockdown, Dan, Eric, and Catherine continued to read new revisions and helped me toward the finish line. I never would have reached it without them. A final word of gratitude must go to Eric, who has been an extraordinary mentor. My sincerest thanks to my department chairs Steven Justice, Genaro Padilla, and Katherine O'Brien O'Keeffe and department administrators Linda Fitzgerald and Joemari Cedro for their support. Charlie Altieri, Amanda Jo Goldstein, Dorothy Hale, Victoria Kahn, Grace Lavery, Colleen Lye, David Marno, Kent Puckett, Poulomi Saha, and Dora Zhang read portions of my manuscript and helped me think through some of its most difficult problems. Additionally, I would

Acknowledgments

like to thank Elizabeth Abel, Oliver Arnold, Mitchell Breitwieser, Cecil Giscombe, Marcial Gonzalez, Kevis Goodman, Kristin Hanson, Lyn Hejinian, Jeffrey Knapp, David Landreth, Steven Lee, Fiona McFarlane, Sue Schweik, Namwali Serpell, Katherine Snyder, and Elisa Tamarkin for their advice and encouragement. I am indebted to all my students at Berkeley—especially those in my graduate seminars in the fall of 2016, spring of 2019, and fall of 2020. My thanks to Dylan Furcall and Emily Sutton in particular, as well as my research assistant Ari Oppenheimer. I am grateful for the fellowships and research support I received from the Townsend Humanities Center (under the direction of Timothy Hampton), the Division of Arts and Humanities, and the Office of the Vice Provost for Faculty. I would also like to offer special thanks to several colleagues, both inside and outside the English department, whose friendship and intellectual generosity have meant so much: Danika Cooper, Shamik Dasgupta, Chiyuma Elliott, Julia Fawcett, Andrew Leong, Duncan MacRae, Kristin Primus, and Emily Zazulia.

This book has also been made stronger by colleagues at other institutions, as well as friends outside literary study. In the spring of 2018 I was invited by Nancy Armstrong to present some of my ideas about literary minds at Duke University's *Novel* Symposium. My deepest gratitude to Nancy, the symposium's other speakers and respondents (Rey Chow, Leigh Claire La Berge, John Marx, Rita Monticelli, Lloyd Pratt, and Kenneth Warren), and the graduate students who put the symposium together. I am similarly indebted to Deidre Lynch and Evelyne Ender, whose suggestions had lasting effects on my project as a whole. Extra thanks to Ted Martin, who has been making me a better thinker and writer since 1999. Additionally, I would like to thank Sam Alexander, Michael Allan, Magalí Armillas-Tiseyra, Michaela Bronstein, Angus Brown, Sanders Creasy, Jed Esty, Laura Fisher, Jennifer Fleissner, Andrew Gaedtke, Chris Grobe, David James, Michael LeMahieu, Kate Marshall, Paul Saint-Amour, Blakey Vermeule, Timothy Wientzen, and Karen Zumhagen-Yekplé for conversation and encouragement over the years. A special note of gratitude to Wendy Chang, Joey Coleman, Erika Dahlin-Lee, Joshua Honeyman, Jessie Lee, Ari Stern, Juliette Wallack, and Fran White for their friendship and care.

It has been a great pleasure working with Johns Hopkins University Press. Somehow, despite the pandemic and lockdown, my editor Catherine Goldstead still managed to make this book happen. My sincere thanks to Catherine, to series editor Doug Mao, and to the anonymous reader who offered such helpful feedback on my manuscript. I would also like to thank the editors and publishers of *ELH*, *NOVEL: A Forum on Fiction*, and *PMLA*, where very early versions of some of this book's ideas first appeared. My thanks as well to the Estate of Samuel Beckett and the librarians at Trinity College, Dublin, where I was able to examine the unpublished writings of Samuel Beckett and Harold Pinter.

Finally, I want to express my gratitude to my family. I think everyone is ready to hear me stop talking about behaviorism and logical type-errors—I'll do my best. My thanks to my sister Julia Gang for doing the illustrations for chapter 3 and bringing Beckett's *Eleutheria* to life. This book is dedicated to JHEJ and AEJJKAE: Jeanette, Hy, Esther, and Jesse and Arthur, Ellen, Joanna, Julia, Kent, Asher, and Ezra. Without them I don't know who, what, or where I would be.

Behaviorism, Consciousness, and the Literary Mind

Introduction
Literary Experience and the Concept of Mind

> How does the philosophical problem about mental processes and states and about behaviourism arise?——The first step is the one that altogether escapes notice. We talk of processes and states and leave their nature undecided.
>
> —Ludwig Wittgenstein, *Philosophical Investigations* (1953, §308)

> Psychology as the behaviorist views it is a purely objective experimental branch of psychology. Its theoretical goal is the prediction and control of behavior. Introspection forms no essential part of its methods, nor is the scientific value of its data dependent on the readiness with which they lend themselves to interpretation in terms of consciousness. The behaviorist, in his efforts to get a unitary scheme of animal response, recognizes no dividing line between man and brute.
>
> —John Broadus Watson, "Psychology as the Behaviorist Views It" (1913, 158)

This book shows the ways that behaviorism—through its arguments against dualism, introspection, innate knowledge, and even the existence of consciousness—shaped how twentieth-century writers and readers imputed mental properties to texts. It shows the ways that behaviorism encouraged these writers to manipulate the perceived relations between linguistic objects and mental phenomena. For figures such as I. A. Richards, the New Critics, Samuel Beckett, Harold Pinter, and J. M. Coetzee, behaviorism raised a difficult and intriguing question: if inanimate objects such as novels and poems have no mental properties—that is, no qualities that would give them phenomenal experience or induce them to follow psychological rules—then why do we perceive them as if they do? For that reason, this book isn't really a history or genealogy. To be clear: I stand by the historical claims and narratives offered in the following chapters—drawing connections between the histories of psychology, rationalism, empiricism, and the past hundred years or so of literature and literary study in English. But these historical claims and narratives are mostly means to an end. At its core, this is a book about the logical relations between minds and texts, and how literary criticism might talk about those relations more meaningfully and effectively.

To do that, this book develops and advocates a behavioristic sensibility for analyzing literature and its concepts. As an approach to human psychology, or as a doctrine within analytic philosophy of mind, behaviorism is problematic for a number of reasons. Over the course of the twentieth century, behaviorist philosophers and psychologists—including John Broadus Watson, B. F. Skinner, Carl Hempel, Ludwig Wittgenstein, Gilbert Ryle, and W. V. O. Quine—made various arguments against consciousness's usefulness as a concept and, at times, the existence of consciousness itself. What we perceive as mental states and interiority, some claimed, were really just misrecognized effects created by nonmental phenomena, such as behavior, physiology, language use, bad logic, and so on. As Watson wrote in *Behaviorism* (1924), "thinking is nothing but talking to ourselves" (191)—that is, a set of "muscular habits" onto which we have projected the myth of interiority. But at the risk of sounding naive, or believing too much in mentalistic folk psychology, my own experiences tell me this is not the case. While I grant the power of stimulated reflexes and conditioned behaviors, I know I have a mind. I am able to perform intentional actions. I am reasonably certain that my thoughts aren't just silent speech (if only by virtue of my possessing some thoughts that aren't fully verbalized or grammatical). And while I know my own mind better than I know the minds of other people, if only because I know my mind by different means, I am confident that they have minds and inner lives like my own. Lastly, while I know that all this mental talk must come down to neurons and synapses in the end, such reductive explanations don't seem to offer meaningful accounts of either phenomenal experience or observed behavior (whether my own or those of other people). For these reasons and others, behaviorism really doesn't work very well as a psychological or philosophical program.[1]

My decision to bring behaviorism to literary study, therefore, might seem baffling. Several questions present themselves. If texts don't have the same mental properties as people, then why use an admittedly obsolete psychological model to talk about them? Also, isn't it somewhat contradictory to reject behaviorism as a psychological doctrine but assert its critical value for thinking about literature? And how can you justify talking about different kinds of literary objects and concepts—whether novels, poems, speakers, styles, intentions, and so on—as if they all present us with the same kind of logical problem?

Let me begin answering these questions by drawing a set of distinctions between two concepts that will reappear throughout this book: *actual minds* and *literary minds*.[2] Actual minds—as represented by my recent, and somewhat hammy, appeal to folk psychology—generally have the capacity for phenomenal experience. Actual minds can frequently be represented through language, but they aren't linguistic objects. Indeed, while actual minds often seem amenable to linguistic representation, language and thinking follow different kinds of rules. Conventional wisdom would have it that *literary minds* are linguistic approximations of such actual minds. But is it even fair to call them approximations? This is a point Ann Banfield raises in *Unspeakable Sentences: Narration and Representation in the Language of Fiction* (1982). As she explains, "Represented consciousness is not a 'realistic reproduction' of the mind at work.... Rather its contents are hypothetically reconstructed and represented in a language sensitive to its various modes" (209). Insofar as literary texts are linguistic objects that follow linguistic rules, they can only offer us linguistic representations of what are (at least in part) nonlinguistic phenomena. This means they can only provide linguistic abstractions of mental states and properties, which necessarily have a conventional rather than imitative relation to actual mental states and properties.[3] Sometimes these abstractions comprise the "minds" of implied authors, as distinct from the actual minds of actual writers, or the "minds" of novelistic characters and poetic speakers. But they can also be more fragmentary or partial. For while actual minds must be embodied and attributed, this isn't true of literary minds. All a literary mind needs is a small amount of language that either purports to represent a mental state or implies the existence of mental activity; it isn't necessary for this language to be embodied by, or attributed to, a thinking subject. When we refer to a character's mind, or a poem's affect, or what a novel wants, we are referring metonymically to these kinds of linguistic representations.

The trouble is that these linguistic representations, these literary minds, often feel *real* or *actual*.[4] This is the defining feature, and problem, of literary minds. Somehow, we perceive characters, narrators, poetic speakers, and even bits and pieces of written style as if they too possess mental properties or follow mental rules. We do this even though we know it can't possibly be the case. This is even true of theatrical performance to an extent, as actors, who do in fact possess mental states and properties, use linguistic utterances and gestures to make it seem like their characters are following psychological rules rather than a script. (My focus in this introduction is primarily the imputation of mental properties and mental rule-following to aspects of written language. In chap. 3, however, it will indeed be the logical problems of mind entailed, and circumvented, by dramatic performance.) In all of these cases the linguistic abstraction of a mental phenomenon somehow becomes tantamount to perceiving the phenomenon itself. Cribbing David Chalmers's assertion that the emergence of subjective experience from physical matter is the "hard problem of consciousness," we might even say that the apparent emergence of mental properties from language is the "hard problem of literature."[5]

And that is why, in examining the logical relations between minds and texts, I have turned to behaviorism. The difficulty of using behaviorism to talk about humans is that we actually have minds. Linguistic objects, on the other hand, do not. Nonetheless, they create the appearance of minds and mental rule-following. Necessarily, these literary minds must be misrecognized effects of the text's nonmental phenomena (although this misrecognition can be both intellectually meaningful and enjoyable). Therefore, what limits behaviorism as a psychological or philosophical program is precisely what makes it apt for literary study. *If behaviorism is a protocol for analyzing the nonmental origins or causes of seemingly mental phenomena, then literary texts—which, along with their contents, are imputed with mental properties they couldn't possibly possess—are its ideal objects of analysis.* It's not a contradiction to reject behaviorism as a psychological program while asserting its critical value. Instead, it's a recognition that some of behaviorism's ideas are worth holding onto if, and only if, those ideas are brought to bear on appropriate objects of analysis. And as critical interest in the sciences of mind grows, as certain cognitive and scientific paradigms become entrenched in literary study, such analysis is essential. Today our discipline finds itself in a position not unlike the one described by Wittgenstein above. We talk of the mental processes and states we perceive when reading—but we leave the nature of these literary minds undecided and act as if they're just like our own. We blur even further the distinctions between aesthetic experience and the objects of such experience. My hope is to throw some light onto this phenomenon and reveal the crucial, and frequently overlooked, conceptual relations that make literary minds so peculiar and so extraordinary.

These are not the sorts of intellectual ambitions we usually associate with behaviorism. Instead, behaviorism is most famous for its theories of conditioning and psychological control. And while psychology moved beyond behaviorism a long time ago, the experiments of John Broadus Watson and B. F. Skinner still loom over cultural memory. Even now, Skinner's "superstitious" pigeons and Watson's "Little Albert," which I will describe later in this introduction, can feel like imminent threats to free will and interiority. The twentieth century's literary and critical records reflect this, particularly with respect to fiction.[6] Despite B. F. Skinner's dreams of a behaviorist utopia—culminating, perhaps, in his novel *Walden Two* (1948)—behaviorism has long been a key component of dystopian fiction. In *The Snooty Baronet* (1932), Wyndham Lewis focused on the relationships between behavioristic psychology, automation, and totalitarian politics. Aldous Huxley's *Brave New World* (1931) offered an even darker view. There, in the World State of the future, nearly every aspect of life is determined by the conditioning citizens undergo as infants. According to the director of the Central London Hatchery and Conditioning Centre, the coupling of linguistic and physical stimuli allowed by "hypnopaedia" constitutes "the greatest moralizing and socializing force of all time" (28). In *A Clockwork Orange* (1962), Anthony Burgess provided a parallel vision. The state-administered Ludovico Technique—a twisted version of B. F. Skinner's operant conditioning—steered Alex Delarge away from crime. But it did so at great cost: it detached Alex's intentions from his behaviors and thereby diminished his capacity as a moral agent. Dr. Brodsky, his treating physician, didn't think that this diminution was important. "We are not concerned with motive, with the higher ethics. We are only concerned with cutting down crime" (141). Alex became the eponymous clockwork orange: made of organic flesh, perhaps, but determined mechanistically just the same.

Behaviorism, however, isn't always cast as the tool of oppressive social order and control. Some writers have represented it as a source of social disorder, and even resistance. Throughout Richard Wright's *Native Son* (1940), Bigger Thomas is bombarded by the negative stimuli of the status quo—by poverty, by racism, by brutality. But whereas Alex Delarge was conditioned into obedience, Bigger is conditioned into violence and upheaval. As Wright explained in "How Bigger Was Born" (1940), Bigger was one among "many variations to this behavioristic pattern" (437). "Conditioned as his organism is," Wright wrote, Bigger Thomas "will not become an ardent, or even lukewarm supporter of the *status quo*" (446). More recently, and in a lighter vein, Paul Beatty's novel *The Sellout* (2016) entertained the possibility that behaviorism could help individuals contend with that same racist status quo. Under the guise of advancing "Liberation Psychology," the narrator's father recreates the "Little Albert" experiment, which John Watson and Rosalie Rayner described in their article "Conditioned Emotional Reactions" (1920). As Watson and Rayner conditioned the infant "Little Albert" to fear anything white and fluffy, the narrator's father conditions his son to fear anything, well, *white*—namely, the police, Middle America, economic liberalism, and the Republican Party. "When I was seven months old," we read, "Pops placed objects like toy police cars, cold cans of Pabst Blue Ribbon, Richard Nixon campaign buttons, and a copy of *The Economist* in my bassinet, but instead of conditioning me with a deafening clang, I learned to be afraid of the presented stimuli because they were accompanied by him taking out the family .38 Special and firing several window rattling rounds into the ceiling" (29). Typically, we think of political resistance as something voluntary and intentional. But given the right kind of psychological conditioning, Beatty implies, that needn't be the case.

These novels, and others like them, represent one aspect of behaviorism. But as might be inferred from my discussion of actual minds and literary minds, this book focuses on a different, often more abstract, set of concerns. That's not to say that I'm uninterested in conditioning and stimulus-response physiology; they appear in nearly every chapter. Nor is it to say that this book is aloof to the human costs and political concerns associated with behaviorism or the imputation of mental states (this is particularly important in the chapter on J. M. Coetzee's fiction, Chomskyan linguistics, and the interiority of colonial subjects). But on the whole, I am less concerned with behavioristic techniques than with the concepts behind them and how such concepts might apply to literary minds rather than actual ones. Therefore, in the next section of this introduction, I offer a very brief history of psychological and philosophical behaviorism, connecting Watson's deterministic program to the philosophical behaviorisms of Hempel and Wittgenstein. Different concepts and theories from this history will be revisited throughout this book in greater detail. My goal here is to give an overview of behaviorism's development between roughly 1900 and 1950. This overview will culminate in what is the intellectual heart of this book: Gilbert Ryle's critique of mind-body dualism and the idea of the *category-mistake*.

"A purely objective branch of experimental psychology"

When Watson published "Psychology as the Behaviorist Views It" in 1913, experimental psychology was dominated by the theories of Wilhelm Wundt. Many consider Wundt the originating figure in experimental psychology.[7] Building on Gustav Fechner's *psychophysik*, which measured the psychological effects of physical stimuli, Wundt conceived of a methodology whereby mental states could be analyzed in an experimental setting. The primary mode of experimentation was introspection. Test subjects would be exposed to stimuli and then asked to analyze their own responses—breaking higher-order mental states into successively simpler thoughts and sensations, or "images." Wundt founded the first psychological laboratory at the University of Leipzig in 1879. By 1913, there were more than eighty across Germany, Great Britain, and the United States. Most were modeled on Wundt's approach—and many were founded or managed by Wundt's former students.[8] Not every psychologist followed Wundt's example. The functionalists—including William James, John Dewey, and James Angell—were influential exceptions. And in 1911 Edward Lee Thorndike published *Animal Intelligence*, which suggested protocols for behavioral reinforcement and argued that both human and animal behaviors could be explained without recourse to unseen "magical agencies" (241). Nonetheless, by 1913, experimental psychology was a fundamentally introspective discipline.

In "Psychology as the Behaviorist Views It," Watson rejected Wundt's approach categorically. Like Thorndike, Watson's training was in animal behavior and learning. He completed his dissertation at the University of Chicago under the functionalist Angell and the physiologist Jacques Loeb, who studied animal and plant tropisms. Insofar as it relied on introspection and employed concepts such as "consciousness," Watson argued, psychology could not be considered a natural science. In contrast, behaviorism would "throw off the yoke of consciousness" (160) and redefine psychology as an objective and more strictly empirical discipline. Its primary experimental method would involve the observation of behavioral responses to stimuli, rather than relying on subjective accounts of experience. Watson's explanation of acceptable methods raises an important point about behaviorism's development. While classical conditioning has become synonymous with behaviorism, it's missing from "Psychology as the Behaviorist Views It." It wasn't part of Watson's original formulation. In *The Work of the Digestive Glands* (1897), Pavlov showed that he had been able to induce new reflexes in dogs through associative learning. Dogs, he claimed, have an unconditioned reflex (i.e., inborn reflex) that causes them to salivate when presented with food. By pairing the presentation of food with an additional stimulus (such as the sound of a buzzer), Pavlov trained his test subjects to associate one with the other. As a result, the dogs would salivate when they heard the buzzer, with or without the presentation of food.[9] It was only in the years immediately following "Psychology as the Behaviorist Views It," however, that Watson realized the applicability of Pavlov's research (and that of Vladimir Bekhterev) to behaviorism.[10] As Watson explained in a letter to the psychologist Ernest Hilgard, "I had worked the thing out in terms of *Habit* formation. It was only later, when I began to dig into the vague word *Habit*, that I saw the enormous contribution Pavlov had made, and how easily the conditioned response could be looked upon as the unit of what we had been calling *Habit*."[11]

The aforementioned "Little Albert" experiment constituted Watsonian behaviorism at its most Pavlovian (and dystopian). In 1919, Watson and his graduate assistant Rosalie Rayner hypothesized that classical conditioning could be used to induce emotional responses. Their test subject was a nine-month-old infant, "Albert B." As they explained in "Conditioned Emotional Reactions," Albert was chosen because of his availability (his mother worked in the hospital) and his "stability": "He was on the whole stolid and unemotional. . . . We felt that we could do him relatively little harm by carrying out such experiments" (1–2). The degree of short- and long-term harm done to Albert remains a point of debate. After establishing that a loud noise induced fear in Albert, Watson and Rayner repeatedly paired that noise with different white stimuli. Now Albert started crying whenever he perceived something white—whether a rat, a rabbit, a fur coat, or even Santa Claus. For Watson and Rayner the significance of this was twofold. First, it seemed to confirm their hypothesis that emotional reactions could be induced through classical conditioning. Second, and perhaps more importantly, it called into question the very nature of emotional response itself. "It is probable," Watson and Rayner concluded, "that many of the phobias in psychopathology are true conditioned emotional reactions either of the direct or transferred type" (14). Many of the "emotional disturbances" encountered in adults, they claimed, could be attributed to classical conditioning rather than purely emotional or neurotic causes. The mentalistic explanations favored by psychologists and psychoanalysts were neither necessary nor correct.

In the aforementioned *Behaviorism*, Watson extended this reasoning considerably. In so doing he began to translate behaviorism from a psychological program into a philosophical doctrine. Whereas his earlier writings had offered qualified critiques of mentalistic reasoning, Watson now asserted that consciousness didn't exist at all. This argument was substantially different from the one that William James offered in "Does Consciousness Exist?" (1904). "Consciousness," James wrote, "connotes a kind of external relation, and does not denote a special stuff or way of being. *The peculiarity of our experiences, that they not only are, but are known, which their 'conscious' quality is invoked to explain, is better explained by their relations—these relations themselves being experiences—to one another*" (486; italics in the original). Watson, however, dispensed with mental talk entirely. Insofar as Wundt replaced the term "soul" with the term "consciousness" (5), he claimed, experimental psychology was predicated on the fictions of religious dogma. As I mentioned earlier, *Behaviorism* concluded that any so-called "mental" phenomena were in fact misinterpreted behaviors or bodily processes. "By 'memory' then," Watson wrote, "we mean nothing except the fact that when we meet a stimulus again after a long absence, we do the old habitual thing (say the old words and show the old visceral—emotional—behavior)" (190). If thinking "is nothing but talking to ourselves," then it stands to reason that memory would constitute merely the persistence of conditioned verbal behaviors.

Watsonian behaviorism was but one phase in psychological behaviorism's development. In the wake of Watson's reliance on physiology and arguments against metaphysics, other psychological behaviorisms began to emerge. Skeptical of what he described as Watson's "mere Muscle Twitchism,"[12] Edward Chace Tolman advocated an approach he termed *purposive behaviorism*. Most behaviors, he claimed, have a specific purpose or goal. Therefore, no behaviorist could justify excluding (or denying the existence of) mental content. As he explained in *Purposive Behavior in Animals and Men* (1932), every behavior possesses "the character of getting-to or getting-from a specific goal-object or goal-situation" (10). Without determining that "goal-object," it's impossible to predict or control the behavior in question. In contrast, Clark Hull attempted to deduce a systematic theory of behavior exclusively from S-R physiology, classical conditioning, and habit reinforcement. Moreover, in books such as *Mathematico-Deductive Theory of Rote Learning* (1940) and *Principles of Behavior: An Introduction to Behavior Theory* (1943), Hull claimed that psychological laws could be expressed meaningfully in quantitative terms.

The most influential of the new behaviorists, of course, was Burrhus Frederic (B. F.) Skinner, who dispensed with many of behaviorism's arguments against the existence of consciousness. Instead, Skinner—who described his project as "radical behaviorism"—was most invested in behaviorism as a philosophy that, when applied, could make tangible improvements in people's lives. As he explained in *About Behaviorism* (1974), "A way of life which furthers the study of human behavior in its relation to [its] environment should be in the best possible position to solve its major problems. This is not jingoism, because the great problems are not global. In the behavioristic view, man can now control his own destiny because he knows what must be done and how to do it" (277). Skinner's utopian novel *Walden Two*—originally, he wanted to be a writer, not a psychologist—imagined what such a destiny might look like. According to the novel's protagonist, Frazier, the intellectual foundations of such a utopia are easy to understand and hard to disagree with. "The questions," he explains, "are simple enough. What's the best behavior for the individual so far as the group is concerned? And how can the individual be induced to behave in that way? Why not explore these questions in a scientific spirit?" (95).

At the center of this utopian vision was Skinner's theory of operant conditioning. In contrast to Pavlovian classical conditioning, which induced involuntary behaviors ("respondents") through stimulus generalization, operant conditioning used associative learning techniques to encourage test subjects to perform specific voluntary behaviors ("operants") without induction. Operant conditioning therefore had a significant precursor in Thorndike's law of exercise and law of effect. The former stated that the more frequently a stimulus elicits a particular response, the more likely that response is in the future; the latter stated that voluntary behaviors accompanied by pleasant experiences are more likely to be performed—and voluntary behaviors accompanied by unpleasant experiences are less likely to be performed.[13] In operant conditioning, however, there was no singular eliciting stimulus, as this implied a one-to-one correspondence between stimulus and response. Instead, Skinner understood his test subjects to be interacting dynamically with broadly stimulating environments, which might allow for any number of possible associations and operants. A famous example was described by Skinner's article "'Superstition' in the Pigeon" (1948). A hungry pigeon is placed in a cage. A mechanism is attached to the cage that can insert, or retract, a food hopper at programmed intervals. "The bird," Skinner wrote, "happens to be executing some [operant] response as the hopper appears; as a result it tends to repeat this response" (168). If the pigeon was turning clockwise when the hopper appeared, then it would repeat this behavior to make the hopper reappear—as if the behavior caused the appearance of food. The more the hopper's appearance corresponds to clockwise turning, the more likely the pigeon is to repeat this behavior. In effect, operant conditioning makes the bird "superstitious," confusing correlation with causation.

Skinner's examples of operant conditioning, however, weren't restricted to feeding pigeons or building utopias. In *Verbal Behavior* (1957), he argued that language use was fundamentally an operant behavior—and that language acquisition was therefore an example of operant conditioning. When children imitate verbal behaviors (i.e., utterances), he theorized, these imitations are subjected to positive and negative reinforcement until they are performed correctly and in the correct circumstances. In his 1959 review of *Verbal Behavior*, however, Noam Chomsky argued that language acquisition couldn't be explained by such a theory. As a rule, children are able to use and understand examples of language that they have never encountered before—and which, therefore, have never been subject to operant conditioning. "The young child," Chomsky explained, "has succeeded in carrying out what from a formal point of view, at least, seems to be a remarkable type of theory construction. Furthermore this task is accomplished in an astonishingly short time, to a large extent independently of intelligence, and in a comparable way by all children. Any theory of learning must cope with these facts" (57). In short, a child's fluency in a given language could not be explained by stimulus history alone; Chomsky later labeled this the "poverty of the stimulus."[14] The only possible explanation, he explained, was that humans have an innate ability to sort and make sense of linguistic data. Chomsky's nativist argument was a turning point in the sciences of mind— and marked psychological behaviorism's imminent decline as an explanatory paradigm.

Psychology, however, was not the only discipline that behaviorism shaped. By the 1950s, analytic philosophy of mind was dominated by logical behaviorism—bearing many of the anti-mentalistic and anti-metaphysical commitments of Watsonian behaviorism but without any of the methodological baggage. The person most responsible for introducing behaviorism to philosophy was Bertrand Russell. Russell emphasized that he was not a behaviorist himself—he believed in the existence of consciousness and in its utility. Nonetheless, *The Analysis of Mind* (1921) shows the degree to which Russell took Watson's claims seriously. "The inference that other people have something non-physical called 'mind' or 'thought,'" Russell suggested, is "unwarranted" (29). Something like the "unconscious," he explained, wasn't an entity unto itself but "merely a causal law of behavior" (88). In *An Outline of Philosophy* (1927)—which he wrote in consultation with Watson—Russell remained ambivalent about behaviorism's categorical rejections of consciousness and introspection. Nonetheless, he proclaimed that behaviorism's contributions could not be ignored. Behaviorism and pure physiology, he wrote, are "vital to a proper understanding of philosophy, since they are necessary for an objective study of knowledge and inference" (33). "I do not fundamentally agree with [behaviorism's rejection of consciousness]," Russell explained later in that same volume, "but I think it contains more truth than people suppose, and I regard it as desirable to develop the behaviorist method to the fullest possible extent" (73).

Russell's ambivalent advocacy for behaviorism changed the landscape of philosophy. (It also changed the landscape of psychology; late in life, Skinner confessed that it was Russell who drew him to behaviorism rather than Watson.[15]) As Laurence Smith suggests in *Behaviorism and Logical Positivism: A Reassessment of the Alliance* (1986), it was Russell who brought behaviorism to the logical positivists. There, in the wake of Ludwig Wittgenstein's *Tractatus Logico-Philosophicus* (1922), Watson's ideas found a reasonably receptive audience in Rudolf Carnap, Carl Hempel, and Otto Neurath. Of these three, Carnap was the least impressed. Despite its physicalism, Carnap explained in *The Logical Structure of the World* (1928), behaviorism nonetheless misrepresented the "epistemic relations" between sensations and concepts (96). Neurath and Hempel were more enthusiastic. For Neurath, behaviorism created a foundation for a new generation of sociologists. As he wrote in "Sociology in the Framework of Physicalism" (1931), "social behaviorism" provided a vocabulary for predicting both individual and group action: "Within the framework of social behaviorism it is a perfectly meaningful statement to say that human groups encourage individual human beings to adopt certain ways of action and inhibit them in respect to others" (89). Without any mentalistic or metaphysical distractions, this "social behaviorism" was compatible with Carnap's thesis that all knowledge was theoretically translatable into a language of physical description.

In thinking about behaviorism's development as a philosophical program, however, the most significant of the logical positivists was Carl Hempel. Building on Watson's work, as well as that of Carnap and Neurath, Hempel developed a "logical behaviorism" that was methodologically and disciplinarily distinct from "psychological behaviorism." As he wrote in "The Logical Analysis of Psychology" (1935), "Logical behaviorism claims neither that minds, feelings, inferiority complexes, voluntary actions, etc., do not exist, nor that their existence is in the least doubtful. It insists that the very question as to whether these psychological constructs really exist is already a pseudoproblem" (20). By Hempel's reasoning, the goal of logical behaviorism was to determine the logical and epistemological entailments of seemingly mental phenomena. As such, logical behaviorism wasn't a psychological theory but rather a logical theory about the content of psychological propositions and how those propositions could be expressed more fundamentally in nonpsychological (i.e., "physical") terms. In that way, Hempel's logical behaviorism wasn't restricted to *behavior* at all. Instead, it was about displacing the epistemological priority of mentalistic concepts and explanations and then reframing such concepts and explanations in a reductive physicalist system.

It was this recasting of mental concepts in nonmental terms that became the fundamental gesture of philosophical behaviorism in the 1940s, 1950s, and 1960s. But whereas the logical positivists sought out a physicalist framework for mental phenomena, a later generation of logical behaviorists sought a primarily linguistic framework for these same phenomena. But there were differing opinions about the nature of language's relation to problems of mind. Some, like W. V. O. Quine, insisted that language had a special logical purchase on these problems—and that linguistic analysis could yield important insights. As he explained in "Mind and Verbal Dispositions" (1975), "A theory of mind can gain clarity and substance . . . from a better understanding of the workings of language, whereas little understanding of the working of language is to be hoped for in mentalistic terms" (84). In *Philosophical Investigations* (1953), Wittgenstein also argued for the necessity of such linguistic analysis. But if linguistic analysis could clarify certain problems of mind, he claimed, it was only because those problems were themselves produced or exacerbated by linguistic convention. "'Are you not really a behaviourist in disguise? Aren't you at bottom really saying that everything except human behavior is a fiction?'—If I do speak of a fiction, then it is a *grammatical* fiction" (§307). As an example, let's imagine two people riding in a car with an unreliable transmission. The car stops suddenly; the driver says, "I'm sorry the car is misbehaving." Obviously, this is a figure of speech. The driver hasn't actually imputed intentions to the car. Nonetheless, it is idiomatic and grammatical for the driver to use a psychological predicate ("misbehaving") to group together a range of unseen—and possibly unrelated—mechanical problems. Where there were once a worn clutch, a cracked manifold, and a broken fan belt, there is now a single agent performing a seemingly cohesive and intentional action. Or, as Wittgenstein explains, "Where our language suggests a body and there is none: there, we should like to say, is a *spirit*" (§36).

In *The Concept of Mind* (1949), Gilbert Ryle makes a parallel point—speculating that Cartesian dualism itself, "the dogma of the Ghost in the Machine" (5), originated in linguistic error.[16] In the seventeenth century, Ryle suggests, René Descartes struggled to find a vocabulary for bridging mental and physical phenomena. "How can a mental process, such as willing, cause spatial movements like the movement of the tongue?" (9). As a scientist and mathematician, Descartes readily accepted the mechanics of Galileo. But as a religious man, Descartes couldn't accept that the "soul"—immaterial, eternal, divine—was made of the same stuff as flesh or earth, or subject to the same physical laws. His solution, Ryle explains, was as follows:

> Still unwittingly adhering to the grammar of mechanics, he tried to avert disaster by describing minds in what was merely an obverse vocabulary. The workings of minds had to be described by the mere negatives of the specific descriptions given to bodies; they are not in space, they are not motions, they are not modifications of matter, they are not accessible to public observation. Minds are not bits of clockwork, they are just bits of not-clockwork.
>
> As thus represented, minds are not merely ghosts harnessed to machines, they are themselves just spectral machines. (9)

If something has no physical properties, then physical predicates can't be applied to it. I can't say, "That vat is full of belief," because beliefs are nonphysical concepts and therefore can't fill physical vessels. (In contrast, a textual representation of those beliefs could potentially fill something physical.) Similarly, I can't say, "His soul is on the second floor but not the third," because if souls have no physical properties then they can't have locations either. And yet these are precisely the kinds of mistakes Ryle sees in Descartes. By describing souls through "the grammar of mechanics," Descartes created the expectation that these nonphysical entities acted as if they did possess physical properties ("spectral machines"). This expectation was so pervasive, Ryle claims, that it was even present in the early (Watsonian) behaviorists, who replaced talk of "inner-life" with talk of inner mechanisms (300). Ryle concludes that any such mind-body dualism amounts to a *category-mistake*: "It represents the facts of mental life as if they belong to one logical type or category (or range of types and category), when they actually belong to another" (6). The sentence "His soul is on the second floor" would be an example of such a Cartesian category-mistake. And as I hope to show in the next section, the sentence "I want Clarissa Dalloway to be as happy as I am" would be too.

The Category-Mistake

My claim is that mind-body category-mistakes are logically fundamental to our perceptions of literary minds. In this sense, the category-mistake isn't a "mistake" in the conventional sense—it's not *bad*, per se. In *Character and Person* (2015), John Frow warns against "the category error of abstracting character from its textual existence and treating it as though it had an independent existence" (vi). But I would argue that the perception of a character having an "independent existence" or a mind comparable to my own is precisely what so many readers experience. By definition literary texts possess linguistic and physical properties and can use those properties to represent mental phenomena. But these texts don't actually possess mental properties or operate by those kinds of rules. So when we perceive minds like our own in these texts, or when we assume that literary minds and actual minds are meaningfully comparable, we are imputing mental phenomena to nonmental substances. In effect, we are misattributing properties across category boundaries. As I mentioned earlier, this is why behaviorism—a protocol for determining the nonmental origins of seemingly mental phenomena—is so well suited for thinking about literature. My hope is to extrapolate from Ryle's version of behaviorism a model for analyzing the mental phenomena that seem to emerge through the act of reading literature—and for analyzing the assumptions and claims of contemporary cognitive literary criticism.

Such extrapolation, however, is not without its difficulties. Nowhere in *The Concept of Mind* does Ryle explain what he means by "category." Instead, the discussion of category-mistakes focuses on examples. But it's hard to abstract from these examples what Ryle's notion of "category" or "type" might be (he uses these two terms interchangeably). Claiming that mind and body are the same logical type, Ryle notes, is not unlike taking a tour of a university—the dorms, the library, the academic departments—and then asking which building contains the university (6). Universities are different types of concepts from dorms; the dorms are physical buildings on a campus, but the university is a conceptual relation among that campus's buildings. Another example comes from Charles Dickens's *The Pickwick Papers* (1837), despite Ryle's famously slavish devotion to Jane Austen: "She came home in either a flood of tears or else a sedan chair" (*Concept of Mind*, 11).[17] It's possible to arrive in either a flood of tears or a sedan chair—and you could conceivably do both these things at the same time. But you can't arrive in them in the same way. Here the category-mistake rests on zeugma, with both terms constrained by preceding the same verb phrase. But what exactly do universities and mind-body dualism have in common with riding tearfully in a sedan chair? "When two terms belong to the same category," Ryle explained, "it is proper to construct conjunctive propositions embodying them" (11). And yet without a definition of "category" Ryle's sense of propositional propriety—or impropriety—only gets us so far.

Ofra Magidor's *Category Mistakes* (2013) is helpful here. As Ryle himself acknowledged, categorization had preoccupied philosophy for thousands of years—from Aristotle's *Organon* (fourth century BCE) to Kant's *Critique of Pure Reason* (1781). But according to Magidor, Ryle's sense of categories had a more recent origin: Bertrand Russell's theory of "logical types" (7-8). Magidor points to the following passage from Russell's *Principles of Mathematics* (1903): "Every propositional function $\varphi(x)$—so it is contended—has, in addition to its range of truth, a range of significance, i.e., a range within which x must lie if $\varphi(x)$ is to be a proposition at all, whether true or false. This is the first point of the theory of types; the second point is that ranges of significance form *types*, i.e., if x belongs to the range of significance of $\varphi(x)$, there is a class of objects, the *type* of x, all of which must also belong to the range of the significance of x" (Russell, 523). To put things more concretely, let's take the sentence "I love all literature." This proposition is false; I don't love *all* literature, and I doubt that anyone does. But even though it's false, the proposition still works logically. A false proposition is no less functional than a true one. As long as enjoyment and reading literature are attributed to something within the given "range of significance," the sentence still produces meaning (even if that meaning isn't true). By Russell's reasoning, and by extension Ryle's, a category or logical type would be any set of concepts that entail the same range of significance and that can sustain the same kinds of predicates. I don't love all literature, but there's no logical reason I couldn't.

Therefore, there are several crucial differences between Ryle's understanding of "category" and that of Aristotle or Kant. First, Ryle's categories are logical insofar as they are *semantic* and *syntactical*. In contrast, Aristotle's were a mixture of ontological, epistemological, and logical concepts: substance, quantity, quality, relation, place, date, posture, state, action, passion. Kant used some of these names too, although his categories served a primarily epistemological function: unity, plurality, totality ("quantity"); reality, negation, limitation ("quality"); substance and effect, cause and effect, reciprocity ("relation"); possibility, existence, necessity ("modality"). Second, Ryle claimed in his early essay "Categories" (1938) that the advantage of a logico-semantic understanding of categories is that it is generalizable to new, previously unknown examples. Aristotle and Kant only posited a finite number of categories (10 and 12, respectively). In Aristotle's system, Ryle wrote, one could categorize predicates through the interrogatives that could be applied to those predicates: "Any two predicates which satisfy the same interrogative are of the same category and any two which do not satisfy the same interrogative are of different categories" (179). The trouble was that Aristotle—constrained by the nontechnical vocabulary of ancient Greek—offered even fewer interrogatives than he did categories. So unless the difference between two predicates is precisely that of "how," "why," "when," and so on, there's no way to represent that difference. Ryle was even less generous to Kant. The theory of categories in *The Critique of Pure Reason*, he wrote, gives no vocabulary at all to "exhibit or symbolize type-homogeneities and heterogeneities in abstraction from the concrete factors which exemplify them. Nor does he explain how they are established" (187). This accusation against Kant's system doesn't actually seem to be true. But by Ryle's reckoning Kant emphasized categorical content over the logical relations between categories—meaning that one couldn't move from specific type-heterogeneities to more general criteria for distinguishing categories.

The criterion Ryle settled on was "absurdity." By "absurd," however, he didn't merely mean the bizarre or outlandish. Instead, Ryle's absurdities were closer to J. L. Austin's *infelicities*—referring to the logical and pragmatic failures of a given sentence or, in Austin's case, a performative utterance.[18] "Only expressions can be affirmed or denied to be absurd," Ryle wrote in "Categories," as "Nature provides no absurdities" (189). Ryle's absurdity was exclusively a logical and linguistic property. If a sentence appeared absurd, this meant that type-incongruities were present. Knowing the categorizations of particular concepts, therefore, wasn't necessary. Instead, all you needed was a sense of how a particular concept was used in particular propositions and whether it was used successfully. As Ryle explained, "To ask the question To what type or category does so-and-so belong? is to ask In what sorts of true or false propositions and in what positions in them can so-and-so enter?" (188). The culmination of Ryle's essay was the following method for determining type-incongruities:

> Two proposition-factors are of different categories or types, if there are sentence-frames such that when the expressions for those factors are imported as alternative complements to the same gap-signs, the resultant sentences are significant in the one case and absurd in the other. It is tempting but not quite correct to say, as the converse of this, that two factors are of the same type if there is any case where both can fill the same gap. For 'I' and 'the writer of this paper' can be alternative nominatives to hosts of significant sentences but both cannot fill the gap in ' . . . never wrote a paper'. It follows that, though nearly, it is not quite, true to say that every gap-sign in its context in a determinate sentence-frame indicates the category of all its possible complements. (190)

Let's try this method out. Our sentence-frame will be "_____ loves all literature." Anything that can be inserted into "_____" is a gap-sign. According to Ryle, the way to determine a type-incongruity is to complete the same sentence-frame with two different gap-signs. All other aspects of the sentence-frame—speaker, audience, context, sense, and so on—stay constant. Insofar as they don't change the sense of the sentence, verb conjugations in the sentence-frame can vary as needed (I love, you love, she loves, people love, etc.). "I love all literature," "You love all literature," and "She loves all literature" are all logically sound but (most likely) factually false. *Loving* is an action that people can perform, and, as Deidre Lynch shows in *Loving Literature: A Cultural History* (2015), it's an action we've been performing with respect to novels since the eighteenth century. That's when the application of the predicate "love" to literature became conventionalized. Therefore, these propositions function logically even though, as I mentioned before, they are most likely untrue.

But if we change the gap-sign to "book," everything changes. The sentence "Book loves all literature" is absurd. That the predicate "love" applies to "literature" is irrelevant. Instead, the issue is that books don't have phenomenal experience; they can't *love*. The sentence "Book loves all literature" is neither true nor false but rather absurd. So we conclude that, with respect to this sentence-frame, "people" and "I" are potentially members of a shared logical category but "book" is not. But this doesn't mean that "book" and "I" are always logically incomparable. Logical comparability is dependent on the sentence-frame. If our sentence-frame were "_____ is in the library," then all three of our gap-signs would likely be members of the same logical category. This sentence isn't necessarily true, but it works logically. Each of the gap-signs possesses physical properties and can sustain the predicates in question. They also follow conventional rules about the sorts of things libraries contain. There might be neither people nor books in the library, but there's no logical reason there couldn't be. Indeed, we can even bring this back to mind-body dualism. Ryle's point is that we mistakenly treat "mind" as if it were comparable to "body" by talking about it as if it followed physical laws. But there are frame-sentences whereby "mind" and "body" would be logically comparable. The most obvious one would be "I have a _____." Insofar as "mind" and "body" are both things a person can possess (a point Watson would dispute), the sentence presents no logical difficulty. At the same time, given the broadness entailed by "I have a _____," the comparison between "mind" and "body" isn't hugely meaningful. The frame-sentence doesn't impute any properties to "mind" and "body" beyond my ability to have them. What "mind" shares with "body" here it also shares with "sedan chair," "belief," "cat," and so on.[19]

Since the publication of *The Concept of Mind*, Ryle's idea of the category-mistake has been the subject of considerable discussion, particularly with respect to whether such mistakes have semantic meaning or not.[20] For my purposes here, however, we don't need to get into that. Instead, as my sentence-frames thus far have shown, it's possible to use Ryle's method to track the logical differences between literary minds and actual minds with respect to the use of mental predicates. Let's try the following pair of sentence-frames, both of which will feature the same gap-signs as they oscillate between literary experience and interpersonal interactions: "I want

_____ to experience happiness" and "_____ wants people to experience happiness." Our gap-signs will be "you," "Clarissa Dalloway," "the disembodied omniscient narrator," "*Mrs. Dalloway*," and "Virginia Woolf." Here are all the possible permutations of sentence-frames and gap-signs:

1. I want <u>you</u> to experience happiness.

2. I want <u>Clarissa Dalloway</u> to experience happiness.

3. I want <u>the disembodied omniscient narrator</u> to experience happiness.

4. I want <u>*Mrs. Dalloway*</u> to experience happiness.

5. I want <u>Virginia Woolf</u> to experience happiness.

6. <u>You</u> want people to experience happiness.

7. <u>Clarissa Dalloway</u> wants people to experience happiness.

8. <u>The disembodied omniscient narrator</u> wants people to experience happiness.

9. <u>*Mrs. Dalloway*</u> wants people to experience happiness.

10. <u>Virginia Woolf</u> wants people to experience happiness.

Only one of these sentences appears absurd outright—no. 4. "I want *Mrs. Dalloway* to experience happiness" seems to violate the most obvious of type-distinctions. We might guess that it has something to do with the name being italicized. As I mentioned earlier, books can't have minds or phenomenal experiences, even if they ostensibly contain entities that do seem to possess these properties. So sentence no. 4 produces the effect of logical absurdity, while the other nine sentences do not. But that doesn't mean these other sentences are free of suspicion. Ryle's method can't prove type-homogeneities definitively, but it should alert us when concepts are grouped inappropriately. Given the ontological and metaphysical differences among "you," "Clarissa Dalloway," "the disembodied omniscient narrator," "*Mrs. Dalloway*," and "Virginia Woolf," it stands to reason that these terms wouldn't be comparable to each other in this situation. Granted, "you" and "Virginia Woolf" both describe real people with subjective experience. Yet I would never say that I know "your" mind the same way I know that of "Clarissa Dalloway." Nor would I suggest that I know Clarissa Dalloway's mind the same way I know that of a disembodied omniscient narrator.

And novels don't have minds at all. But these sentences don't produce the feeling of incomparability or absurdity that they should.[21] Moreover, you would expect the absurdity of no. 4 to entail the absurdity of no. 9—and yet it doesn't. You can't want something if you don't have phenomenal experience.[22] For example, cookbooks contain recipes, but it would be wrong to say that cookbooks *want* people to make the recipes they contain, or that the recipes want anything at all. Somehow, despite the italicization of the title, "*Mrs. Dalloway* wants people to experience happiness" dodges that absurdity. And it does this without any indication that this use of "want" is metaphorical, or that the novel's title is metonymic for authorial psychology. Indeed, there's nothing *logically* problematic about saying, "*Mrs. Dalloway* wants people to experience happiness but Virginia Woolf does not." If the title were necessarily metonymic for authorial psychology, then we wouldn't be able to say that an author and her novel want different things. Similarly, if the novel's ability to "want" were metaphorical, then the sentence wouldn't imply that the predicate applies to "Virginia Woolf" and "*Mrs. Dalloway*" equally and in the same way.

Cognitive Criticism and the Literary Mind

Has my appeal to Ryle's method backfired? Most of the sentences that should have produced absurdity didn't. And it's that *lack* of absurdity that's very much my point. If Ryle's method doesn't apply to sentences describing literary experience, then what must be true about the concepts and relations that constitute such experience? What must be true about the similarities between minds and texts we perceive so readily, or about the fictional minds that feel just like our own?

I think we're left with one possibility: *language (in this case, literary language) can engineer the perceived logical comparability of minds and texts, and linguistic objects within those texts, while it also circumvents or disables the absurdity such category-mistakes typically produce.*[23] Logically, we know that this perception of comparability can't be a condition of our literary experiences (even though we do learn to anticipate its future occurrences). Therefore, it must be an effect of our reading—a product of our grammatical fictions, so to speak. If literature seems to have a special purchase on problems of mind, then this purchase must itself be the result of literary artifice. This conclusion is congruous, I believe, with other recent accounts of literary experience. In *The Lyric in the Age of the Brain* (2016), Nikki Skillman suggests that it was literary form itself that allowed poets such as Robert Lowell and

A. R. Ammons to compare consciousness and lyric poetry. "As poets explore the implications of the conceptual identity of mind and brain through concrete transformations of poetic form," she writes, "they are often playfully, solicitously, often ingeniously conscious of the timeless analogies between the verbal, sensual aspects of the poem and the human body, between the irreducible, inspirited 'meaning' of the poem and the immaterial soul" (46). In Deidre Lynch's *Loving Literature*, the logical comparability of literary minds and actual minds is explicitly a product of the imagination. "We don't treat literature as a thing," she writes, "but as a person: lovers of literature construct the aesthetic relation as though it put them in the presence of other people" (8). The idea that minds and texts do the same sorts of things, or that characters and actual people follow the same psychological rules, is as fictional as the story being read and loved.

On the whole, however, contemporary cognitive criticism has moved in the opposite direction. Instead of seeing logical comparability as a perception created by literary experience, many critics have proceeded as if, or even stipulated specifically, that minds and texts are the same type of concept, despite the ontological and epistemological differences between them. Moreover, this perceived comparability is often identified as the reason that literature can simulate minds at all. The reasoning goes like this: if literary minds feel real, or if literary worlds are engrossing, it must be because minds and texts work in similar ways. But if we acknowledge that literary minds must have linguistic origins, and that these minds are a different *type* of concept than actual minds, then we know that this reasoning can't be right. Despite its appeals to empirical data and scientific rigor, much cognitive criticism has actually blurred the lines between aesthetic objects and the way those objects are experienced. Therefore, in offering the following emblematic examples from cognitive literary study, my aim isn't to single out any particular critic. Nor is it to survey, or dismiss, the field in its entirety. Instead, my goal is to show the ways that category-mistakes are fundamental to different conversations in cognitive literary criticism and to highlight the logical and epistemological problems that emerge as a result.

It is worth pointing out, however, that while "cognitive science" is a young discipline, dependent on new technologies, the impulse toward "cognitive" criticism or commentary is nothing new. Nearly every generation has had its own version—from Sidney's *Defense of Poesy* (1595) and Coleridge's *Biographia Literaria* (1817) to I. A. Richards's *Principles of Literary Criticism* (1924) and the Chomsky-inspired criticism of Ohmann and Freeman in the

1960s.[24] Around the beginning of the twenty-first century, modern cognitive literary study was reenergized by two pioneering books: Elaine Scarry's *Dreaming by the Book* (1999), which juxtaposed literary experience to various psychological experiments and concepts, and Lisa Zunshine's *Why We Read Fiction: Theory of Mind and the Novel* (2006), which brought "theory of mind" research to the critical mainstream.

To be clear: the aforementioned category-mistake of minds and texts did not originate with Scarry or Zunshine. As I shall show in this book's remaining chapters, that category-mistake is much older and far more ingrained. But the perceived comparability of minds and texts is a central point in both these books, as is the similarly perceived comparability between linguistic knowledge and sensory data. For Scarry, such comparability is why literary imagery appears so vivid—and why different writers, using different techniques, can nonetheless induce daydream-like images in their readers. The "mysterious consistency" of these images, she claims, comes "from the qualities of mental life itself. The same practice turns up in the *Illiad* and in *Anna Karenina* because Homer or Tolstoy is giving us a transcription, in verbal form, of the images as they come fully-blown into the mind, and in doing so, each encodes the formal properties of those envisioned pictures on the page so that we can reconstruct the pictures. In effect, writers give us a transcript of how the brain works" (244). In trying to explain why poetic language creates vivid images, Scarry invariably treats "language" and "image" and "brain" as if they were all the same type of concept. The issue lies in the term "transcription," which typically refers to a written record of spoken language. It's possible to transcribe a movie's dialogue or a court case. But is it possible to transcribe an "image" or "how the brain works"? Neither "image" nor "brain" is a linguistic concept—so if one were to "transcribe" them, it's not clear what information would be written down. But in order to explain why images and language seem interchangeable, and why language affects our brains in the way it does, Scarry has little choice but to apply the same predicate to all the concepts involved. What is being "transcribed" here, however, is not the preterit comparability of these ideas—including the apparent epistemological comparability between images and texts—but rather the *experience* of comparability that emerges from reading Homer and Tolstoy. Like the mental properties we perceive in novel characters, the images we perceive in poems—the words on the page that really feel like they possess visual content—also rely on a category-mistake. A similar point might also be made about Scarry's assertion of the epistemological comparability between minds and flowers. In a gesture that recalls Ryle's criticism of Cartesian syntax, Scarry describes mental processes in a decidedly botanical grammar of mechanics: "In the independence of their motions," she explains, flowers "perhaps provide a model for the sovereign motion of mental images" (161). *Dreaming by the Book*, however, doesn't only compare minds and flowers; texts are compared to flowers too, although on compositional rather than epistemological grounds. "Flowers," she writes, "are implicitly present in paper and cloth because both are made from vegetable matter. When we write with ink on paper, vegetable matter is being set down on top of vegetable matter" (161). It's hard to dispute this physicalism. But is such physicalism meaningful, or is it closer to being a token physicalism?[25] Despite the compositional similarities between flowers and books, it's hard to imagine a predicate that would apply to both concepts equally and yet maintain the qualities Scarry values about either one.

The comparison between different types of concepts is more implicit in Zunshine's *Why We Read Fiction*. But as Zunshine employs "theory of mind" (ToM) to explain novelistic form, the comparison is no less central.[26] The term "theory of mind" dates back to David Premack and Guy Woodruff's paper "Does the Chimpanzee Have a Theory of Mind?" (1978). But there is continued disagreement among psychologists and philosophers about what ToM actually entails. As Alvin Goldman explains in *Simulating Minds: The Philosophy, Psychology, and Neuroscience of Mindreading* (2006), there are three competing explanations for how ToM works: *theory-theory*, which says that people have (or acquire) a general theory for thinking about other minds; *rationality theory*, which says that people use logical reasoning to deduce what other people are thinking; and *simulation theory*, which says that people think about what they would be thinking in a given scenario and then apply that to other people (4). Zunshine's sense of ToM is closest to *theory-theory*, as shown by these comments on Woolf's *Mrs. Dalloway* (1925):

> How much prompting do we need to begin to attribute a mind of her own to a fictional character? Very little, it seems, since any indication that we are dealing with a self-propelled entity (e.g., "Peter Walsh has come back") leads us to assume that this entity possesses thoughts, feelings, and desires, at least some of which we could intuit, interpret, and, frequently, misinterpret. Writers exploit our constant readiness to posit a mind whenever we observe behavior when they experiment with the amount and kind of interpretation of the characters' mental states that they supply themselves and that they expect their readers to supply. (22)

In saying that novels activate the ToM apparatus, Zunshine isn't *necessarily* assuming comparability between minds and texts. But she is assuming comparability between literary minds and actual minds, as well as between different types of knowledge—namely, the comparison between sensory knowledge and linguistic abstractions or descriptions of such sensory knowledge. Typically, we wouldn't say that we know Peter Walsh's thoughts the same way that we know the thoughts of actual human beings. There is an enormous difference between seeing a behavior and reading a description of one. Therefore, in order to accept Zunshine's claim that both observations and descriptions activate ToM, we need to be able to explain why the epistemological differences between observations and descriptions don't matter. One potential explanation would be the "constant readiness" hypothesis offered by Zunshine. The ToM apparatus, we're told, is so hypersensitive that it can be activated by nearly any decontextualized reference to behavior or mental state. But if this were true, it stands to reason that our ToMs would be going off constantly. This would also negate Zunshine's own claim that novels have a special ability to activate our ToM. If we accept "constant readiness" as an explanation, there's no reason that poems, newspaper articles, tweets, and stop signs wouldn't also have this special ability. If the constant readiness hypothesis were true, this very paragraph could potentially activate your ToM mechanism. (My belief is that it will not, or at least not in the same way as meeting in person.) This leads us to a second potential explanation: that there's something about novelistic *form* that's uniquely suited to stimulating the ToM apparatus. But this isn't an explanation at all, as it returns us to the epistemological differences between literary minds and actual minds. In effect, both these explanations rely on category-mistakes —on the critic's ability to compare, however implicitly, terms that are not in fact logically comparable.

Some critics, however, don't let these comparisons remain implicit. In his essay "Reminding Modernism" (2011), David Herman suggests that modernist literature isn't so much an "inward turn" but rather comparable to phenomena described by theories of enactive cognition. Varela, Rosch, and Thompson coined the term in *The Embodied Mind* (1992): "We propose as a name the term *enactive* to emphasize the growing conviction that cognition is not the representation of a pregiven world by a pregiven mind but is rather the enactment of a world and a mind on the basis of a history of the variety of actions that a being in the world performs" (9). In other words, we sense not the world-as-it-is but rather a synthesis of stimuli, memories, and habits. And this is a cognitive theory that Herman sees as being especially applicable to modernist literature: "The modernists emphasized the tight coupling between mind and world, the nexus between intelligent agents and the environments they seek to navigate. Indeed, these narrative methods can be compared to experimental methods that aspire to what researchers in the cognitive sciences have come to call ecological validity ... a trait shared by research models that allow the analyst to approximate how intelligence operates in the wild" (264). Broadly speaking, Herman's argument is that modernist literature is more "enactive" than other kinds of literature. But saying that literature is enactive or embodied—or extended or embedded, for that matter[27]—doesn't mean that minds and texts suddenly possess the same properties, or that they can sustain the same kinds of predicates. Our sense of cognition is broadened, perhaps, but the logical and epistemological constraints of the literary object remain in place. As an example, we can turn to Herman's claim that "narrative methods can be compared to experimental methods." Initially there's something appealing about this point. Instead of stating a relationship of identity, which would have a heavier logical burden (i.e., narrative methods *are the same as* experimental methods), Herman is only stating a relationship of comparison. On that basis, he implies that modernist novels also "aspire" to ecological validity (or at least something similar). The trouble is that this analysis relies on the assumption that narrative "methods" and experimental "methods" refer to the same types of things. If narrative methods were meaningfully comparable to experimental methods, then the objects examined by those methods would also be logically comparable—in this case, modernist novels and minds. Per Herman's argument, there would be the added stipulation that modernist novels are more comparable to minds than other kinds of novels. But in this instance, we know that these terms aren't comparable either logically or epistemologically—or even physically. Therefore, if we do perceive such comparability, and if modernist novels do seem to aspire to ecological validity, it must be an effect of our reading rather than a condition of it.

Some cognitive critics, however, have become wary of such mind-text comparisons. In *What Literature Teaches Us about Emotion* (2011), Patrick Colm Hogan urges us against conflating literary representations of emotion with empirical studies of the same phenomenon: "The overt, literal claims made about emotion in literary works have no special theoretical status. Such statements may operate as part of the overall simulative effect of the work. But they are not, in general, comparable to scientific hypotheses about emotion" (23-24). We also find in Hogan's work explicit attention to whether concepts are comparable to each other. In *Beauty and Sublimity: A Cognitive Aesthetics of Literature and the Arts* (2016) he concludes that *beauty* and *sublime* are "comparable concepts, even if they are not identical," as both terms "are distinct varieties of aesthetic response, or, more precisely, different complexes of emotion that bear on aesthetic feeling" (34). And yet even Hogan is unable to avoid projecting the mental predicates of literary experience onto the textual object itself. Here, too, mental properties seemingly emerge from linguistic and physical concepts, as if literary representations of emotion and affect somehow exceed their ontological and epistemological entailments. Such represented emotions might have no "special theoretical status," but they do seem to have a special *logical* and *psychological* status. In *Literature and Emotion* (2018), Hogan suggests that a "more appropriate name for fiction emotions [emotions elicited by art] would be *simulation emotions*" (101). Somehow, the representation of mental states amounts to "simulation"—despite the differences between sensation and description I described earlier. As a result, Hogan is able to characterize literary texts as nearly able to sustain the same kinds of mental predicates as authors and readers. "In the context of simulation," he writes, "there is no reason why a literary work could not draw on authentic, emotional experiences while still producing a work that is unique with its own particularity of emotion" (88).

Words and Minds

As I mentioned, I'm not looking to single out any individual critic. Nor am I looking to dismiss cognitive criticism as a whole (for reasons that will become clear shortly). Instead, I want to make two interrelated points. The first is to reiterate the extent to which category-mistakes are embedded in how we read literature and how we talk about literary minds as if they were just like our own. Despite the ontological and epistemological differences between literary minds and actual minds, between psychological rules and literary or linguistic rules, category-mistakes allow us to talk about them as comparable phenomena. They do this even though these minds are different types of concepts, following different kinds of rules, that are unable to sustain the same kind of mental and physical predicates. Ryle's sentence-frame method confirms this, while also revealing that singular logical structure that allows us to impute mental states to characters, narrators, styles, and even textual objects as if they had minds like our own. Moreover, as we saw in the examples of cognitive criticism above, these category-mistakes aren't unique to problems of mind. Any imputation of nonlinguistic properties to a linguistic object must also rely on a category-mistake. The formal mechanisms that allow us to perceive affects in texts, or images in poems, are vastly different. But the logical relations entailed by these perceptions are very much the same. One effect of literary reading is to misattribute certain properties of aesthetic experience to the object itself, even if the object in question cannot sustain the predicates in question. (This bears an important similarity to the "affective fallacy" described by Wimsatt and Beardsley, which I will return to in chap. 1.)

This misattribution leads me to my second point. The goal of cognitive literary study, as I understand it, is to examine the physiological and neurological structures that enable literary experience. That is a valuable goal. But I would maintain that this goal is only attainable—or meaningful—if a certain kind of conceptual work precedes it. Some of this necessary conceptual work, as seen in a book like Jonathan Kramnick's *Paper Minds: Literature and the Ecology of Consciousness* (2018), concerns the state of literary study as a discipline and its potentially reductionist relation to the sciences. As Kramnick explains, the world doesn't follow only one set of rules. Instead, "minds and behavior, literature and literary history, cells and organisms, mark out separate kinds of things with different constituents in play and varied techniques for their explanation" (21). But in addition to this kind of disciplinary work, many of our future conceptual analyses must focus on the literary mind itself: what it is, what it isn't, and why we perceive it in the ways we do. We cannot study how literature affects the brain unless we have a clear sense of the metaphysical and epistemological differences between the concepts "literature" and "brain," or "language" and "mind." This point seems so obvious as to be unnecessary. And yet, as so much literary experience belies this point, it bears repeating if we seek a naturalistic or logically sound account of why we perceive novels, poems, and plays in the ways we do. In novels and poems, literary minds share neither substances nor laws with actual minds (let alone actual brains). In plays, literary and actual minds might have substances in common, but they still follow different kinds of rules and generally comprise different concept types. We must avoid the unwitting comparison of unlike concepts, even though it is such a comparison that literary reading and going to the theater encourage us to make. Obviously I'm not suggesting that we have access to literary objects as things-in-themselves—to perfect, unmarked texts unencumbered by the distortions of subjectivity. But I think we can distinguish many of the entailments and properties of literary objects from the entailments and properties of how we experience those objects. And one way to do that, I believe, is to read behavioristically: to understand that any perceived mental phenomena in literary texts must have nonmental origins; to understand the category-mistake itself as enabling writers to circumvent or exacerbate the logical and empirical problems entailed by representing mental life; to weigh our perceptions as readers against what must be true about those perceptions. To read behavioristically, therefore, is to take behaviorism not as a critical method but as a critical sensibility that would strengthen the logical and epistemological foundations of literary study more broadly. It's an awareness that counters our actual experiences of literary minds with the necessarily nonmental mechanisms that such literary minds entail—and also with the mind-body category-mistakes our experiences rely on.

And even though I think this sensibility would benefit literary studies today across periods, genres, and national traditions, I nonetheless think that the best way to exhibit it here is through behaviorism's own literary history—through writers who encountered behaviorism meaningfully and who brought it to bear on their critical and creative practices. But while the writers I discuss here all encountered behaviorism during their careers, that was not my sole criterion for selecting them. Instead, I chose these writers because of how they instrumentalized these encounters with behavioristic doctrine—because of the ways they subsequently revealed the hard work of perpetuating literature's mentalistic illusions, as well as the critical value of manipulating or even shattering those illusions. So even as the following chapters examine fundamentally different moments from behaviorism's development, from Watson's emotional reflexes to Ryle's category-mistakes to Quine's indeterminacies, it is this spirit—or should I say behavior—that runs through them all.

In chapter 1, "Behaviorism and the Beginnings of Close Reading," I place behaviorism, along with the mind-body category-mistake, squarely at the beginnings of modern poetic criticism. Following a discussion of John Watson's notion of "behavior," I show the ways in which I. A. Richards translated behaviorism into a protocol for reading poetry. Turning his classroom into an ersatz laboratory, Richards trained his students to respond to poetry without appealing to authorial psychology—that is, without the application of psychological predicates to poems. At the same time, Richards himself professed a concept of poetry that yoked psychological, visual, and haptic properties to poetic form. Richards's aspirations to scientific knowledge led some to worry about the reductionism inherent in his methods—as well as worrying about the affective content that Richards assigned to poetic experience. Accordingly, critics such as Cleanth Brooks and W. K. Wimsatt translated Richards's psychologism into a literary formalism—and translated his affective concept of poetry into a strictly semantic one, such that neither psychological nor empirical predicates applied. This sequence of transformations, I show, has contributed to the longevity of the intentional fallacy as a critical problem, as has literary criticism's reluctance to talk about psychological language more generally.

Following the previous chapter's examination of poetic criticism, my second chapter, "Inner Sights," turns to fiction and how Samuel Beckett adapted behaviorist criticisms of introspection. Over the first ten years of behaviorism, Watson went from rejecting introspection entirely to claiming that it was a form of internal sensory knowledge. This was a point that Beckett investigated as well. For Beckett, behaviorism was a contemporary proxy for debates going back to the seventeenth century—when empiricist philosophers rejected the infallible, disembodied *cogito* of Cartesian philosophy and concluded that self-knowledge was a kind of sensory knowledge. These ideas are the crux of Beckett's novels *Murphy* (1938) and *Molloy* (1951). Over the course of *Murphy*, both Cartesian reflection and introspective psychology become the objects of ridicule. This occurs until *Murphy* suddenly supplants introspection with what it calls "vicarious autology." In *Molloy*, Beckett uses the paired characters of Molloy and Moran—who might or might not be aspects of the same person—to suggest that empiricist and behaviorist notions of introspection aren't opposed to rationalist notions at all. Instead, Beckett presents them as the logical result of believing in an infallible *cogito*. In this chapter's final section I show the ways in which Beckett's dissolution of the distinctions between observation and introspection changes the entailments of psychological language in novels and guides us toward the philosophical concerns Beckett examined in his plays.

Accordingly, in chapter 3, "Mental Acts," I move to drama. As I mentioned earlier, drama, by virtue of its live actors and the physicality of the treater, has a different relation to mind-body category-mistakes than written texts. Nonetheless, I show the centrality of such mistakes in the plays of Beckett and Pinter. For while both playwrights acknowledged the physicalism of the theater, they also worked toward representing purely "mental" actions onstage. Following a history of behaviorism's engagement with epistemological mind-body dualism, I begin with Beckett's plays *Eleutheria* (1948) and *Krapp's Last Tape* (1957), both of which use a divided mise-en-scène to stage mental events, attempting to give such events physical properties while also distinguishing them epistemologically from more typical theatrical actions. In *The Birthday Party* (1955) and *The Dumb Waiter* (1957) Pinter used the demarcation between onstage and offstage to similar effect. But whereas Beckett actually attempted to give mental events a physical reality onstage, Pinter used the possibility of such realization to manipulate the expectations of both characters onstage and the audience. In the chapter's conclusion I build on this parallel between actor and audience minds to revisit the differences between novelistic and dramatic psychology and suggest that dramatic minds are no less dependent on category-mistakes than their written counterparts.

In chapter 4, "The Form of Thought," I return to fiction and stylistic criticism through the work of J. M. Coetzee. In the late 1950s and 1960s, behavioristic accounts of language acquisition were overtaken by the innatist and transformational theories of linguists such as Noam Chomsky. Drawing a parallel between Chomskyan linguistics and stylistics, critics such as Richard Ohmann argued that authorial mental content could be deduced from literary style in the same way that deep grammatical structures could be derived from surface transformations. In his linguistics dissertation on Samuel Beckett, however, Coetzee argued that such efforts relied on a deterministic and imitative relation between grammar and mental operations. Moreover, they neglected the fundamental logical disjunction between language and thought—such that mental representation itself necessitates something like a category-mistake. These ideas are recapitulated in Coetzee's *Waiting for the Barbarians* (1980) and *Foe* (1986). In these novels the narrators struggle with what they perceive to be the inaccessibility of the colonized subject's mind. However, both eventually realize that racism and colonialism only heightened a priori gaps between language and thought—and eventually learn that their own minds are not as transparent or expressible as they once thought. And in addition to taking up the logical difficulties posed by mental representation, *Waiting for the Barbarians* and *Foe* contend with the moral difficulties as well, asking readers to think about what might be gained or lost by avoiding mental representation entirely.

1 Behaviorism and the Beginnings of Close Reading

No one doubts that poets have minds. Nonetheless, literary critics have struggled to talk about those minds for the better part of a century—and especially since 1946. That was when W. K. Wimsatt and Monroe Beardsley first published "The Intentional Fallacy," which stated that authorial mental states couldn't be inferred from poems—and didn't need to be. "There is a gross body of life, of sensory and mental experience," they wrote, "which lies behind and in some sense causes every poem, but can never be and need not be known in the verbal and hence intellectual composition which is the poem" (*Verbal Icon*, 12). A decade later, in *Literary Criticism: A Short History* (1957), Wimsatt and Cleanth Brooks made the same point but even more directly: "The poem is before us and is susceptible to analysis, but the psychological goings-on turn out to be below the surface and out of sight" (620). The biographical and psychological lead-up to the poem, they tell us, is irrelevant. What matters is the poem itself and nothing else.

Since the 1950s, this position has suffered a number of prominent repudiations.[1] In "Against Theory" (1982), Steven Knapp and Walter Benn Michaels argued that authorial intention was knowable insofar as "intention" was just another word for a text's semantic meaning. "The mistake made by theorists," they wrote, "has been to imagine the possibility or desirability of moving from one term (the author's intended meaning) to a second term (the text's meaning), when actually the two terms are the same" (724). In *Must We Mean What We Say?* (1969), Stanley Cavell asserted neither identity nor epistemological parallelism between intended meaning and perceived meaning. Nonetheless, he insisted on the logical necessity of the former, even if readers only had evidence of the latter. "The category of intention," Cavell wrote, "is as inescapable (or as escapable with the same consequences) in speaking of objects of art as in speaking of what human beings say and do: without it we would not understand what they are" (198). Our very concepts of language and art, we infer from Cavell, depend on the concept of intention (although, as I will address later on, it's not clear whether intention and authorial intention are always comparable concepts). Granted, some authorial intentions are more knowable than others. But even if such intentions were completely unknowable, it still wouldn't mean that those intentions were any less logically necessary.

Despite these criticisms, Wimsatt and Beardsley's critical prohibition remains largely in effect. Since the 1940s, nearly every critical generation has found new reasons to ignore authorial mental states. In "Form and Intent in the New Criticism" (1971), Paul de Man argued that the New Critics had largely ignored "the intentional structure of literary form" (27). The version of intention we encounter in "The Intentional Fallacy," he wrote, was a distortion—something like "a physical model . . . a transfer of a psychic or mental content that exists in the mind of the poet to the mind of a reader, somewhat as one would pour wine from a jar into a glass" (25). Insofar as it identifies the misattribution of physical properties to mental phenomena, my discussion of Wimsatt and Beardsley later on will resonate with de Man's comments. In the same essay about the New Critics, however, de Man also suggested that authorial intention was still of limited interest for literary criticism. Literature, he wrote, "does not fulfill a plenitude but originates in the void between intent and reality. The imagination takes its flight only after the void . . . literature begins where the existential demystification ends and the critic has no need to linger over this preliminary stage" (34-35). In their essay "Surface Reading: An Introduction" (2009), Stephen Best and Sharon Marcus rejected much of de Man's assessment. At the same time, Best and Marcus asked that we pay new attention to the texts in front of us. And in that way they also turned us away from the "gross body of life, of sensory and mental experience" behind every text. "We remain intrigued by [de Man's] observation," they write, "that poetry is the 'foreknowledge' of criticism, and that the interpreter therefore 'discloses poetry for what it is' and articulates 'what was already there in full light'" (11). In "Close Reading and Thin Description" (2013), Heather Love made a parallel point, but in a more sociological and psychological register. Literary criticism, she claimed, "might forge an expanded defense of reading by considering practices of exhaustive, thin description . . . forms of analysis that describe patterns of behavior and visible activity but do not traffic in speculation about interiority, meaning, or depth" (404).

Others, however, have disputed the concept of "intention" itself. Authorial intention hasn't necessarily been the focus of these discussions. But they're relevant here just the same. In *Parables for the Virtual: Movement, Affect, Sensation* (2002), Brian Massumi suggested that intentional actions were as dependent on affect and involuntary response as on anything else. "In the circus of synesthesia," he wrote, "you never really know what act will follow.... Experience, normal or clinical, is never fully intentional. No matter how practiced the act, the result remains at least as involuntary as it is elicited" (191). In "The Turn to Affect: A Critique" (2011), Ruth Leys rebuked Massumi's position and criticized what she saw as the "anti-intentionalism" of affect theory in both the sciences and the humanities. "What the new affect theorists and the neuroscientists share," she wrote, "is a commitment to the idea that there is a gap between the subject's affects and its cognition ... such that cognition or thinking comes 'too late' for reasons, beliefs, intentions, and meanings to play the role in action and behavior usually accorded to them" (443). Many took issue with this accusation of "anti-intentionalism."

Responding to Leys, Jonathan Flatley argued that "affects and moods may not be directly subject to intentions ... but this does not mean that there is no way to exert agency in relation to our affects and affective experiences, only that such agency is mediated, variable, and situated."[2] As it leaves open the possibility of mental causation, this version of intention seems more moderate than Massumi's. But Flatley's sense of affective mediation still leaves us unable to consider the possibility or content of authorial intentions. And even in its moderate position it renders "intention" an unusable concept. The consensus among Massumi, Leys, and Flatley is that affects are noncognitive phenomena; in the same way that they aren't caused by thoughts, or representative of thoughts, affects aren't fully cognizable either. So let's imagine an intentional action, *A*. If my affects mediate *A*, but I only have limited control over (and imperfect cognitive access to) those affects, then this means that I could only ever have imperfect knowledge of *A*. But this creates a logical problem. For while it's entirely conceivable that I might execute *A* imperfectly, or perform some other action accidentally, it's both a category-mistake and a contradiction to say I don't know my own intentions, whether in part or in whole. If I don't know my own intentions, then, by definition, they aren't intentions at all—they're something else. Or, to put it another way: it's entirely possible, even probable, that a reader might guess a poet's intentions incorrectly. We do this all the time. It's logically absurd, however, to say that about the poet herself.

My own attitude toward authorial intention is likely clear by now. In her book *Intention* (1957), Elizabeth Anscombe defined intentional actions as "the ones to which the question 'Why' is given application" (24). Unsurprisingly, Anscombe excluded those actions wherein self-knowledge is mitigated or mental causation is absent (i.e., reflexes). Like Cavell, I believe that this application of "Why?" is methodologically essential, and logically necessary, to our work as literary critics—even if our own answers to the question are wrong. But my goal here isn't to offer yet another repudiation of the intentional fallacy or anti-intentionalism. Instead, I'd like to make an argument for how these problems with authorial intention began, why they persist in the ways they do, and the stakes entailed therein. My claim is that the intentional fallacy—along with the other hallmarks of close reading, such as the affective fallacy and the anti-historicism associated with the New Critics—originated in a sequence of critics adapting Watsonian behaviorism for the purposes of literary study.[3] This chapter, therefore, gives behaviorism a central place in the development of modern Anglo-American critical practice and in the foundations of literary study as a discipline. Moreover, this chapter shows the different layers of mind-body category-mistakes embedded in such critical practice—and the ways behavioristic psychology became a tool for defining, and determining the entailments of, poetic language. In the 1920s, as Watson's ideas expanded into analytic philosophy, Ivor Armstrong (I. A.) Richards synthesized behaviorism into an interpretive protocol he termed "practical criticism." As such, Richards treated poems as if they were *behaviors*, in the Watsonian sense of the term: observable actions to be studied without recourse to unobservable mental states. Poems couldn't be read as descriptions or indices of authorial mental states, such that certain mental predicates had no place in critical language. But by virtue of poetry's ability to hijack sensory perception, Richards argued, poetry could effectively simulate visual and auditory content. Certain aspects of poetic language were therefore comparable to these nonlinguistic phenomena, as he granted poetry the special ability to impute properties across logical types. In the 1930s and 1940s, Richards's "practical criticism" met with strong resistance from critics such as John Crowe Ransom, Allen Tate, and the aforementioned Brooks, Wimsatt, and Beardsley. Wary of Richards's scientism and interest in the physiological effects of poetry, these critics stipulated a strictly semantic (i.e., nonaffective, nonpsychological) concept of poetic language—while nonetheless adapting many of Richards's concepts and methodological innovations. In that way, Richards's behaviorism-inflected practical criticism found itself the object of the New Critics' own behaviorism-inflected critique. The intentional and affective fallacies weren't problems solved by the New Critics so much as they were symptoms of the complicated, inconsistent logic of formalism itself—a formalism that is perpetuated today.

In order to prove these claims, I divide the rest of this chapter into four sections. In the first, I turn to the concept of behavior and demonstrate the way Watson's approach to that concept evolved over the course of his career. Initially he suggested that "behavior" could be defined without any reference to consciousness, such that mental predicates could not be used to describe observed actions. Only a year later, however, Watson insisted that mental states themselves were just misperceived behaviors, albeit internal ones. But these claims about the nature of behavior were not without controversy—even among psychological behaviorists. In the second section of this chapter, I show the ways that Richards, despite his criticism of Watson's "ontological" arguments, translated behaviorism into a protocol for reading poetry. Turning his classroom into an ersatz laboratory, Richards trained his students to respond to poetry without appealing to authorial psychology—that is, without the application of psychological predicates to poems. At the same time, Richards himself professed a concept of poetry that attributed psychological, visual, and haptic properties to poetic form. As I show in this chapter's third section, Richards's aspirations to scientific knowledge led some to worry about the reductionism inherent in his methods—while also worrying about the affective content that Richards assigned to poetic experience. Accordingly, critics such as Cleanth Brooks and W. K. Wimsatt transformed Richards's psychologism into a literary formalism—turning his affective concept of poetry into a strictly semantic one, such that neither psychological nor empirical predicates applied. Given this tortured history of obsolete psychology and disciplinary infighting, some might be tempted to get rid of close reading altogether. In this chapter's final section, however, I argue for the continued necessity of close reading, while also identifying some of the reasons for the intentional fallacy's critical longevity.

The Study of Behavior

Watson, of course, wasn't the first psychologist to privilege the study of behavior over that of consciousness. In *Animal Intelligence: Experimental Studies* (1911), Edward Lee Thorndike offered a similar perspective. Psychology's reliance on introspection, he claimed, had been detrimental in a number of ways. Like Watson, Thorndike was concerned about the accuracy of introspective data—a topic I will discuss in greater detail in chapter 2. But he was even more concerned about how such data were given priority over behavioral observation. Among Wundtian psychologists, he wrote, "there was a tendency to an unwise, if not bigoted, attempt to make the science of human nature synonymous with the science of facts revealed by introspection" (3). Within the disciplinary parameters of psychology, behavioral observation could be used to confirm introspective data, but it could never challenge them. This was particularly problematic for animal psychologists, Thorndike explained, as animals couldn't give verbal accounts of their experiences. As a result, behavioral observation was devalued as a research protocol, even though it was easier to analyze. In *Animal Intelligence*, Thorndike sought to correct this, redefining experimental psychology as the objective science of *behavior*, and avoiding any talk of introspection or subjective experience. "Behavior is predictable," he wrote, "*without recourse to magical agencies.... Every response or change in response of an animal is then the result of the interaction of its original knowable nature and the environment*" (241-42; italics in the original).

Thorndike's sense of behavior, however, was far more capacious than we might expect—and certainly more nuanced than Watson's (or, later on, Richards's). As an object of psychological study, Thorndike claimed, behavior needed "to include all that biology includes under the term 'behavior,'" as well as "all that common sense means by the words 'intellect' and 'character'" (5). In contrast to Watson's complete severing of behavior from mental state, Thorndike's version of behavior was closer to what we might think of as "conduct" or "disposition." Indeed, even though he insisted on the primacy of observable behavior, Thorndike was committed to studying the eponymous "intelligence" of animals. In order to compare the inferential capacities of dogs and cats, Thorndike designed a crate with a large opening on the side; the door to this opening was controlled by a lever on the inside of the crate. A hungry dog or cat would be placed inside the crate, and a dish of food would be placed outside the crate. But while the hungry animal could see and smell the food, it couldn't reach it. The test was to see how long it would take the animal to press the lever initially—and then how long it would take for the animal to repeat this behavior (an example of the aforementioned laws of exercise and effect). Would the animal, Thorndike asked, infer the lever's function and then press it? Or it would it only act instinctively and, after hitting the lever accidentally several times, gradually associate it with the opening of the door? The answer, he concluded, was a combination of instinct, accident, and association: "No one who has seen the behavior of these animals when trying to escape could doubt that their actions were directed by instinctive impulses, not by rational observation. It is then absolutely the case that a dog or cat *can* open a door closed by a thumb latch or button, merely by the accidental success of its natural impulses" (73). Compared to cats, dogs were more likely to associate pressing the lever with opening the door. But neither, Thorndike concluded, showed any evidence of inferential reasoning.

Thorndike's discussion of the practical inseparability of behaviors and mental states gives us a sense of how extreme Watsonian behaviorism really was. While it was premised on the rejection of experimental introspection, "Psychology as the Behaviorist Views It" wasn't strictly an argument about methods. It was also an anti-metaphysical argument about the kinds of predicates that could or could not be used for behavioral description. In his introductory textbook *Essentials of Psychology* (1911), the psychologist Walter Pillsbury offered the following definition of psychology: "Mind is known from man's activities. Psychology may be most satisfactorily defined as the science of human behaviour" (1). As we might infer from Thorndike, Pillsbury's attention to behavior was perhaps unusual—particularly as Pillsbury studied human, rather than animal, psychology. Nonetheless, Pillsbury's psychology was thoroughly mentalistic in its orientation. But in "Psychology as the Behaviorist Views It," Watson seized on Pillsbury's definition—and left out the part about "mind is known from man's activities." "I believe," Watson wrote, "we can write a psychology, define it as Pillsbury, and never go back upon our definition: never use the terms consciousness, mental states, mind, content, introspectively verifiable, imagery, and the like" (166). Indeed, Watson's sense of psychology couldn't have been further from Pillsbury's. By Watson's account, no psychologist could ever say that "mind is known from man's activities"—because psychology wouldn't have words for "mind" or "know." Some of the phenomena generally denoted by these terms would be given physical descriptions. Others, however, wouldn't be described at all; they would fall outside psychology's language and its purview as a discipline. Either way, psychologists would be unable to employ mentalistic language to describe or explain the organism actions they observed. Therefore, "Psychology as the Behaviorist Views It" didn't just sever behavior from mental states methodologically. It attempted to do so logically as well, making it impossible for psychologists to assert any kind of conceptual or otherwise inferred relation between behavioral and mental phenomena.

The logical difficulties posed by the application of psychological predicates will reappear throughout this chapter (and, indeed, throughout this book). But it's worth noting that Watson's ideas on the subject continued to evolve after 1913. Only a year later, in *Behavior: An Introduction to Comparative Psychology* (1914), Watson maintained behaviorism's methodological core: the observation, prediction, and control of *behaviors*—organism actions without reference to or reliance on mentalistic concepts. But now the very concept of behavior had expanded, subsuming many of the mentalistic concepts that "Psychology as the Behaviorist Views It" had rejected. It wasn't enough to suggest that psychology *ought* to restrict itself to the study of observed behavior. Instead, Watson felt the need to proclaim that the objects of Wundtian psychological study—"centrally aroused sensations" or mental "images" (16) accessed through introspection—were in fact part of behaviorism's purview even though they were (*a*) mental and (*b*) unobservable. Watson's solution to this problem was to argue that these mental images weren't *mental* at all. Instead, they were "implicit" behaviors. Typically, Watson explained, we think of behavior as "explicit"—as involving large muscles and entailing visible actions. But there are also internal actions "involving only the speech mechanisms (or the larger musculature in a minimal way) . . . it goes on without adequate bodily portrayal" (19). The Wundtian image was such an implicit behavior—as was thinking more generally. In the same way that a reflex arc could circumvent (or "arc") the cerebral cortex entirely, Watson argued, the activity we call thinking primarily happens through the larynx and tongue. The only difference between speaking and thinking, he claimed, was that the former was voiced and the latter was not. And because "thinking" is silent and ostensibly private, we assume that it must be a different kind of action than speaking. But Watson had faith that this misperception of thinking and speaking would dissipate soon. Once psychology had the technological ability to monitor implicit behaviors, he believed, the reclassification of mental phenomena as behaviors would be inevitable: "Words spoken or faintly articulated belong really in the realm of behavior as do movements of the arms and legs. If implicit behavior can be shown to consist of nothing but word movements (or expressive movements of the word-type), the behavior of the human being as a whole is as open to objective control as the behavior of the lowest organism" (21). In other words, there was fundamentally no difference between human psychology and that of nonverbal animals. Even more importantly, there was relatively little about the mental life of humans that could not be studied as "behavior."

A Behaviorist Poetics

Watson's claims generated a fair amount of controversy, even among those sympathetic to behaviorism's aims. Some took aim specifically at his definitions of foundational concepts. In *Purposive Behavior in Animals and Men* (1932), the behaviorist Edward Chace Tolman claimed that Watson had failed to notice a key distinction among behaviors—that of *molecular* and *molar* actions (7).[4] Molecular behaviors, such as the twitching of a leg muscle, could in fact be explained through reflex conditioning. Molar behaviors, he claimed, are purposive—even intentional—and enact a new relationship between the test subject and his or her environment. The problem, Tolman argued, was that Watson acted like all behaviors have the same kinds of causes and follow the same sets of rules. Some behaviors, Tolman claimed, were in fact irreducible to their physiology—such that psychology's value as a discipline was similarly irreducible. Forty years before Fodor's token physicalism and Davison's mind-body supervenience, there was Tolman's defense of molar behavior: "An act *qua* 'behavior' has distinctive properties all its own. These are to be identified and described irrespective of whatever muscular, glandular, or neural processes underlie them. These new properties, thus distinctive of molar behavior, are presumably correlated with, and, if you will, dependent upon, physiological motions. But descriptively and per se they are other than those motions" (8).

In contrast, books such as Bertrand Russell's *The Analysis of Mind* (1921) attacked the ontological questions raised by Watson's ideas—although there were aspects of behaviorism that Russell praised. Watson, in fact, had helped Russell revise an early draft of *The Analysis of Mind*. As Russell wrote in the preface, "My thanks are due to Professor John B. Watson and to Dr. T.P. Nunn for reading my MSS. at an early stage and helping me with many valuable suggestions" (6). Nonetheless, Russell dismissed Watson's rejection of consciousness categorically. It was absurd, Russell argued, to define consciousness only as a misperception of habits, behaviors, and reflexes. This sense of consciousness, he claimed, would force behaviorists into a methodological double bind: in order to practice behavioristic psychology, one had to possess and access the very faculties whose existence Watson denied. "Images without beliefs," Russell wrote, "are insufficient to constitute memory; and habits are still more insufficient. The behaviourist, who attempts to make psychology a record of behaviour, has to trust his memory to make the record" (160). For Russell, Watson's rejection of consciousness amounted to a practical impossibility, even as he remained sympathetic to behaviorism's other aims.

I. A. Richards mirrored this critique in two early writings: *The Meaning of Meaning* (1923), which he coauthored with C. K. Ogden, and a review of Watson's *Behaviorism* that appeared in the March 1926 issue of the *New Criterion*. In *The Meaning of Meaning*, Ogden and Richards criticized Wundtian introspection and Watson's arguments against consciousness simultaneously. In studying how people perceive linguistic signs, they wrote, "we need neither confine ourselves to arbitrary generalizations from introspection after the manner of classical psychology, nor deny the existence of images and other 'mental' occurrences to their signs with the extreme Behaviorists" (22). Richards's review of *Behaviorism* for the *New Criterion* developed this critique. On the one hand, Richards admired Watson's focus on observable behavior and the insistence that such "behaviour should be conceived in terms of itself" (84). For these reasons, behaviorism was already preferable over psychoanalysis or Wundtian introspection. On the other hand, Richards thought that Watson's "ontological" argument—his denial of the existence of consciousness—was absurd and impractical. This denial, Richards wrote, "does not follow from [consciousness's] unobservable nature. We may not observe consciousness, but we have it or are it. . . . And in fact many of our observations of other things require it. In this respect the point of the behaviourist is hardly so much a point of view as a mistake" (83). In order for behaviorism to be useful or even coherent, Richards concluded, it would have to discard its ontological claims and restrict itself to the analyses of observable phenomena.

My claim here, of course, is that Richards's practical criticism amounted to such a behaviorism—defining the literary text as a behavior, to which psychological predicates could not be applied. And as I shall show, Richards wasn't entirely successful at escaping Watson's ontological arguments either, particularly with respect to the mental states of his students. On the whole, Richards's relationship to Watsonian behaviorism was a vexed one, vacillating between enthusiasm and caution. As he wrote in *Practical Criti-*

cism, "Damage is very likely already being done by elementary courses in Behaviourism and stimulus-response psychology. Yet it is not the inquiry which is harmful, but the stopping short of the inquiry" (303). My emphasis on behaviorism's relation to practical criticism, however, goes against the grain of most critical accounts.[5] The critical consensus seems summed up by Richards's biographer, Richard Russo. At best, Russo claims in *I. A. Richards: His Life and Work* (1989), Richards was "lured not by the premise but the promise of behaviorism" (175). Generally, Richards's contributions are attributed to other discourses. In *The Physiology of the Novel: Reading, Neural Science, and the Form of Victorian Fiction* (2007), Nicholas Dames sees Richards perpetuating the Victorian psychologies of George Henry Lewes and Alexander Bain, while also building on the neurology of Charles Sherrington, the psychology of William James, and the philosophy of G. E. Moore (249). Joseph Glicksohn and Chanita Goodblatt have disputed these kinds of influences on Richards. Instead, they have suggested that Richards was powerfully indebted to Gestalt psychology—particularly the work of Kurt Koffka. As they write in "Reclaiming I. A. Richards" (2014), Richards's work "should be viewed in the terms of a cognitive psychology that is familiar with both the Würzburg school and its outgrowth, the Gestalt school" (184).[6] The influence of behaviorism and Pavlovian physiology on Richards, they claim, has been overstated.[7]

I don't dispute the influence that Sherrington, James, Lewes, Bain, or Koffka had on Richards (although I remain unconvinced that he was first and foremost a Gestalt theorist of literature). There are key aspects of Richards's criticism, however, that can't be attributed to these influences: his aversion to analyzing authorial psychology and his categorical distrust of introspection. As he wrote in *Principles*, two years before his review in the *New Criterion*,

> Whatever the psycho-analysts may aver, the mental processes of the poet are not a very profitable field for investigation. They offer far too happy a hunting-ground for uncontrollable conjecture. Much that goes to produce a poem is, of course, unconscious. Very likely the unconscious processes are more important than the conscious, but even if we knew far more than we do about how the mind works, the attempt to display the inner workings of the artist's mind by the evidence of his work alone must be subject to the greatest dangers. . . . Nearly all speculations as to what went on in the artist's mind are unverifiable, even more unverifiable than the similar speculations as to the dreamer's mind. The most plausible ex-

planations are apt to depend on features whose actual causation is otherwise. (29-30)

Given Richards's rejection of Watson's ontological argument, the recognition of "unconscious processes" here is unsurprising. Nonetheless, Richards's reasoning is decidedly behavioristic. It matches both Watson's critique of introspection and his insistence on the study of observable phenomena. It also points to a somewhat surprising intersection between behaviorism and psychoanalysis, with both discourses dismissive of introspective self-knowledge. Literary critics, he explains, have two ways of knowing the "mental processes of the poet." Either they can infer the "inner workings" of her mind through her poems, or they can turn to the poet's self-reports (if those are available). But both of these strategies, Richards suggests, are unsatisfactory. Any attempt to know the poet's mind through their poetry would be necessarily speculative and unverifiable. Richards even goes as far as suggesting that the poet's mind is less verifiable—less analyzable—than that of a dreamer. Relying on the poet's self-knowledge is no more productive. As it's "very likely the unconscious processes are more important than the conscious," the poet wouldn't have conscious access to the mental states in question. The introspective self-knowledge of the critic, however, doesn't seem to be an issue for Richards (or, at least, not yet).

In that way, *Principles* laid the groundwork for *Practical Criticism*'s development of a behaviorist poetics, where poems are analyzed without reference or recourse to authorial mental states. But while *Principles* supported this claim on primarily empirical grounds, *Practical Criticism* adds an additional justification premised explicitly on language processing. When we encounter a linguistic utterance, Richards explains, one of two things usually happens. If the utterance fails to make sense, as might be true of "the ravings of mania or the dream maunderings of a neurotic," we use the method of the "alienist," or psychiatrist. In those cases we try to interpret the language in question by imagining the mental processes that produced them. But linguistic utterances that make sense—that signify, parse, and follow convention—are processed very differently:

> Whenever we hear or read any not too nonsensical opinion, a tendency so strong and automatic that it must have been formed along with our earliest speech-habits, leads us to consider *what seems to be said* rather than the *mental operations* of the person who said it. . . . Ordinarily we at once try to consider the objects his words seem to stand for and not the mental goings-on that led him to use the

words. We say that we "follow his thought" and mean, not that we have traced what happened in his mind, but merely that we have gone through a train of thinking that seems to end where he ended. (6)

According to Richards, readers and listeners induce semantic meaning from the particularities of "sensical" utterances rather than by trying to infer the mental state of the speaker or writer. This process, we're told, is automatic—such that the consideration of verbal behaviors without reference or recourse to mental states is neither abnormal nor unnatural. Instead, it's the typical state of affairs. The behavioristic separation of word and mind, Richards claims, is so ingrained that it must have "been formed along with our earliest speech habits." When both speaker and listener are of sound mind, this is how semantic meaning is processed. The alternative is only necessary when "some very special circumstance calls us back" (6-7) to the presumed mental states of the speaker, whether because of linguistic peculiarity or psychiatric pathology.

But while poetry surprises us and challenges us, as we infer from Richards, such difficulties are not so great as to require the alienist's methods. Instead, *Practical Criticism* developed an interpretive protocol based on the reader who can make no reference to authorial mental states—who gleans meaning only from "*what seems to be said* rather than the *mental operations* of the person who said it.*" To test the effectiveness of this protocol, Richards transformed his classroom at Cambridge into a would-be laboratory. In the spring of 1926, just as his review of Watson appeared in the *New Criterion*, Richards's "Practical Criticism" seminar at Cambridge instantiated many of Watson's arguments against introspective psychology (and, at times, veered toward the ontological arguments that Richards had attacked). In the seminar, Richards presented his students with radically decontextualized poems—with no titles, author names, identifying marks, or clues about their origin. Such decontextualization, Richards hoped, would make psychological speculation impossible and force students to restrict their analyses to the poetic text exclusively. After reading each poem, students presented Richards with a written analysis of the text; these written analyses became *Practical Criticism*'s main body of evidence. As his students analyzed the verbal behaviors of unknown and unknowable poets, the students themselves produced verbal behaviors, which Richards in turn analyzed as such. The only difference was that Richards allowed himself to refer to the minds and mental faculties of his students, although he tended to do so in terms of habit, stimulus, and response.

Behaviorism and the Beginnings of Close Reading 45

We can see this in *Practical Criticism*'s discussions of what Richards labeled "Poem 3" and "Poem 6." Let's consider two versions of the first four lines of "Poem 3." The first is how the poem first appeared in print (fig. 1); it is a facsimile of John Donne's *Poems* (1633), published two years after the poet's death.[8] The second is how Richards presented it to his seminar (as copied from appendix D of *Practical Criticism*):

> At the round earth's imagined corners blow
> Your trumpets, angels, and arise, arise
> From death, you numberless infinities
> Of souls, and to your scattered bodies go. (352)

These are the opening lines of Donne's "Holy Sonnet IV," which Richards mislabels as "Holy Sonnet VII." In appendix C of *Practical Criticism*, Richards explains how he tailored the poem to the demands of the experiment. His notes are as follows: "*Poem 3*. JOHN DONNE (1573). *Holy Sonnets VII*. Probably composed in 1618. The modernized spelling was adopted in the interests of the experiment" (350). By Richards's reasoning, the anachronistic spelling of the 1633 edition—"imagin'd," "Angells," "numberlesse"—would have invited his students to speculate about authorship and, in turn, speculate about authorial psychology. As a result, Richards scoured the text typographically and removed any identifying marks.

This procedure, however, wasn't exclusive to seventeenth- and eighteenth-century authors. More recent works, such as George Manley Hopkins's "Spring and Fall: To a Young Child," which was written in 1880 but first published in 1918, were also scoured of their identifying marks. This was the hidden identity of "Poem 6," which underwent even more drastic redaction than "Poem 3." A facsimile of the first edition appears in figure 2.[9] The following version is the one Richards presented to his seminar:

> Margaret, are you grieving
> Over Goldengrove unleafing?
> Ah! as the heart grows older
> It will come to such sights colder
> By and by, nor spare a sigh
> Though worlds of wanwood leafmeal lie;
> And yet you will weep and know why. (353)

The most glaring difference between these versions is that Richards has omitted the third and fourth lines of the poem. Richards never addresses

> **IV.**
>
> At the round earths imagin'd corners, blow
> Your trumpets, Angells, and arise, arise
> From death, you numberlesse infinities
> Of soules, and to your scattred bodies goe,
> All whom the flood did, and fire shall o'erthrow,
> All whom warre, death, age, agues, tyrannies,
> Despaire, law, chance, hath slaine, and you whose eyes,
> Shall behold God, and never tast deaths woe,
> But let them sleepe, Lord, and mee mourne a space,
> For, if above all these, my sinnes abound,
> 'Tis late to aske abundance of thy grace,
> When wee are there; here on this lowly ground,
> Teach mee how to repent; for that's as good
> As if thou'hadst seal'd my pardon, with thy blood.

Figure 1. From John Donne's "Holy Sonnet IV" (in Donne, *Poems*, 34).

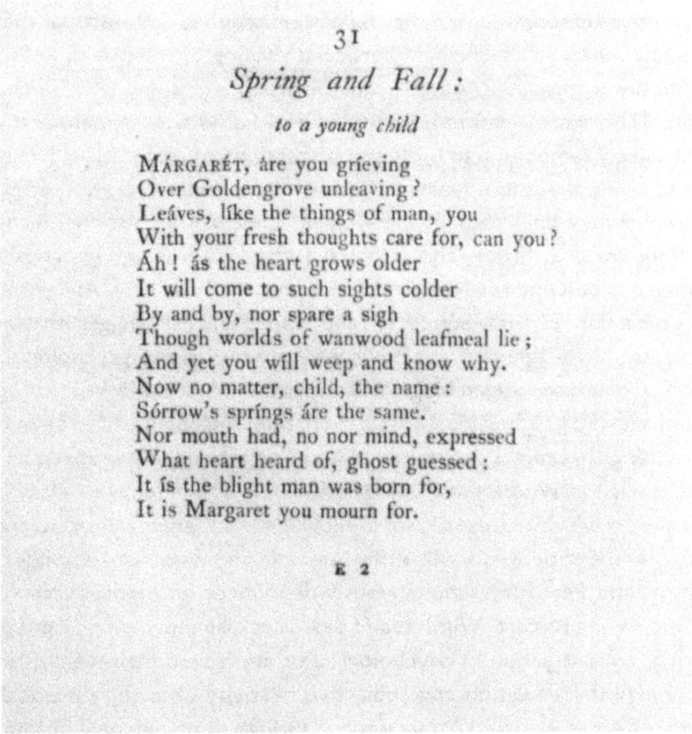

Spring and Fall:

to a young child

MÁRGARÉT, áre you gríeving
Over Goldengrove unleaving?
Leáves, líke the things of man, you
With your fresh thoughts care for, can you?
Áh! ás the heart grows older
It will come to such sights colder
By and by, nor spare a sigh
Though worlds of wanwood leafmeal lie;
And yet you will weep and know why.
Now no matter, child, the name:
Sórrow's springs áre the same.
Nor mouth had, no nor mind, expressed
What heart heard of, ghost guessed:
It ís the blight man was born for,
It is Margaret you mourn for.

Figure 2. From Gerard Manley Hopkins's "Spring and Fall: To a Young Child" (in Hopkins, *Poems of Gerard Manley Hopkins*, 51).

their absence. Without more information it's hard to say whether the omission is intentional (would comments on Margaret's "fresh thoughts" constitute a kind of psychological speculation?) or an unforced error. He also neglects to mention the change of "unleaving" to "unleafing." Instead, his comments on "Poem 6" are largely restricted to the removal of Hopkins's rhythmical markings. This removal was made for both methodological and interpretive reasons—preserving the aforementioned "interests of the experiment" but also advancing a particular reading of the poem. Referring specifically to the line "And yet you will weep and know why," Richards writes, "This mark I omitted, partly to see what would happen, partly to avoid a likely temptation to irrelevant discussions. Without it, 'will' may be read as giving the future tense, as [Student #13] reads it" (79). If we go by his commentary on "Poem 3," the avoided "irrelevant discussions" Richards mentions are likely history and authorial psychology. The anti-historical bias so often attributed to the New Criticism looms overhead here. And yet Richards's redactions of "Holy Sonnet IV" and "Spring and Fall" suggest that some of this anti-historical bias was actually a by-product of anti-psychologism. If historical data encouraged biographical speculation, and biographical speculation allowed psychological speculation, then the poem had to be purged of anything that might seem unmodern. This reasoning was made all the more explicit in Wimsatt and Beardsley's essay "The Affective Fallacy," despite the essay's resolute criticism of Richards as an "affective" or psychologistic literary critic. (As I will show later on, this was not the only time Wimsatt and Beardsley simultaneously denounced and reproduced Richards's ideas.) At its core, Wimsatt and Beardsley claimed, historical criticism was just an abstraction of psychological or affective criticism—displacing psychological speculation and subjective relativity onto the historical archive. "Affective criticism," they wrote, "though in its personal or impressionistic form it meets with strong dislike from scholars, yet in its theoretical or scientific form finds strong support from the same quarter. The historical critic, if not much interested in his own personal responses or in those of his students, is intensely interested in whatever can be discovered about those of any member of Shakespeare's audience" (*Verbal Icon*, 28).

Richards, however, was intensely interested in the responses of his students. But it would be a mistake to say that his approach to these responses was entirely mentalistic. While he certainly engaged in psychological speculation about each response's author, this speculation was preoccupied with the automatic, ready-made quality of his students' ideas. Richards termed these "stock responses." He points to Student #15's analysis of "Poem 3" as an example: "Mouthfuls of words. Has no appeal whatsoever. Make a good hymn—in fact, that's the way the meter goes. Too religious for one who doesn't believe in repenting that way" (43). This student's reading of the poem, Richards explains, was overwhelmed by his automatic response to the text's religious content—so much so that the student misapprehends the poem's objective features. "That a stock response," Richards writes, "elicited merely by the religious subject-matter, should be able to make a sonnet sound like a hymn is a fact that surely stretches our notions of the mind's power over matter" (43). Richards is being a bit dramatic about the "mind's power over matter" here, and maybe a little coy. But his explanation of the mechanisms behind stock responses requires no notional stretching at all. When a poem activates a stock response, he writes, "the button is pressed, and then the author's work is done, for immediately the record starts playing in quasi- (or total) independence of the poem which is supposed to be its origin or instrument" (14). Earlier I discussed Richards's rejection of the "ontological" component of Watsonian behaviorism. But here, as he speculates about the nature of stock responses, he portrays a mind overrun by automatic, unthinking processes. The metaphor of the phonograph is a significant one. When we press the "button" on Richards's proverbial phonograph, we do not suppose that the machine in front of us has any understanding or phenomenal experience of the music it plays. Richards believes his students to be analogous to such a machine: their critical efforts are less products of thinking or reasoning than they are of a "button" being pressed and reflexes kicking into gear.

Richards's abnegation of critical mental states was therefore less complete, and less categorical, than his abnegation of creative or poetic mental states. But the overall behaviorism of Richards's efforts—his rejection of mentalistic language to talk about verbal behaviors, his attenuation of intentional action and mental causation—is clear enough. As I will show later in this chapter, it was precisely these aspects of Richards's work that Wimsatt and Beardsley transformed into "The Intentional Fallacy." But in terms of this book's larger trajectory, Richards's methods are an early example of how writers used behaviorism to reconceive the attribution of mental properties to language and form—whether they prohibited the attribution of mental properties entirely or misattributed those same properties across category lines. As we have seen, the former was a key dimension of *Practical Criticism*'s methodological protocols. The latter, I suggest, inhered in Richards's sense of poetic experience, as well as the physiological and epistemological differences he perceived in poetic language and nonpoetic language.

The nature of poetic experience and language, of course, were the main topics of *Principles of Literary Criticism*, which drew on behaviorism as well as Pavlovian physiology, Sherringtonian neurology, and Gestalt psychology. This appeal to science would be one of the reasons that Richards was criticized by the American New Critics, who insisted that Richards had sought physiological solutions to formal problems. Richards maintained, however, that literary criticism had an obligation to keep up with advances in psychology and neurology. In so doing, critics had the opportunity to correct some of the misconceptions that had become commonplace in literary study. First and foremost among these was the separation of "aesthetic" or "poetic" experience from other kinds of experience. This separation, Richards claimed, could be traced back to Kant. "All modern aesthetics," he wrote, "rests upon the assumption . . . that there is a distinct *kind* of mental activity present in what are called aesthetic experiences. . . . Thus arises the phantom problem of the aesthetic mode or aesthetic state, a legacy from the days of abstract investigation into the Good, the Beautiful, and the True" (11-12). But the "aesthetic state," Richards maintained, was neither neurologically nor epistemologically different from other types of experience. Returning us to some of the ideas I raised in my introduction, Richards claimed that aesthetic experiences were neurologically similar and comparable to nonaesthetic experiences, even if they appeared necessarily dissimilar and incomparable. "When we read a poem, or look at a picture, or listen to music," he explained, "we are not doing something quite unlike what we were doing on our way to the Gallery or when we dressed in the morning. The fashion in which experience is caused in us is different, and as a rule the experience is more complex and, if we are successful, more unified. But our activity is not of a fundamentally different kind" (17). By this account, the difference between looking at a poem and getting dressed in the morning, or eating a donut, is one of degree rather than type. If these experiences feel different to us, we infer from Richards, it's because of "complexity" or the number of neurons used rather than different parts of the brain being engaged, or different bodily organs being activated.[10]

But despite claiming that reading a poem and getting dressed are the same kind of experience, Richards also claimed that poetry was irreducibly distinct from other types of language use. The semantic content of a poem, he claimed, was inseparable from both the poem's form and the sensory stimuli produced by reading. Additionally, poetic language wasn't denotative, in contrast to scientific and philosophical propositions.[11] In *Science and Poetry* (1926), Richards announced that poems made *pseudo-statements* rather than *statements*. These pseudo-statements weren't factually "true" but psychologically "true" in that they reproduced in readers the experiences of the poet. The pseudo-statement, therefore, transmitted a different kind of data than standard propositions. If scientific and philosophical statements conveyed meanings, the poetic pseudo-statement conveyed experience itself. Or, as Richards explained, "It is never what a poem *says* which matters, but what it *is*. . . . The words will reproduce in [a reader's mind] a similar play of interests putting him for the while into a similar situation and leading to a similar response" (25-26). Typically, we would say that knowing an object empirically and reading a description of such empirical knowledge are not epistemologically comparable. In short, they are different types of experiences. But in Richards's scheme, the sensory stimuli of the poem could overcome this epistemological difference, such that the linguistic representation of the object would be tantamount to experiencing the object firsthand.[12] The language of philosophy could only transmit propositional meaning. The language of poetry, however, could re-create any number of nonlinguistic perceptions—including visual imagery, smells, tactile sensations, and so on. As long as the poet correctly anticipated the reader's responses to stimuli, the poem could effectively transfer mental states from one person to another—despite possessing no mental properties, or subjective experiences, of its own.

What we see in *Principles* and *Science and Poetry* is a set of scientific and formal explanations as to why poetry can turn one type of knowledge into another and then transmit subjective experience by way of paper and ink. This, I believe, gives new significance to one of the more memorable moments in *Principles*: Richards's neurological "hieroglyph" of a line from Robert Browning's "Pan and Luna" (1880) (fig. 3). Richards stresses that this picture is not a mimetic representation of the nervous system. "The spatial relations of the parts of the diagram," he explains, "are not intended to stand for spatial relations between parts of what is represented" (*Principles*, 117). But in giving us this particular image of "Arcadia, Night, a Cloud, Pan, and the Moon" stimulating a reader's mind, Richards implies that there is a necessary *physiological* cause for poetry's ability to transform one type of knowledge into another. If poetry allows linguistic representation to be tantamount to empirical experience, the reasoning goes, it's because that's how

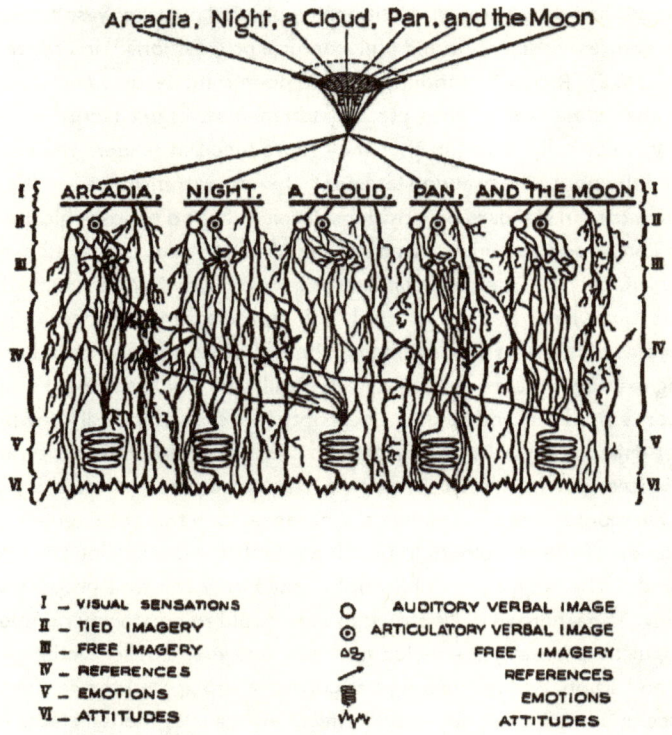

Figure 3. I. A. Richards's neurological "hieroglyph" of a line from Robert Browning's "Pan and Luna" (Richards, *Principles of Literary Criticism*, 116).

our brains function—processing poetic stimuli automatically and beyond the scope of our interventions. Immediately after the line enters the eye, it is processed as a "visual sensation" (I). This sensation, however, immediately elicits "tied imagery" (II) from the poem and associated "free imagery" (III); imagery here refers not to visual data per se but to sensory impressions more broadly. These sensory impressions are then connected to "references" (IV)—nonsensory "thinkings" (117) in the mind that are semantically associated with the line of poetry. These thinkings and sensory impressions then elicit "emotions" (V) and "affective-volitional attitudes" (VI). In effect, Richards sees Browning's line not just mixing linguistic knowledge with empirical knowledge but mixing cognitive mental states with noncognitive states as well (i.e., affect). But any epistemological or logical differences between these different states, we infer, would be quickly superseded by the overall experience of reading the poem.

Richards offers a similar step-by-step analysis of poetic perception in *Science and Poetry*. There he shows the extent to which poetic language can misattribute properties across category lines—and how essential this misattribution is to poetic experience. But whereas *Principles* claimed that this misattribution occurred as a result of the reader's psychological associations, *Science and Poetry* illustrates that we actually perceive these misattributions as if they were qualities of the poem itself. This is most obvious in Richards's discussion of Wordsworth's "Composed upon Westminster Bridge, September 3, 1802" (1807), which relies on a sequence of metaphors to illustrate the categorical misattributions entailed by reading the poem. When we read, Richards explains, "the first things to occur . . . are the sound of the words 'in the mind's ear' and the feel of the words imaginarily spoken. These together give the *full body*, as it were, to the words, and it is with the full bodies of words that the poet works, not their printed signs" (12). The most obvious categorical misattribution here is "the mind's ear." This phrase is no more metaphorical or catachrestic than the phrase "the mind's eye"—it just isn't conventionally idiomatic. As a result, it defamiliarizes an aspect of poetic reading we might otherwise take for granted: even when we read silently, poems have empirical (namely, aural) qualities —as if our minds somehow had *ears*. To read the poem, therefore, is to experience sounds where none ought to exist. As a result of these sounds, the poem's words acquire physical properties—a "*full body*"—that they wouldn't have otherwise. This misattribution of properties shapes the reader's visual experiences as well. Even as the poem's words are cast across the retina, what the reader sees are "pictures . . . not of words but of things for which the words stand; perhaps of ships, perhaps of hills; and together with them, it may be, other images of various sorts. Images of what it feels like to stand leaning on the parapet of Westminster Bridge" (12). Richards's slippage between visual "images" and sensory "images" here is amusing. But it's also important in its own right, perhaps. Either the poem's visual content has somehow acquired haptic content, or different types of information really do become interchangeable through poetic experience, despite the logical and epistemological differences they entail.

Paradoxes and Fallacies

As might be inferred from contemporary cognitive criticism, Richards's scientific, affective concept of poetry has proven incredibly durable.[13] During the 1930s and 1940s, however, many critics were ready—and eager—to consign *Principles of Literary Criticism*, *Practical Criticism*, and *Science and Poetry* to the ash heap of critical history. Richards's appeals to science and affective psychology were of particular concern. William Empson, who had been Richards's student at Cambridge, thought that his former teacher's reductionism precluded meaningful commentary on what was unique and important about poetry. As he wrote in *Seven Types of Ambiguity* (1930), "It would be tempting to say I was concerned with science rather than with beauty; to treat poetry as a branch of applied psychology. But, so far as poetry can be regarded dispassionately, so far as a critic has made himself dispassionate about it, so far as he has repressed sympathy in favor of curiosity, he has made himself incapable of examining it" (314). The American New Critics were even less forgiving than Empson. In "The Present Function of Criticism" (1940), the former Fugitive poet Allen Tate claimed that Richards's writings were replete with the "hocus pocus" of psychology, neurology, and Pavlovian physiology. Richards's work, he explained, bore "the elaborate charts of nerves and nerve-systems that purport to show how the 'stimuli' of poems elicit 'responses.' . . . How many innocent young men—myself among them—thought, in 1924, that laboratory jargon meant laboratory demonstration!" (9). In *The New Criticism* (1941), John Crowe Ransom's position was somewhere between Empson's and Tate's. "When you think of a thing as the cause of something else," he wrote, "you waive interest in it for itself. To Richards the object known in a poem—whether its status be that of a real or of an illusory object—is preferably a mere stimulus that produces first a set of emotions, and presently a set of attitudes" (15). Looking back to the diagram of "Arcadia, Night, a Cloud, Pan, and the Moon," we can at least confirm that Ransom doesn't misrepresent Richards's ordering of stimulus responses.[14]

For the purposes of examining behaviorism's place in critical history, as well as the category-mistakes entailed by Richards's poetics and perpetuated by his detractors, there are two New Critical concepts I want to focus on here.[15] The first is Cleanth Brooks's notion of poetry as "paradox," which he raised in *The Well Wrought Urn* (1947). The second is the aforementioned intentional fallacy, which William K. Wimsatt and Monroe C. Beardsley described in "The Intentional Fallacy" (1946) and later reprinted in *The Verbal Icon* (1954). These critics rejected Richards's scientism and psychologism wholeheartedly, as well as the logical peculiarities of his affective poetics. To replace this poetics, Brooks and Wimsatt and Beardsley offered purportedly semantic concepts of poetic experience. When we read a poem, they argued, we are not responding to the physiological stimuli that comprise words and forms. Instead, we are perceiving the poet's ideas through the poem's layered—and at times contradictory—semantic meanings. And yet, as they attempted to attribute poetic experience to meaning, both Brooks and Wimsatt and Beardsley failed to avoid following Richards's example, although they failed in different ways. Brooks's paradoxical notion of poetry—which wasn't paradoxical at all—amounted to a sly reconfiguration of Richards's affective poetics and the logical reasoning behind it. In contrast, Wimsatt and Beardsley attempted to quash Richards's affective poetics by replicating Richards's own behavioristic rejection of authorial mental states, thereby precluding the application of mental predicates to poetic language.

Like Tate and Ransom, Wimsatt and Beardsley were utterly disdainful of Richards's theories. Brooks, however, was more measured in his critique. As he wrote in *The Well Wrought Urn*, "My purpose is not to welcome Richards as a returned prodigal. Richards is not a renegade but a pioneer who started out from a different set of assumptions" (266). For Brooks, the most fundamental of these assumptions was Richards's belief that literary criticism could be objective (a belief shared by Wimsatt). In contrast, Brooks conceded that the analyses in *The Well Wrought Urn* could be "hopelessly subjective" (217). But if literary critics wished to avoid relativism, and wished to maintain poetry's separation from other types of language use, such subjective judgment was essential. Therefore, "for better or for worse, the judgments are rendered, not in terms of some former historical period and not merely in terms of our own, the judgments are very frankly treated as if they were universal judgments" (217). This is the imperious, anti-historical, almost intellectually decadent sensibility so many of us associate with the New Critics—synthesizing, perhaps, Richards's methodological bias against historical speculation with Brooks's own peculiar Kantianism. But as John Guillory notes, this might have been part of Brooks's strategy to place poetry outside the reaches of the scientific disciplines and logical positivism. "Brooks' theory," he writes, "concedes a very great deal to the epistemological tyranny of science (really, to the positivist 'philosophy of science' regnant between the wars), but only because that concession is strategic, because scientific truth has already been stigmatized as the origin of our dissociated modernity."[16]

But Brooks's commitment to subjective knowledge might have been less strategic, and more contradictory, than Guillory indicates. Or as Gerald Graff sums it up (if a little glibly), *The Well Wrought Urn* comprises "Ricardian psychologism in new trappings."[17] For while Brooks rejected Richards's affective poetics and ambitions of scientific objectivity, his own methods and conclusions were nearly identical. And far from being "hopelessly subjective," his discussions of poetic language seemed to discount the subjective experience of reading entirely. His analysis of paradox is a prime example. In the first chapter of *The Well Wrought Urn*, Brooks announced that "the language of poetry was fundamentally the language of paradox" (3). Whereas scientists make propositional statements about the world, he reasoned, the poet is not so logically restricted. In a poem, Brooks wrote, "terms are continually modifying each other, and thus violating their dictionary meanings" (9). Paradox and multiple, incompatible meanings are therefore inevitable. But in contrast to Richards's affective poetics—which entailed the categorical misattribution of mental and physical predicates—this language of paradox is disembodied. There's no indication that a poem such as Wordsworth's "Composed upon Westminster Bridge," which Brooks examined in detail, would transmit or evoke anything extrasemantic. Richards's diagram of Browning's "Pan and Luna" imagined a version of the nervous system that could account for poetry's ability to simulate all sorts of nonlinguistic phenomena. In Brooks's analysis, however, the poet's words "modify" each other in an undefined space, so to speak. This space is neither physical nor mental. Modification occurs neither on the written page nor in the minds of writer or reader. Instead, Brooks presents this modification as occurring within an ethereal, hypostatic world of idealized language use. There the meanings of the poem proliferate freely and paradoxically, without either logical or psychological constraint. Think of a poem, Brooks seems to tell us, when you aren't there.[18]

The difficulty with Brooks's disembodied world of paradox, however, is that it, too, is predicated on physiologically affective poetics. But whereas Richards claimed that poetry's ability to simulate nonlinguistic properties was a perception created by poetry, Brooks claims that the unity of poetic form can sustain physical and psychological predicates. The language of poetry, it seems, isn't that of *paradox* but that of *category-mistake*—a relation comprising the misattribution of properties across category lines rather than one of contradictory semantic meanings. This is apparent in Brooks's reading of "Composed upon Westminster Bridge"—a poem he describes as containing "some very flat writing and some well-worn comparisons" (5). Nonetheless, he concedes that the poem is successful. The question is *how* it achieves that success: "The reader may ask: Where, then, does the poem get its power? It gets it, it seems to me, from the paradoxical situation out of which the poem arises. The speaker is honestly surprised, and he manages to get some sense of awed surprise into the poem. It is odd to the poet that the city should be able to 'wear the beauty of the morning' at all. Mount Snowden, Skiddaw, Mont Blanc, these wear it by natural right, but surely not grimy, feverish London" (5-6). When Brooks suggested that the "language of poetry was the language of paradox," and that poetic words violate their dictionary meanings continually, the implication was that paradox was a property of language. A phrase can contain a paradox, but a bridge, or an epoch, can't. This is congruous with the concept of paradox we get from philosophy: a paradox is any statement wherein the veridicality of the statement implies its falsity (and vice versa). In short, you can't prove the claim *Q* without also proving the claim *not-Q*. Conversely, any attempt to prove *not-Q* would also prove *Q*. A famous example would be Epimenides's paradox, also known as the paradox of the Cretan liar. In "Mathematical Logic as Based on the Theory of Types" (1908), Bertrand Russell explained it in the following way: "The simplest form of this contradiction is afforded by the man who says 'I am lying;' if he is lying, he is speaking the truth, and vice versa" (222). In other words, the Cretan liar can't tell the truth without lying and can't lie without telling the truth. Accordingly, Brooks's analysis of Wordsworth's paradoxes raises some serious problems. First, while it's possible for a statement to be paradoxical, a situation can't be so. In saying that the poem's "power" emerges from the speaker's "paradoxical situation," Brooks has made paradox a problem of psychology rather than language or form—as both "power" and "situation" refer to psychological phenomena. At best, we might speculate that the situation on the bridge has *reminded* the speaker of feelings associated with linguistic and logical paradoxes. If so, poetry's own supposedly paradoxical qualities are largely beside the point.[19]

And that leads to a second serious problem raised by Brooks's reading of "Composed upon Westminster Bridge." Even if we were to grant the notion that situations can be "paradoxical," we run into the problem that neither the situation nor the line describing it bear any sign of paradox. There's nothing about London "wear[ing] the beauty of the morning" that suggests we can't assert this line's veridicality without also implying its falsehood. Instead, what Brooks seems to be pointing to is a peculiar combination of catachrestic metaphor and irony—a combination entailing the unexpected and defamiliarizing misattribution of properties sliding across logical type-boundaries. In other words, it's a layering of category-mistakes. In the same way that situations aren't typically "paradoxical," cities don't typically "wear" things. Furthermore, "beauty" isn't something one can wear. It's an abstract concept noun, such that one can possess "beauty" as one possesses "integrity" or "dignity." But to *wear* either of those properties, as one would a scarf or a shoe, is to attribute physical properties to an abstraction. Moreover, the very phrase "paradoxical situation" comprises the application of a logical-linguistic predicate to "situation"—which, as shorthand for the speaker's subjective experience of said situation, is a psychological concept. In effect, the poem itself becomes able to sustain psychological predicates, although in very small amounts. This is not to suggest that the poem has something like subjective experience—only that Brooks is able to attribute to the poem the sort of properties that language doesn't usually have. As he suggests, the speaker "manages to get some sense of awed surprise into the poem." Along those lines, Brooks's hypothetical reader does not ask, "*Why* does the poem have such a powerful effect on me?" (my emphasis). Instead, they ask, "*Where* . . . does the poem get its power" (my emphasis)—suggesting that this hypothetical reader has also conflated their psychological experience of the poem with the poem itself.

These same issues are presented by Brooks's central emblem for poetic form: John Donne's "well wrought urn." As Douglas Mao has shown, this New Critical tendency to see poems as "things" was central to the critical enterprise—a tendency that remains today. As Mao explains in "The New Critics and the Text-Object" (1996), the New Critics' "attachment to thingly reticence" became a way of distinguishing poetry from other forms of language and a "privileging of the poem's resistance to transparency" (248). This strikes me as right. But I would maintain that it's important to see Brooks's "urn" not merely as a *thing* but as a *linguistic thing* that, somehow, possesses nonlinguistic properties. In the case of the "well wrought urn," which originates in Donne's poem "The Canonization" (1633), Brooks describes said urn as sustaining not only physical predicates but visual ones as well. Responding to the lines "We'll be in sonnets pretty roomes; / As well a well wrought urne becomes / The greatest ashes, as halfe-acres tombes,"

Brooks writes that Donne's poem "is both the assertion and the realization of the assertion. The poet has actually before our eyes built within the song the 'pretty room' with which he says the lovers can be content. The poem itself is the well wrought urn which can hold the lovers' ashes" (17). If the poem comprised semantic meaning exclusively, then the "realization" of the "assertion" would simply be the assertion itself. But here, this "realization" is rendered as both a physical space ("pretty roomes") and something we can see ("the poet has before our eyes"). Granted, these physical and visual properties are perhaps metaphorical (and not unrelated to the Italian *stanza* meaning "room"). Even so, what matters is that Brooks's poetic experience has allowed him to bypass the logical absurdity that would otherwise be produced by saying, "Inside this poem there are several pretty rooms."

This was precisely the type of "error" that Wimsatt and Beardsley sought to correct in "The Affective Fallacy." There they castigated Brooks and Richards for their reliance on affective psychology (this was especially the case with Richards), as well as their conflation of psychological and linguistic phenomena. As Wimsatt and Beardsley explained, "The Affective Fallacy is a confusion between the poem and its *results* (what it *is* and what it *does*)" (21; italics in the original). Or, put another way, the affective fallacy is the categorical misattribution of perceived nonlinguistic phenomena, such as feelings or visual images, to linguistic objects (i.e., poems or novels). For Richards, this misattribution was, of course, what made poetic language special and powerful; Brooks largely shared this notion (although he was cagey about it). But for Wimsatt and Beardsley, such misattribution made it increasingly difficult to talk about poetry itself—redirecting the critic's attention to issues that had no direct bearing on poetic structure or meaning. Their point wasn't to deny that people experience literary language as somehow simulating nonlinguistic properties. Instead, it was to insist that any experiential predicates (I feel, I see, I hear, etc.) be restricted to descriptions of experience and eliminated from descriptions of literary objects themselves. As they explained, "Vividness is not the thing in the work by which the work may be identified, but the result of the cognitive structure, which *is* the thing. . . . The opaque accumulation of physical detail in some realistic novels has been aptly dubbed by Middleton Murry 'the pictorial fallacy'" (33). Such a "fallacy" wasn't merely inappropriate for criticism. By Wimsatt and Beardsley's reasoning, such misattributions couldn't exist in criticism at all. By virtue of their subjectivism and confusion between object and experience, they comprised a different intellectual mode entirely. As an example, Wimsatt and Beardsley turned to Brooks's chapter on Tennyson's "Tears, Idle Tears" (1847) in *The Well Wrought Urn*. "The last stanza," Brooks wrote, "evokes an intense emotional response from the reader" (174). Wimsatt and Beardsley counter, however, that, "this statement is not really a part of Brooks's criticism of the poem—rather a witness of his fondness for it" (34). In other words, it isn't close reading but rather literary appreciation.

In that way, "The Affective Fallacy" imbued Wimsatt and Beardsley's earlier essay "The Intentional Fallacy" with new significance. At its core, "The Intentional Fallacy" comprised a behavioristic response to the psychological, affective criticisms of Richards and Brooks. But despite Wimsatt and Beardsley's antipathy toward Richards's methods, "The Intentional Fallacy" mirrored Richards's own turn to behaviorism in *Practical Criticism*. As I showed earlier, *Practical Criticism* centered on Richards's adaptation of Watsonian behaviorism to redefine poems as analyzable behaviors—removing any reference to authorial consciousness. "The Intentional Fallacy" fundamentally reproduced this gesture, with "intention" functioning as a synecdoche for the broader class of authorial mental states. In effect, Richards's argument for the exclusion of authorial mental states from criticism found new life in Wimsatt and Beardsley: "the design or intention of the author is neither available nor desirable as a standard for the work of literary art" (3).[20]

The easiest way to see the behaviorism in "The Intentional Fallacy" is to throw the essay into relief. For as Wimsatt and Beardsley note, "The Intentional Fallacy" was not the first time they had teamed up to write about the problems entailed by authorial or artistic intention. "The present writers," they explain, "in a short article entitled 'Intention' for a *Dictionary* of literary criticism, raised the issue but were unable to pursue its implications at any length" (3). The dictionary in question was *The Dictionary of World Literature* (1943), edited by Joseph Twadell Shipley. Unlike their later essay, Wimsatt and Beardsley's dictionary entry doesn't dismiss the value or accessibility of authorial intention. Instead, it makes three points about the methodological difficulties posed by authorial intention: first, that inferring authorial intention usually requires both "internal" textual evidence and biographical evidence, although this hardly precludes the possibility of getting the intentions wrong; second, that any inference of intention must be corroborated by the literary text in question; and third, that the term "intention" has two frequently overlapping meanings—one referring to a text's *actual* meaning and the other referring to the *intended* meaning the author might have had in mind (329). The only "intentional fallacy" in Wimsatt and Beardsley's dictionary entry is one confusing aboutness (or *intentionality*, perhaps, in Franz Brentano's sense) with intent. As a rule, we cannot say that two similarly themed poems necessarily have the same intention, or that one poem realizes this intention better than the other. "A commonly occurring type of judgment," they wrote, "implies that two works have the same 'subject,' while one expresses it better than the other. . . . The fallacy arises if we then proceed to take the abstraction as the 'what' of the poems and to treat everything else in them as the 'how' to be judged with reference to the 'what'" (329). Let's take Donne's "The Canonization" and John Keats's "Ode on a Grecian Urn" (1819) as examples. As Cleanth Brooks would remind us, both of these poems are, at some level, about urns. This shared "what," however, can't be interpreted as a shared intention. Nor does it imply that every detail in these poems is somehow urn oriented.

These claims are profoundly different from the ones Wimsatt and Beardsley would make three years later. If the earlier dictionary entry outlined some of the methodological difficulties of inferring authorial intention, "The Intentional Fallacy" was broader in its purview. This is apparent from Wimsatt and Beardsley's attempt to define "intention": "'Intention,' as we shall use the term, corresponds to *what he intended* in a formula which more or less explicitly has had wide acceptance. 'In order to judge the poet's performance, we must know *what he intended*.' Intention is design or plan in the author's mind. Intention has obvious affinities for the author's attitude toward his work, the way he felt, what made him write" (4). Insofar as it makes "intention" an unusable concept, this is a terrible definition—an attempt, perhaps, to disable the very concept in question. As the excerpt begins, Wimsatt and Beardsley's sense of intention is so narrow ("what he intended") that it actually comprises a tautology. But as the discussion progresses, their sense of intention becomes both enormous and nebulous. As descriptions of an author's relation to a literary text, "plan" and "design" are no less ambiguous than "intention." Furthermore, the statement that "intention has obvious affinities for the author's attitude toward his work" casts doubt on what kind of knowledge intention actually comprises. If intention has obvious affinities for these attitudes, does that mean that intention itself is not such an "attitude" toward the text? If intention is not such an attitude, does it comprise propositional knowledge at all? If so, what is that knowledge about? By defining intention so sloppily, and by grouping it with similar (poorly defined) phenomena, Wimsatt and Beardsley transform intention from an executable idea to a broader class of concepts and phenomena—

including not only "what he intended" but also plans, designs, attitudes, the way the writer felt at the time of writing, and so on. Instead of speaking to a poet's intention to write a poem in a specific way, such that the poem might be read in equally specific ways, intention is now the term given to *any* mental state the poet has with regard to that poem. Essentially what "The Intentional Fallacy" prohibits isn't just the inference of authorial intention but any psychological language at all. Here, as in Richards's *Practical Criticism*, the poem is fundamentally a behavior—an observable human action to be analyzed without recourse or reference to mental states, even though no one assumes that the behavior in question is involuntary or unintentional.

This similarity to Richards extended into the justification Wimsatt and Beardsley offered for dismissing the relevance of authorial mental states. As I mentioned earlier, Richards claimed that his critical approach was based on how people perceive semantic meaning in ordinary conversation: "Whenever we hear or read any not too nonsensical opinion, a tendency so strong and automatic that it must have been formed along with our earliest speech-habits, leads us to consider *what seems to be said* rather than the *mental operations* of the person who said it" (*Practical Criticism*, 6; italics in the original). This notion takes a somewhat different form in "The Intentional Fallacy," part of which I quoted earlier: "There is a gross body of life, of sensory and mental experience, which lies behind and in some sense causes every poem, but can never be and need not be known in the verbal and hence intellectual composition which is the poem. For all the objects of our manifold experience, for every unity, there is an action of the mind which cuts off roots, melts away context—or indeed we should never have objects or ideas or anything to talk about" (12). Like Richards, Wimsatt and Beardsley ultimately justify the abnegation of authorial intention by appealing to what they see as the habits or automatic mechanisms of consciousness. But whereas Richards's justification was grounded in language use, Wimsatt and Beardsley speculate about the nature of perception more broadly. When a poet writes a poem, they claim, "there is a gross body of life, of sensory and mental experience" that contributes to the poem's existence. When someone reads that poem, however, that material isn't available. The reason that material is unavailable, however, has nothing to do with the nature of poetry or even of language. Instead, by virtue of being perceived "as a unity," the reader's mind itself "cuts off roots" and "melts away context." Ultimately, Wimsatt and Beardsley end up even more behavioristic than Richards—and preposterously so. In "The Intentional Fallacy," it's not just poetry that's cut off from mental states but *all objects of perception*—whether texts, behaviors, clouds, or closet doors. In an effort to prevent application of psychological predicates to literary texts, Wimsatt and Beardsley manufacture an absurd critical reality where such predicates apply to nothing at all. It is not the authorial mind that "cuts off roots, melts away context," but rather the critical one.

Unintended Consequences

My aim here has been to show behaviorism's contributions to Richards's practical criticism and, through Richards's influence, American New Criticism. Thus far, however, my own indebtedness to Richards and the New Critics has gone unacknowledged. I don't think the critics I've discussed would agree with many of my points—particularly with respect to my analyses of literary minds and the logical mechanisms that enable them. At the same time, my identification of the problems entailed by close reading has itself relied on a version of close reading. For that reason I think it's only fair to ask, given what I've shown about the behavioristic foundations of Richards's practical criticism, Brooks's paradoxes, and Wimsatt and Beardsley's fallacies, how can I justify close reading as a critical practice? And this is to say nothing of close reading's political and institutional histories—including its instrumentalization as a means of exclusion and cultural control.[21] Might it be incumbent on me to reject close reading as a methodology and replace it with something else?

Certainly, this chapter has made no secret of close reading's shortcomings. Nonetheless, I do believe that close reading is an important critical and pedagogical tool. And I believe this not in spite of close reading's relation to behaviorism but because of it. Given how easily both readers and professional critics impute mental properties to language, as well as the crucial role such imputation plays in our perceptions of literature, there is value in a method that tries to separate psychological concepts from critical ones (even if that effort is sometimes unsuccessful and/or done for the wrong reasons). Moreover, many of the logical and formal problems I've described in this chapter—problems both identified and created by Richards, Brooks, and Wimsatt and others—were produced not by the presence of behavioristic reasoning in close reading but rather by attempts to mask or misapply that reasoning. The intentional fallacy is an example of this. We perceive authorial intentions all the time; if we didn't, then we wouldn't have a critical prohibition against doing so. Our perceptions of these intentions might be right or wrong, but there's no logical problem (i.e., category-mistake or contradiction) in saying that a text gives the impression of its author having worked toward a particular goal. The difficulties begin when a stronger determinative relation between thought and language is asserted, or when it's assumed that language and thought follow the same kinds of rules and sustain the same kinds of predicates. This is what Richards did when he claimed that language could actually transmit the mental states of poets to readers—even as he also treated poems as isolatable behaviors. Wimsatt and Beardsley countered this category-mistake with their own. Instead of correcting Richards's error in its specificity, they rejected all psychological content in critical language. They suggested that seeing language as *representing* authorial mental states is just as much a fallacy as seeing language *containing or delivering* authorial mental states. At one level Wimsatt and Beardsley were indeed reminding us of the crucial distinction between the actual minds of authors and literary minds—that is, those figures in texts that appear to have mental properties or follow mental rules. But at another level, Wimsatt and Beardsley fundamentally confused the issue by treating actual minds and literary minds as if they were the same type of phenomenon.

This confusion is one of the reasons that the intentional fallacy has proven so enduring, and frustrating, as a critical problem. But I think there are other reasons too—reasons more specific, perhaps, to the concept of authorial intention itself. As I showed early in this chapter, recent reassertions of the intentional fallacy have coincided with a broader rejection of intentional action by affect theorists. Like Cavell, I maintain that semantic meaning relies on an assumption of intentional action. Nonetheless, I think one of the other reasons the intentional fallacy has proven so durable a problem is the continual comparison of "authorial intention" with other uses of "intention." For while they are related thematically and semantically, they are nonetheless different kinds of concepts entailing different properties and logical relations. A person can intend to write a certain way or intend to get across a certain meaning or effect. But you would never say "I have an authorial intention" unless, perhaps, you intended to become an author (and even then the sentence sounds absurd). This is because "authorial intention" is not something that "I" can possess, even if the "I" in question is also an author. Critical appeals to "authorial intention" only ever refer to a set of third-person psychological propositions inferred or reconstructed after the fact. In effect, "authorial intention" is a special kind of mental property that only certain *literary* minds (such as implied authors) can possess but that actual minds cannot. The authorial mind implied by a text such as *The Well Wrought Urn* can have an authorial intention. And we might be able to make certain inferences about that intention. But that refers to a fundamentally different type of phenomenon than the intention Cleanth Brooks had as he wrote his book. And like the logical errors I described above, it is this continued confusion between literary and actual minds—between the properties of consciousness and the properties of textuality—that has kept the fallacy alive for so long.

2   Inner Sights

It's hard to talk about problems of mind in Samuel Beckett's writings without talking about René Descartes.[1] This isn't to say that other philosophers weren't of importance to Beckett (including Spinoza, Leibniz, Geulincx, and Schopenhauer). Nor is it to say that Beckett accepted or hewed to Descartes's ideas uncritically—far from it. But versions of these ideas do persist in Beckett's texts. Even as Beckett exposes the problems entailed by certain Cartesian concepts—the paralyzing cycle of doubt, the peculiar logic of mind-body dualism, the fallibility of the infallible *cogito*—these same concepts somehow prove inescapable. Hugh Kenner makes a version of this point in his seminal *Samuel Beckett: A Critical Study* (1961). By Kenner's rationale, "Beckett would seem to be the first person to have read the *Discourse de la Méthode* as what it is, a work of fiction" (81). But despite this presumed fictionality, Kenner shows the extent to which Beckett's characters must nonetheless contend with the indignities of Cartesian life. In *Molloy* (1951), Kenner explains, the character Moran is hardly a "Cartesian Centaur, body and mind in close harmony." Instead, as his legs stiffen, he becomes "a mere intelligence fastened to a dying animal" (124). This intelligence, Kenner reminds us, has problems too. The self-knowledge that Moran trusts above all else, the *cogito*, becomes a noisy source of confusion—and might even be "piped into him by other beings" (131). The eponymous protagonist of *Murphy* (1938) faces a related set of problems. Murphy seeks to separate his mind from the physical world entirely. What makes this possible, Kenner suggests, is not only Descartes's ontological separation of mind and body but also the occasionalism of Arnold Geulincx (who was Descartes's student and whom Murphy refers to specifically). Murphy's separation of mind and body, Kenner writes, "follows, for Geulincx, from the fact that I do not know how I lift my hand: and *Quod nescis quomodo fiat, id non facis:* because you do not know how it was done, you did not do it" (84). Because Murphy does not know how his mind and body are connected, the reasoning goes, they must not be connected at all—even though, as Murphy concedes, they *must* be.

Given this odd persistence of Cartesian concepts in his writings, it stands to reason that Beckett wouldn't have much use for behaviorism. Beckett criticizes Descartes's ideas, yes, but the framework of mentalistic philosophy partly remains. Moreover, as I showed earlier, behaviorism and Cartesianism don't usually go together. But what I argue in this chapter is that Beckett actually found behaviorism to be a valuable proxy for his interest in, and concerns about, the Cartesian *cogito*. (I will focus on behaviorism's critique of dualism more extensively in the next chapter, where I discuss Beckett's plays and those of Harold Pinter.) Behaviorism was able to do this for Beckett because of its multiple critiques of introspection. Initially behaviorists such as John B. Watson and E. L. Thorndike rejected introspection as a scientific method. As Watson argued in "Psychology as the Behaviorist Views It," it was precisely the reliance on introspection that prevented psychology from being a properly experimental science. "Due to the mistaken notion that its fields of facts are conscious phenomena and that introspection is the only direct method of ascertaining these facts," he wrote, psychology has "enmeshed itself in a series of speculative questions which . . . are not open to experimental treatment" (176). In Watson's *Behaviorism*, however, this methodological rejection evolved into a broader rejection of thinking itself. "What psychologists have hitherto called thought," Watson claimed, "is in short nothing but talking to ourselves. . . . Muscular habits learned in overt speech are responsible for implicit or internal speech (thought)" (191).[2] Therefore, if thinking was in fact "subvocal" speech created by muscle contractions, then knowing one's thoughts was no different than hearing oneself whisper or feeling one's throat twitch. And if that was true, then what psychologists had traditionally called "introspection" was actually an empirical phenomenon. The difference between knowing one's own mind and the mind of someone else was one of degree rather than type. While "you can observe in yourselves only the most elementary forms of response," Watson wrote, "you will find, on the other hand, that when you begin to study what your neighbor is doing, you will rapidly become proficient in giving a reason for his behavior" (11). In other words, Watson concluded that introspection is itself a type of observation—an account of own's own behaviors, sensations, and physiological processes.

For Beckett, the blurry relation between reflective and empirical knowledge was an unresolved problem in Descartes's philosophy. In both *Discourse of the Method* and *Meditations on First Philosophy*, Descartes claimed that empirical knowledge was doubtable in a way that the *cogito* was not. "I have convinced myself," he wrote in the second of the *Meditations*, "that there is absolutely nothing in the world, no sky, no earth, no minds, no bodies. Does it follow that I too do not exist?" (80). The answer to this, Descartes suggested, was no. Even if my perceptions of the world are deceived, I necessarily exist as a being that perceives and thinks (i.e., the *cogito*). But while the existence of the *cogito* can't be doubted, this doesn't mean that the mind can't be fooled. In addition to stipulating that all sensory knowledge is corruptible, Descartes also suggested that true and false sensations are made from the same stuff, so to speak. The qualities of the sensations we experience in dreams, he explained in the first of the *Meditations*, are the same as those we experience while awake (*Descartes: Selected Philosophical Writings*, 77-78). Therefore, actual sensory knowledge of the external world was theoretically indistinguishable from illusory sensations created by the mind itself. Beckett's early poem *Whoroscope* (1930) gestures at this point and anticipates the unlikely, but significant, intersection Beckett found between behaviorism and Cartesianism. As the poem describes a young Descartes waiting for hens' eggs to ripen, it implies that the primary activity of the *cogito* isn't reasoning but the act of being deceived. As he waits, young Descartes blurts out a jumbled synthesis of his own *cogito ergo sum* (I think therefore I exist) and St. Augustine's *Si fallor, sum* (even if I'm mistaken I exist): "*Fallor, ego sum!*" (*Poems 1930-1989*, 6). Translated: I am mistaken therefore I exist. If Augustine continued to exist despite being wrong, this version of Descartes knows he exists *because* he's wrong. Even more importantly, Descartes's jumbled words imply a kind of interchangeability between *cogito* and *fallor*—as if thinking itself were a kind of error. To think is to be wrong; therefore, to be wrong is to have proof of one's own existence—except that such a conclusion, of course, relies on thinking.

In the novels *Murphy* and *Molloy*, this circular logic is sharpened into a more extended critique, as Beckett employs behaviorism's arguments against introspection to attack the infallible *cogito*, as well as mentalistic psychology more generally. In these novels the question isn't just whether introspection is reliable or not. It's also whether thinking might be understood to have sensory properties of its own and whether such properties might be illusions created by introspection and/or the *cogito* itself.[3] In that way, *Murphy* and *Molloy* reveal the broader significance of Beckett's encounters with behaviorism in the 1920s and 1930s—even though it would be a mistake to say that Beckett himself was a "behaviorist." To these ends, the rest of this chapter is divided into five sections. In the first, I offer a deeper explanation of behaviorism's critique of introspection, as well as its (occasionally surprising) historical antecedents. As I mentioned, the issue for Watson and colleagues wasn't merely whether introspection was valid as a scientific practice. Instead, it was also the question of whether introspection was a mental procedure or something epistemologically comparable to behavioral observation. In the second section I examine the ways Beckett instrumentalized aspects of behaviorism's critique in his essays "Dante . . . Bruno . . . Vico . . . Joyce" (1929) and *Proust* (1930); I also reveal Beckett's growing interest in behaviorism through his unpublished psychology notebooks from the early 1930s. In "Dante . . . Bruno" and *Proust*, Beckett seems suspicious of stimulus-response physiology but uses it to justify certain aspects of the writings of James Joyce and Marcel Proust. But it is in the psychology notebooks, written in the few years before he started drafting *Murphy*, where we see Beckett begin to toy with a distinctly behavioristic concept of introspection as a kind of self-observation or sensory activity. In the third and fourth sections I analyze *Murphy* and *Molloy* on these terms, both of which inhabit different aspects of behaviorism's critiques of introspection. Over the course of *Murphy*, both Cartesian reflection and introspective psychology become the objects of ridicule. This occurs until the novel, in a moment of formal upheaval, replaces mentalistic introspection with "vicarious autology"—that is, self-knowledge acquired through the study of other people. Things in *Molloy*, however, are more complicated still. There, the experiences of Molloy and Moran—who might or might not share a physical body—dissolve any perceived opposition between introspection and observation. Instead, Beckett suggests that both rationalism and empiricism/behaviorism result from the fallibility of the supposedly infallible *cogito*. In the concluding section I show the implications of *Murphy* and *Molloy* for thinking about the nature and function of psychological language in novels—and how they point us toward Beckett's career in the theater.

Behaviorism and Introspection

Before getting to behaviorism's critique and redefinition of introspection, it's worth noting that Watson and colleagues were not the first to suggest that self-knowledge might be akin to observation or sensation. Indeed, versions of this point were raised by not only the empiricist philosophers of the seventeenth and eighteenth centuries but also the empiricist psychologists of the nineteenth century—that is, the very experimental psychologists that Watson attacked.

In *An Essay Concerning Human Understanding* (1689), John Locke characterized introspection as an "inner Sense" (2.1.4) comparable to its external counterparts. The ideas received by the mind, he explained, "when it turns its view inward upon itself . . . are as capable to be the Objects of its Contemplation, as any of those it received from foreign things" (2.6.1). David Hume doubted the infallibility of introspective knowledge, much as he doubted there was a cohesive self to be introspected. But he, too, likened self-knowledge to a kind of visual inner sense. The mind, he wrote in *A Treatise of Human Nature* (1739), "is a kind of theatre, where several perceptions successively make their appearance" (253). In effect, having a "mind" amounts to being a spectator in the perceptual theater. But our ability to know these perceptions introspectively doesn't mean that we have introspective access to the mechanisms or processes that make such perceptions possible. "The comparison of the theatre," he continued, "must not mislead us. They are the successive perceptions only, that constitute the mind; nor have we the most distant notion of the place where these scenes are represented, or of the materials, of which it is compos'd" (253).

In *Outlines of Psychology* (1896), Wilhelm Wundt actually credited Locke with establishing "the psychology of the inner sense" (18). Wundt's understanding of introspection, however, was not simply lifted from the British empiricists. Instead, Wundt's methods owed an enormous debt to Franz Brentano's version of associative psychology and the psychophysics of Gustav Fechner, which paired the presentation of physical stimuli with subject self-reporting.[4] As Wundt explained, all higher-order mental phenomena could be broken down into their constituent components or "elements" (28). These elements could then be broken down further: "All psychical compounds may be resolved into psychical elements, that is, into pure sensations and simple feelings" (100). Ultimately, sensation was understood as the foundation of all mental states. But the properties exhibited by these mental states weren't necessarily present in these composite sensations. As if to anticipate Gestalt psychology a few decades later, the wholes and parts of these mental phenomena exhibited different properties. "Thus, a visual idea," he explained, "has not only the attributes of the light sensations and sensations of ocular position and movements contained in it, but it has also the attribute of spatial arrangement of the sensations, a factor not present in the elements themselves" (100).

These relations were conceivably knowable through introspection—but only if test subjects had a clear sense of proper introspective technique. Scientific introspection (*Selbstbeobachtung*), Wundt claimed, was not the same thing as ordinary inner experience or self-knowledge (*innere Wahrnehmung*). Instead, scientific introspection examined the same kinds of objects as other empirical modes of investigation. "Outer and inner experience," he wrote in *Outlines*, "do not indicate different objects but *different points of view*" of a shared set of objects (2; italics in the original). It therefore had the same credibility, and limitations, as empirical observations of the external world. For that reason, it was suitable as an experimental methodology. As Wundt explained, "Psychology has, like natural science, *two* exact methods: the experimental method, serving for the analysis of simpler psychical processes, and the observation of general mental products, serving for the investigation of higher psychical processes and developments" (23-24). After undergoing intensive training in scientific introspection, Wundt's test subjects could experience a sequence of physical stimuli and then introspectively examine the sensations and perceptions these stimuli produced. When trained correctly, these subjects possessed a set vocabulary for describing immediate sensations, as well as the relation between those sensations and more abstract mental phenomena.[5]

Wundt's students—including Oswald Külpe, James Cattell, G. Stanley Hall, and Edward Titchener—largely followed his methodology and set up similar psychological laboratories around the world. But there were key differences between Wundt and his students. This was particularly true of those in the Würzburg School, which was directed by Külpe and included psychologists such as Karl Bühler, Narziß Ach, Karl Marbe, and Henry Watt. First, the Würzburgers relaxed Wundt's restrictions about the types of introspection permitted and the types of thoughts that could be examined scientifically. As Külpe explained in *Outlines of Psychology* (1893), "sensations" weren't indivisible phenomena. Instead, each sensation could be broken down into "four attributes: quality, intensity, duration, and extension" (29). Second, and perhaps more importantly, the Würzburg laboratory claimed to find experimental proof of "imageless" thoughts—of mental states, accessed through introspection, that had neither empirical content nor referent. In "Versuche über Abstraktion" (Testing Abstraction; 1904), Külpe explained, "I attach importance to the statement that there are intractable abstractions in phenomenal consciousness. . . . The test subjects believed that they saw no colors or objects but indeterminacy" (67).[6]

With respect to behaviorism's critiques of introspection, Wundt and the Würzburg School were important for several reasons. Most obviously, it was Wundtian introspection that Watson rejected as being unscientific in "Psychology as the Behaviorist Views It." And while it's tempting to see some similarity between Watson and Wundt on the observational nature of introspection, it cannot be stressed enough that their theories were in fact mutually exclusive. Fundamentally, Wundt's introspective method was a means for examining *consciousness*—a concept that, except as it could be explained as a mislabeling of physiological and behavioral processes, Watson rejected as having neither value nor existence. By the 1930s, however, fewer behaviorists were making such extreme claims. A new, more moderate generation of psychologists emphasized the primacy of observable behavior but acknowledged the potential value of introspection, as well as its status as mental action (at least in part). In *Purposive Behavior in Animals and Men* (1932), Edward Chase Tolman suggested that while some knowledge could be gleaned from introspection, it "present[s] . . . nothing which, theoretically at least, cannot be conveyed by other more gross forms of behavior" (244). B. F. Skinner was even more tolerant than Tolman, though he also warned against introspection's limitations. As he wrote in *About Behaviorism* (1974), it was important to "take advantage of the position of the individual as an observer of himself and allow him to report on the mediating linkage between behavior and its antecedent causes" (237). Most of us would consider consciousness to be more than a "mediating linkage." Nonetheless, Skinner's position was still a fairly radical departure from Watson's reduction of thinking to "silent speech."

The comparability of introspection to empirical knowledge, however, did get significant traction among key philosophers of mind in the 1940s and 1950s. Among those philosophers, Ludwig Wittgenstein's account of introspection was perhaps farthest from Watson's—and yet it also concluded that some aspects of self-knowledge were products of observation. In *Philosophical Investigations*, Wittgenstein ventured that many mental phenomena are less private, and more intersubjective, than we might suppose. At the same time, *Philosophical Investigations* generally posited a necessary distinction between introspection and other kinds of knowledge acquisition. "The sentence 'I perceive I am conscious,'" Wittgenstein wrote, "does not say that I am conscious, but that my attention is disposed in such-and-such a way" (§417). Moreover, a concept such as grief proves that such self-perception is epistemologically distinct from observation:

> If you observe your own grief, which senses do you use to observe it? A particular sense; one that *feels* grief? Then do you feel it *differently* when you are observing it? And what is the grief that you are observing—is it one which is there only while it is being observed?
>
> "Observing" does not produce what is observed. (That is a conceptual statement.)
>
> Again: I do not "observe" what only comes into being through observation. The object of observation is something else. (II: 160e)

Let's extend Wittgenstein's reasoning a bit (whether we happen to agree with his conclusions about grief or not). When I observe someone else grieving, their grief can precede my observation, although it doesn't necessarily. Similarly, their grief doesn't necessarily disappear when I stop observing it. The relation between my own grieving and observation, however, is different. By Wittgenstein's reasoning, my grief doesn't precede my awareness of it, nor does it persist once I stop thinking about it. Like intention, my grief is partly constituted by my attention—it produces what it perceives, so to speak. In other words, if I don't know I'm grieving, then I must not be grieving. Therefore, the way I know my grief must be fundamentally different from the way I know other people's grief—or from the way they know mine.[7]

And yet there are some mental phenomena, Wittgenstein acknowledged, that we know through a process akin to self-observation. One such phenomenon was belief, which he discussed in terms of what he called Moore's paradox. In "A Reply to My Critics" (1942), G. E. Moore stated that "'I went to the pictures last Tuesday, but I don't believe that I did' is a perfectly absurd thing to say" (543). And yet, as Moore pointed out, it was entirely possible that a person could go to the movies on one night and not believe that fact the next. The logical absurdity articulated by the sentence doesn't track onto the situation it describes.[8] This absurdity, Wittgenstein claimed, was the result of using the phrase "I believe this is the case" as if it had the same meaning as "This is the case" (II: 162e). When I say, "I believe it is raining," he explained, I'm not just describing my state of mind; I'm also giving an indirect description of my sensory experiences. In that way it's not unlike when "I describe a photograph in order to describe the thing it is a photograph of." But

> then I must be able to say that the photograph is a good one. So here too: "I believe it's raining and my belief is reliable, so I rely on it."—In that case my belief would be a kind of sense-impression.
> One can mistrust one's own senses, but not one's beliefs. (II: 162e)

Wittgenstein does seem to think that certain aspects of self-knowledge are best understood as sensory or empirical. At the same time, he's careful to distinguish belief from sensation epistemologically. If I distrust my senses, then I can say that those senses are wrong. But if I distrust my beliefs, then I don't actually possess those beliefs at all. Instead, Wittgenstein's claim that belief is "a kind of sense-impression" seems predicated on an analogy between observational perspective and logical abstraction. By that reasoning, first-order mental states are to second-order mental states as first-person experience is to third-person observation. Wittgenstein, however, doesn't specify whether this reasoning is unique to belief or true of all second-order states.

Wittgenstein's account, therefore, was not entirely incompatible with the idea that individuals have unique, or even privileged, access to their own minds. In *The Concept of Mind*, of course, Gilbert Ryle rejected this idea outright. "Privileged Access," he claimed, was a myth—a false belief perpetuated by Cartesian dualism and reinforced by a language and culture built on that dualism. If I know my mind better than anyone else, Ryle argued, it's because no one has been more present in my life than I have. I don't have privileged access so much as I have frequent access to perceptions of my conduct and dispositions. To illustrate this, Ryle imagined a speaker giving a lecture to a live audience. "The superiority of the speaker's knowledge of what he is doing over that of the listener," he wrote, "does not indicate that he has Privileged Access to facts of a type inevitably inaccessible to the listener, only that he is in a very good position to know what the listener is often in a very poor position to know" (160). The difference between the speaker's knowledge and the listener's knowledge, therefore, is not one of type but one of degree. And if the speaker and listener share the same type of knowledge, their means of acquiring that knowledge must also be of the same type. The ownership of a given mind doesn't have much of an effect on how that mind can be known.

Accordingly, Ryle suggested that people know *all* minds—self and others

Inner Sights   75

—through a mixture of observation and reasoning. Contrary to Wittgenstein's analysis of grief, Ryle claimed that all seemingly introspective knowledge is predicated, at some level, on self-observation. This wasn't to suggest some sort of detachment between the observer and the observed. Nor was it to deny the existence of mental phenomena (such as memory), or the relative privacy of certain mental phenomena (again, like memory), or the distinction between thinking and sensation. Rather, Ryle's point was that introspection doesn't necessarily draw on so-called mental phenomena at all, but rather on empirically knowable phenomena like reactions, dispositions, and behaviors. "The ascertainment of a person's mental capacities," he wrote, "is an inductive process, an induction to law-like propositions from observed actions and reactions. Having ascertained these long-term qualities, we explain a particular action or reaction by applying the result of such an induction to the new specimen, save where open avowals let us know the explanation without research" (153). We observe ourselves in the same ways we observe other people, Ryle claimed—and we rely on the same set of concepts and rules in doing so.[9]

This conclusion, however, raises a question: if this is what introspection actually entails, then why do so many of us believe otherwise? Wilfrid Sellars's *Empiricism and the Philosophy of Mind* (1956) attempted to answer this question (among many others). *Empiricism* is likely best known for the Myth of the Given, where Sellars argued that all knowledge was epistemically dependent and that, as a result, no piece of knowledge could ever be taken as a "given."[10] But *Empiricism* also offered a corollary myth, the Myth of Jones, which imagined a community of fictional human ancestors called the Ryleans. The Ryleans would be like us in many ways—except for their language. The Rylean language, Sellars explained, lacks conventions for talking about private episodes or experiences. Instead, it is "a language of which the fundamental descriptive vocabulary speaks of public properties of public objects located in Space and enduring through Time" (91). It is a behavioristic language through and through, without any concept of mind or mental phenomena.

One of the Ryleans, Jones, notices something strange. Sometimes, when people act intelligently (i.e., performing actions with intention and purpose), "their conduct is threaded on a string of overt verbal episodes—that is to say, as *we* would say, they 'think out loud'" (102). But at other times, these intelligent actions happen silently. How, Jones asks, could such intelligent actions happen without overt verbal cues? Lacking any vocabulary for talking about covert mental phenomena, Sellars suggested, Jones comes up with a theory where "overt verbal behavior is the culmination of a process which begins with 'inner speech'" (103). And as a result, "the true cause of intelligent non-habitual behavior"—verbal or otherwise—is also described as "inner speech" or "thinking" (103). Jones's theory has two important consequences. First, in assigning the Rylean language of overt phenomena to covert phenomena, Jones's theory necessarily assumes that these phenomena are the same type. In effect, it commits a category-mistake, as it applies physical and linguistic predicates to what might not be physical or linguistic concepts. Second, as Jones tells his friends about his ideas, his theory gains a second function—that of self-description. Once Jones teaches Tom or Dick to recognize the behavioral evidence that supports the statement "Dick is thinking 'p,'" both Tom and Dick "can be trained to give reasonably reliable self-descriptions, using the language of the theory" (106). As they "hear" their silent inner voices, Sellars wrote, "our ancestors begin to speak of the privileged access each of us has to his own thoughts. *What began as a language with a purely theoretical use has gained a reporting role*" (107; italics in the original). By Sellars's reasoning, this was logical proof that the concept of introspection was in fact derivable from the intersubjective language of behavioral observation.

Bad Habits

Like behaviorism's multiple critiques of introspection, Beckett's own engagement with behaviorism had several facets that developed over time. The only explicit mentioning of "behaviorism" in his published works occurs in the novel *Dream of Fair to Middling Women* (1932), which was published posthumously in 1992. There Belacqua is described as "fatally recognizable and willfully cut, so little capable as a behaviourist of versatility did he appear. The hats of friends flew off spontaneously to him as he passed, their arms flared up on his passage" (126). Here behaviorism functions as something of a sight gag. However, at the same time, it also speaks to the lack of mental efficacy and the separation between body and mind that would come to preoccupy so much of *Murphy* and *Molloy*.

But there's evidence that behaviorism became useful for Beckett before *Dream of Fair to Middling Women*—sometimes as an analytical tool, other times as a foil. He encountered behaviorism no later than 1929, when his essay "Dante . . . Bruno . . . Vico . . . Joyce" was published in the collection *Our Exagmination Round His Factification for Incamination of Work in Progress*

(1929). In "Dante . . . Bruno," Beckett took aim at Rebecca West's *The Strange Necessity* (1928), which was a wide-ranging work of criticism that offered commentary on, among other things, Pavlovian physiology, behaviorism, and James Joyce's fiction. For West, Pavlov's work was tantamount to a universal theory of human action—which meant that it functioned as a theory of reading and writing as well. "The basis of all behavior," she wrote, is "the simple reflexes, the inborn instinctive reactions of the nervous system, such as the salivation which happens in a dog's mouth after the introduction of food" (71). West's attitudes toward behaviorism, however, were primarily negative (and also fairly inconsistent). For despite Watson's commitment to Pavlovian physiology, West thought that behaviorism oversimplified the relations between behaviors and "mind" (a concept that West refused to yield). "If [humans] were moved by one force which had no competition but inertia," she wrote, the "mind would not be the complicated instrument that it is," she explained. "Thinking could have become what Dr. John Watson, the apostle of Behaviourism, alleges it to be, a matter of 'tracing paths for action' in the crudest sense" (54).[11] And yet, as Douglas Mao shows in *Fateful Beauty*, as West "attempt[s] to defend subjectivity from behaviorist skepticism, the attempt itself leads West to describe consciousness in a way that resonates with behaviorism's questioning of the priority of mental states" (200). Mao points us to West's discussion of what she terms "mind-consciousness" and "body-consciousness." Insofar as we have a "mind-consciousness" that perceives other minds and a "body-consciousness" that perceives other bodies, she explained, the former "acts less powerfully than the body-consciousness because while [humans] . . . have more or less the same nervous and muscular systems and the same skeletons, each human being has a psychical outfit quite different from every other human being" (*Strange Necessity*, 101). West's reasoning here doesn't hold up very well. But there's little doubt that she privileged behavioral observation over psychological inference (at least when discussing other people).

Embedded in *The Strange Necessity*'s comments on neurology and psychology were West's scathing criticisms of Joyce. Claiming that Joyce suffered from a "cloacal obsession" (50), West maintained that he wasn't very talented either. She argued that the obscenities in *Ulysses*, which had resulted in the novel's censorship in Europe and North America, weren't part of some deliberate or considered "aesthetic process" (10). Instead, they were just the work of an infantile man who reveled in the shock factor of naughty language. "Simply he is gratifying in his maturity the desire to protest against the adult order of things by the closest possible verbal substitutes for the practical actions, originating in the zone against which adults seemed to have such a repressive prejudice" (10). But while Joyce could be blamed for such obscenities, West argued, he couldn't be given credit for the perceived successes of his work. At this moment, the language of stimulus-response physiology and neurology returns in *The Strange Necessity*, mobilized to diminish Joyce's agency as a writer: "*Ulysses* is not as it is because James Joyce chose that it should be so. . . . *Ulysses* is the product of its excitatory complexes of his time, whether derived from art and science or from straight unanalyzed and unsynthesized experience, pressing on the individuality which is called James Joyce" (192). If *Ulysses* was at all worth reading, West seems to have suggested, it was despite Joyce's interference.

In "Dante . . . Bruno" Beckett responds to these criticisms of Joyce in kind—discrediting West by means of the same discourses she used to discredit Joyce. Behaviorism doesn't come up in that essay explicitly, but Pavlov does. As Beckett describes Joyce's work in more psychoanalytic terms, he uses the Pavlovian register for West, as if it were reserved for insult and dehumanization: "When Miss Rebecca West clears her decks for a sorrowful deprecation of the Narcissistic element in Mr. Joyce by the purchase of 3 hats, one feels that she might very well wear her bib at all her intellectual banquets, or alternatively, assert a more noteworthy control over her salivary glands than is possible for Monsieur Pavlov's unfortunate dogs" (*Samuel Beckett: The Grove Centenary Edition*, 4:502). Much as West accused Joyce of immaturity, Beckett misogynistically infantilizes West and characterizes her as a drooling creature of instincts and conditioned reflexes. In *The Strange Necessity*, West gave some degree of agency to Joyce as a writer, even though she concluded that his voluntary contributions to *Ulysses* were obscene, perverted, or dumb. Beckett, however, grants West even less agency. Instead, he implies that she should stop writing about literature and go back to hat shopping.

In "Dante . . . Bruno," however, Pavlovian physiology isn't strictly a vehicle for insults. Beckett argues that reflex conditioning numbs readers to the intricacy and innovation of Joyce's language and reinforces lazy assumptions about the separation between form and content. The reason readers don't understand Joyce, Beckett explains, is that they read so carelessly—"skimming . . . the scant cream of sense"—as to assume that form is less expressive or signifying than content. But separating form and content in this way discards the layers of intellectual material that are frequently embedded into form. As a result, the form becomes nothing but a stimulus—and reading literature becomes little more than a "process of copious intellectual salivation" (502). "That form that is an arbitrary and independent phenomenon," Beckett writes, "can fulfil no higher function than that of stimulus for a tertiary or quartiary conditioned reflex of dribbling comprehension" (502). This separation between form and content is a particular impediment to understanding Joyce, where "form *is* content, content *is* form" (502). It's at this moment that "Dante . . . Bruno" returns us to the category-mistake. At the moment of reading, the representational capacity of Joyce's language becomes tantamount to the actual presence (or properties) of what it represents. Joyce's writing, Beckett explains, is "not *about* something; *it is that something itself.* . . . When the sense is sleep, the words go to sleep. (See the end of *Anna Livia*.) When the sense is dancing, the words dance" (502-3; italics in the original). The effect of this, however, isn't to make *Anna Livia* more difficult or harder to understand. Beckett actually sees this blending of form and content as having "desophisticated language" (504)—using perceived sensory qualities to cut through the abstraction of English diction and making words less susceptible to misinterpretation. "Take the word 'doubt': it gives us hardly any sensuous suggestion of hesitancy, of the necessity for choice, of static irresolution," Beckett writes. "Mr. Joyce," however, "recognizes how inadequate 'doubt' is to express a state of extreme uncertainty, and replaces it by 'in twosome twiminds'" (504).

Behaviorism and Pavlovian physiology play a somewhat different role in Beckett's *Proust*. This role, however, has often been overshadowed by the essay's discussion of Arthur Schopenhauer's *The World as Will and Representation* (1818).[12] And yet, as I hope to show, it's Beckett's interpretation of Schopenhauer that undergirds *Proust*'s behavioristic critique of introspection and memory. In July 1930 Beckett wrote the following note to Tom McGreevy: "I am reading Schopenhauer. . . . An intellectual justification of unhappiness—the greatest that has ever been attempted—is worth the examination of one who is interested in Leopardi and Proust rather than in Carducci and Barrès" (*Letters*, 1:32-33). In *Proust*, however, it's not Schopenhauer's account of unhappiness that matters, but rather that of the "will." Broadly indebted to Kant's metaphysics, Schopenhauer claimed that we're never able to perceive the external world directly (although he also rejected Kant's notion of the thing-in-itself). Instead, what we perceive is an image of our broader attitudes and beliefs about that world—that is, the will—which is then reinforced and made permanent by our own habits of perception. Insofar as the world is "an objectivation of the individual's will," Beckett writes in *Proust*, citing Schopenhauer explicitly, the perceptual relations between individual and world become *habits*—automatic, unaware routines (518). And these routines frequently dull, or distort, our perceptual abilities. "The creature of habit," he writes, "turns aside from the object that cannot be made to correspond with one or other of his intellectual prejudices, that resists the propositions of his syntheses" (518). In other words, it's easier to ignore anomalous perceptions than to change the habits of perception.

But sometimes those perceptual habits can be circumvented. This is what Beckett appreciates about Proust's *memoire involontaire* in *Á la recherche du temps perdu*. As "the laws of memory are subject to the more general laws of habit" (515), voluntary memories are constrained, hidden "in the haze of conception-preoccupation" (517). In contrast, involuntary memories are capable of piercing through this haze, particularly when they recall forgotten experiences. In those cases, Beckett explains, "the central impression of a past sensation recurs as an immediate stimulus which can be instinctively identified with the model of duplication (*whose integral purity has been retained because it has been forgotten*)" (543; italics in the original). The forgotten experience moves past our habits of perception and is experienced again as if it were fresh and new. This, Beckett claims, is the power of Proustian memory—and of Proust's prose as well. But it would be a mistake to see *Proust* strictly in such redemptive terms. For while it presents involuntary memory and literature piercing through perceptual habit, what it offers on the whole is far more pessimistic. Much as "Dante . . . Bruno" suggests that Joyce presents too great a challenge for the conditioned reflexes of "dribbling" readers, *Proust* imagines the human mind as only rarely able to defeat its own habits and previous conceptions. The general state of affairs is one where both memory and introspection are surreptitiously replaced by automatic physiological processes. "Memory," we're told, is "obviously conditioned by perception" (521)—and perception itself is vitiated by habit: "the pernicious devotion of habit paralyses our attention, drugs those handmaidens of perception whose cooperation is not absolutely essential" (516). Returning to *Proust*'s engagement with Schopenhauer, it wouldn't be unfair to say that Beckett effectively replaces "world as will" with the more behavioristic "world as habit" or even "world as conditioned reflex." When we look out into the world, or look into ourselves, we perceive not our "will" but an abstract distortion of our neurological makeup.

Proust was the last time Beckett published anything about behaviorism or reflex conditioning specifically. In his unpublished writings, however, Beckett's engagement with these topics continued through the 1930s. This includes the aforementioned novel *Dream of Fair to Middling Women*, first published after Beckett's death, as well as his psychology notebooks, which were likely written between 1934 and 1935. The notebooks are currently held at Trinity College, Dublin. Recent archival work—such as Matthijs Engelberts, Everett Lloyd Frost, and Jane Maxwell's *"Notes Diverse Holo"* (2006) and Dirk Van Hulle and Mark Nixon's *Samuel Beckett's Library* (2017)—has made the contents of these volumes more widely known. The notebooks themselves, however, remain almost entirely unpublished. For my purposes here, the notes that matter most are those in TCD MS10971/7, folios 7–18, where Beckett summarized Robert S. Woodworth's anti-behaviorist textbook *Contemporary Schools of Psychology* (1931).[13]

Woodworth himself was a well-regarded introspective psychologist at Columbia. Trained by William James and James Cattell (a former student of Wundt's), in 1906 Woodworth proposed the existence of imageless thought independently of the Würzburg School.[14] *Contemporary Schools of Psychology* comprised a detailed introduction to different doctrines of experimental psychology, including Wundt, G. E. Müller, Titchener, Binet, Gestalt psychology, the Würzburg School, and behaviorism. In the section on the Würzburg School (31–42), the research of Külpe, Marbe, Watt, and Ach is discussed in considerable detail. Particular attention is paid to the imageless thought controversy and the relationship between preparatory signals and stimulated responses. Below are Beckett's notes on that section of Woodworth's text:[15]

> The Külpe [crossed out] (1862-1915) School: Marbe, Bühler, Ach, Watt—concerned not with nature of the reaction but with the actual reactive experience, & concluding in the importance of the preparation for reaction—preparation, adjustment, set, Einstellung.
>
> | P (preparatory signal) | S (stimulus) | R (reaction) |
> |---|---|---|
> | / Fore-period | / Main-Period | / |
>
> Most of the effort, active experience & real work takes place in the fore-period.
>   This school agrees with Binet in asserting <u>imageless thought</u>.

> Imageless Thought Controversy: the parting of the ways in
> modern psychological theory. Existentialism arose out of reaction
> against it, Behaviourism reacted by rejecting introspection
> altogether, Gestalt Psychology by objecting to introspection
> as an instrument of analysis & by proposing to abandon mental
> chemistry altogether, sensory elements & thought elements alike.
> (TCD MS10971/7, 7)

Generally, Beckett's notes largely reproduce Woodworth's evenhanded account of the Würzburg School and the imageless thought controversy. Woodworth saw the imageless thought controversy as one of the defining events of experimental psychology. Accordingly, Beckett's notes present the controversy as what precipitated the arrival of psychological existentialism, behaviorism, and Gestalt psychology. However, Beckett's note "Behaviourism reacted by rejecting introspection altogether" leaves out the substantial vitriol Woodworth had for Watson and colleagues. Behaviorism's critique of introspection was particularly galling to Woodworth. If the method of introspective psychology is "unsound," he wrote, then "all scientific observation is unsound, since it makes practically the same demands on the observer" (23). Instead, Woodworth claimed that it was behaviorism that was unsound—comparable, perhaps, to mental illness or even a plague. "The outbreak of behaviorism," he explained, "had its predisposing and its exciting causes, such as the psychiatrist distinguishes in tracing the origin of an attack of insanity" (45). Behaviorism's popularity, Woodworth concluded, had little to do with its success as a scientific doctrine and more to do with its potential as a cultural or political force. In its "boldness, freedom, toughmindedness, and unlimited faith in the ability of science to take charge of human affairs," behaviorism "is a religion to take the place of religion" (92). As a psychological or scientific program, however, behaviorism was irredeemable.

Beckett's notes, however, are no more or less neutral about behaviorism than they are about the Würzburg School. Behaviorism's key points are covered in detail and with Woodworth's objections (and ad hominem attacks) filtered out. Watson's system, Beckett wrote, was the "Rejection ^of 'consciousness' as no less intangible than 'soul' & regarded the 'functional' psychology of William James as merely a compromise between 'structural' psychology [Wundt et al] & the 'truly biological science' of behaviour" (TCD MS10971/7, 7). The notes also offer an account of Pavlov's relationship to behaviorism—"all learned behaviour is a matter of conditioned reflexes. . . . The conditioned reflex gave a great impulse to Behaviourism" (8)—as well as Watson's more unorthodox definition of "thinking," which I discussed earlier in this chapter. "<u>Thinking</u>," the notes read, "is implicit speech reactions, subvocal talking, an implicit sensorimotor performance. The child says something (1) as he does it (2) Inaudibly as he does it (3) Before he does it (i.e. thinks). The implicit behaviour replacing actual manipulation consists mostly of speech movements" (9). Woodworth's text offered an extensive set of counterarguments to Watson's claims on these subjects—"I personally do not accept the equation, thought=speech" (72)—but these counterarguments didn't make it into Beckett's notes.

What did make it into Beckett's notes, however, was a summary of how various psychological behaviorists had started to treat introspection itself as an observable behavior. This section of the psychology notebook is also unusual, as it features Beckett inserting his own conjectures into the material. This is most significant in Beckett's discussion of Max Meyer, an influential psychologist who worked at the University of Missouri from 1900 to 1930. Beckett attributed the following idea to Meyer's monograph *Psychology of the Other-One* (1921): "The scientific value of introspective psychology consists merely in the fact that it aids us in discovering the laws of nervous functioning" (TCD MS10971/7, 10). Beckett's response to this proposition went in a slightly different direction and instead offered a theory of introspection not unlike that of Watson, Ryle, or Sellars. "Introspection," he wrote, "is tolerated only when it occurs in a third party! Typical psychological situation becomes, not P faced by universe, but P studying O faced by universe" (10). Thus conceived, introspection was conceived not only as akin to observation, whether of oneself or of other people, but also as an observable behavior in its own right.

Vicarious Autology

However, this is not the image of introspection we initially encounter in *Murphy*. Instead, as Kenner and others suggest, Murphy's sense of his own mind is inflected by both dualist and occasionalist philosophy.[16] Murphy, who generally tries to avoid gainful employment and whose favorite pastime is tying himself to his rocking chair and looking inward, "felt himself split in two, a body and a mind. They had intercourse apparently, otherwise he could not have known that they had anything in common. But he felt his mind to be bodytight and did not understand through what channel the intercourse was effected nor how the two experiences came to overlap. He was satisfied that neither followed from the other" (66). The operative word here is "bodytight." When Murphy sits in his rocking chair, he enters a mental space, so to speak, that is free of anything remotely physical or sensory. "Murphy's mind," the narrator explains, "pictured itself as a large hollow sphere, hermetically closed to the universe without" (65). This sphere, we read, is divided into three "zones," with each progressive zone bearing less and less reference to the physical world around him. In the first zone, "the pleasure was reprisal, the pleasure of reversing the physical experience" (68), as physical actions in the world are translated into mental actions. In the second zone, this correspondence with the physical world dissolves and Murphy experiences "forms without parallel"—that is, without any kind of physical correlate. In both these zones Murphy feels "sovereign and free." In the third zone, however, "he was not free but a mote in the dark of absolute freedom. He did not move, he was a point in the ceaseless unconditioned generation and passing away of line" (68). There, in the deepest level of his introspection, Murphy is able to experience something like pure abstraction. At the same time he also perceives himself as something like a tiny speck who cannot move himself but is rather moved by the universe itself (à la occasionalist philosophy).

The word "unconditioned," however, is worth thinking about too. For while it invokes the seemingly a priori existence Murphy seeks out in his rocking chair, it also gestures toward one of the novel's other discourses: that of the Würzburg School. Like his reverence for Descartes and Geulincx, Murphy professes enormous faith in the Würzburgers. It's not hard to see a similarity between Murphy's zones and the imageless thoughts that Külpe and colleagues claimed to find through scientific introspection. The significance of the Würzburg School first becomes apparent as Murphy, still working to avoid gainful employment, tries to use its theories to grift food and tea from a waitress. As Murphy spoke to the waitress,

> he paused after this preparatory signal to let the fore-period develop, that first of the three moments of reaction in which, according to the Külpe school, the major torments of response are undergone. Then he applied the stimulus proper.
> "A cup of tea and a packet of assorted biscuits." Twopence the tea, twopence the biscuits, a perfectly balanced meal.
> As though suddenly aware of the great magical ability, or it might have been the surgical quality, the waitress murmured, before the eddies of the main-period drifted her away: "Vera to you, dear." This was not a caress.

Inner Sights 85

> Murphy had some faith in the Külpe school. Marbe and Bühler might be deceived, even Watt was only human, but how could Ach be wrong? (49)

As Matthew Feldman points out in *Beckett's Books: A Cultural History of the "Interwar Notes"* (2006), this description bears a noticeable similarity to folio 7 of Beckett's psychology notebook (104). There, under the heading of "Külpe School," Beckett summarized Ach and Watt's concept of *Einstellung* —or the preparatory signal before the stimulus. By pausing before the stimulus, Murphy believes, he will make the stimulus more intense or effective. And that will make his waitress, Vera, more likely to comply with his requests. But on this point Murphy is as wrong, and as wrongly confident, as he is condescending. If Vera complies with Murphy's requests, it's *despite* his attempts at psychological manipulation—not because of them. As Beckett understood it, the Külpe School was "concerned not with nature of the reaction but with the actual reactive experience" (TCD MS10971/7, 7). But there's no clear indication of how Vera perceives Murphy's request. The phrase "as though suddenly aware" implies that we have less access to her thinking than we, or Murphy, suppose. Her response to Murphy's request is both annoyed and off-topic: "'Vera to you, dear.' This was not a caress." Murphy's later attempts at manipulation continue this pattern:

> With the fresh cup of tea Murphy adopted quite a new technique. . . . "I am most fearfully sorry," he said to Vera, "but would it be possible to have this filled with hot?"
> Vera showing signs of bridling, Murphy uttered winningly the sesame.
> "I know I am a great nuisance, but they have been too generous with the cowjuice."
> Generous and cowjuice were the keywords here. No waitress could hold out against their mingled overtones of gratitude and mammary organs. And Vera was essentially a waitress. (50-51)

Murphy gets yet another free cup of tea this way. But again, it has little or nothing to do with his application of concepts from the Külpe School. As she shows "signs of bridling," Murphy's salvo is "winning" in his mind only. Murphy's belief that she is "essentially a waitress," as if this were a discrete psychological type, reveals the kind of baseless assumptions beneath his efforts. And his theory that no "waitress" could resist the compelling stimulus of the word "cowjuice"—"mingled overtones of gratitude and mammary organs"—tells us far more about Murphy's mind than it does hers. He hasn't revealed her actual psychological associations with the term "cowjuice" but rather projected onto her those associations he thinks she ought to have. In effect, the experimenter has insufficiently separated his associations from those of his test subject. Whether or not his faith in the Külpe School was wrong, whether Marbe and Bühler might actually have been deceived, is beside the point.

A parallel episode in the novel accentuates the absurdity and ignorance of Murphy's position. A few pages after Murphy "adopted quite a new technique" to scam a cup of tea from Vera, he encounters Miss Dew "now experimenting with a new technique" to trick sheep into eating lettuce (60). Unlike Murphy's efforts with Vera, Miss Dew's seem to fail; the sheep won't eat the lettuce. Nonetheless, her experiment throws doubt onto Murphy's reasoning just the same. Her method, we read, "consisted in placing her offering on the ground and withdrawing to a discreet remove, so that the sheep might separate in their minds, if that was what they wanted, the ideas of the giver and the gift. Miss Dew was not Love, that she could feel one with what she gave, and perhaps there was some dark ovine awareness of this, that Miss Dew was not lettuce, holding up the entire works" (60). As Murphy projected his associations onto Vera, Miss Dew projects her concerns about separating the "giver and the gift" onto her sheep. Ostensibly Murphy's efforts were more successful; he did manage to get some free tea. And yet it's implied that, if anything, Miss Dew's theory was slightly less baseless than Murphy's. Murphy got his free tea not because of his "technique" but in spite of it. The narrator, however, grants the distant possibility that Miss Dew was in fact correct in her worries about whether the sheep might confuse giver and gift. The narrator doesn't actually confirm that the sheep refused the gift because of "some dark ovine awareness . . . that Miss Dew was not lettuce." But that possibility is not ruled out either.

When Murphy becomes an orderly at Mental Magdalen Mercyseat (MMM), an inpatient psychiatric hospital, the novel's criticisms of mentalistic psychology intensify and begin extending into the philosophical problems of introspection and self-knowledge I discussed earlier. Most of the patients at MMM, Murphy learns, are either catatonic or delusional. As a result, their treatments focused on reconnecting them with the external world. "The function of treatment," we read, "was to bridge the gulf, translate the sufferer from his own pernicious little private dungheap to the glorious world of discrete particles" (107). Murphy, however, finds this abhorrent. For him, being disconnected from the physical world isn't an illness. Instead, it's a desirable state of affairs—precisely the one he's tried to reach through introspection. Murphy's "experience as a physical and rational being," the narrator explains, "obliged him to call sanctuary what the psychiatrists called exile and to think of the patients not as banished from a system of benefits but as escaped from a colossal fiasco" (108). Far from pitying the patients at MMM, he covets their detached catatonia. He's especially admiring of Mr. Endon, "a schizophrenic of the most amiable variety" (111) who is one of MMM's most disconnected patients. Endon is also suicidal and often tries to kill himself by means of "apnoea"—holding his breath—despite the physiological impossibility of doing so. As his carer, Murphy has a number of opportunities to study Endon closely, and he becomes increasingly jealous of his patient's life. Endon's "languor," we read, "was never so profound as to inhibit all movement. His inner voice did not harangue him, it was unobtrusive and melodious, a gentle continuo in the whole consort of his hallucinations. The bizarrerie of his attitudes never exceeded a stress laid on their grace. In short, a psychosis so limpid and imperturbable that Murphy felt drawn to it as Narcissus to his fountain" (112). The relation between introspection and hallucinated "inner" voices will become more important once we get to *Molloy*. But here neither Murphy nor readers have much access to the content of Endon's hallucinations. Instead, this excerpt's free indirect discourse relays Murphy's impressions of Endon's behavior and his resulting conclusions about Endon's mental life. Studying Endon's largely peaceful body, Murphy decides that his patient's hallucinations are best likened to beautiful music. As Murphy experiences his own motionless introspections pleasurably—"his mind gave him pleasure, such pleasure that pleasure was not the word" (2)—he reasons that the same must be true of Endon's "limpid" psychosis. It's unclear, of course, whether Murphy's characterization of Endon's experience is correct. As was the case with Vera, Murphy has once again projected his desires and associations onto another person. Additionally, Murphy has assumed that there must be some correlation between Endon's "limpid" exterior and the qualities of his mental life.

Murphy's thoughts about such matters, however, soon change. After working at MMM for a while, Murphy finds his own introspective abilities diminishing. This is true not only of his rocking-chair introspections but also of more ordinary cognitive efforts. Murphy, we're told, did not

> think of Celia any more, though he could sometimes remember having dreamt of her. If only he had been able to think of her, he would not have needed to dream of her.

> Nor did he succeed in coming alive in his mind any more. He blamed this on his body, fussy with fatigue after so much duty, but it was rather due to the vicarious autology he had been enjoying since morning, in Mr. Endon and all the other proxies. That was why he felt happy in the wards and sorry when the time came to leave them. (113)

It isn't fatigue that's getting in the way of Murphy's rocking chair pursuits. Instead, Murphy's introspective abilities have been replaced with, or revealed to be a form of, "vicarious autology": knowing oneself by observing the behaviors of others. Recalling Beckett's notes on Max Meyer, the novel has replaced "P faced by universe" with "P studying O faced by universe." When Murphy was observing Vera, his focus was on how to manipulate her; he wasn't considering how Ach and Watt's *Einstellung* might also apply to him. Now, however, as he observes and strives to emulate his catatonic patients, he, in effect, observes analogues to his own introspective efforts. As a result, Murphy's introspections and behavioral observations appear as interchangeable as they are mutually exclusive—yielding the same kinds of results and scratching the same cognitive and emotional itches.

The novel's form experiments with this apparent interchangeability and mutual exclusivity between introspection and behavioral observation. This happens at several moments during the novel's final sections, the last of which I will return to at the end of this chapter. But here I want to focus on Murphy's chess game with Endon, where the novel's omniscient realism is briefly replaced with English chess notation (see figs. 4 and 5 on pages 90–91). English chess notation has no symbols to denote intentions or desires. Instead, it can only describe actions. It abstracts a chess match into a timeline of objects moving across a horizontal plane. It does this irrespective of the players' motivations or designs. So while *Murphy* is built around characters who like to recess into their minds, it also culminates in a figure that records physical movement exclusively and lacks any means of representing mental states. The narrator's pretentious, even cheeky, footnotes work toward this point as well. They emphasize the extent to which the novel itself has temporarily replaced introspective knowledge with behavioral observation—and also the strangeness of a chess game between nearly comatose players, neither of whom knows how to play. In Note A, the narrator explains that "Mr. Endon always played Black. If presented with White he would fade, without the least trace of annoyance, away into a light stupor" (146). Endon, of course, never shows annoyance, as he's always in a light stupor. When he puts Murphy's king in check, Note O explains that he does so without "giving the slightest indication he was alive" (147). But if this angered Murphy, we'll never know. For as we read in Note P, "No words can express the torment of mind that goaded White [Murphy] into this abject offensive" (147). No words can express that torment because, at this moment in the novel, there is no available mode or discourse for referring to mental content.

This change to English chess notation, of course, is only temporary. But Murphy's introspective abilities are never again quite the same. Shortly after he loses the chess game, Murphy accompanies Endon back to his room and tucks him into bed. There he stares into Endon's eyes. But instead of making some kind of emotional connection with his patient, he sees himself reflected and yet "stigmatized in those eyes that did not see him" (150). Murphy observes the image of Endon's placid exterior and, in turn, observes the image of his own. And therein we see the distinctions between private and public phenomena, between introspection and observation, fall away. As he stares into Endon's eyes, as behavioral observation amounts to a kind of self-knowledge, Murphy's own thinking takes on sensory properties. He doesn't think thoughts but hears and speaks them: "Murphy heard words demanding so strongly to be spoken that he spoke them, right into Mr. Endon's face. . . . The relation between Mr Murphy and Mr Endon could not have been better summed up than by the former's sorrow at seeing himself in the latter's immunity from seeing himself" (151). The grammatical complexities of this sentence appear to reflect the psychological muddle of Murphy's thinking. The repetition of "himself" blurs the boundary between self-knowledge and observation. "Seeing" also has two possible meanings here. As Murphy admires and aspires to Endon's condition, it's natural to read "seeing himself" as an expression of psychological identification. This reading, however, doesn't quite work with the "final" seeing. Whether we see the final "himself" referring to Murphy or Endon, the final "seeing" seems inescapably sensory—as if introspection weren't merely psychologically foreclosed upon but grammatically as well. Either way, the possibility of purely mentalistic introspection—of self-knowledge that *isn't* a kind of observation or external behavior—seems to be written out.

The Voice I Listen To

Many critics see *Murphy* and *Molloy* as representing different moments in Beckett's career, with the latter ostensibly amenable to a broader set of phil-

The game, an Endon's Affence, or *Zweispringerspott*, was as follows:

White (MURPHY)	Black (MR. ENDON) (a)
1. P—K4 (b)	1. Kt—KR3
2. Kt—KR3	2. R—KKt1
3. R—KKt1	3. Kt—QB3
4. Kt—QB3	4. Kt—K4
5. Kt—Q5 (c)	5. R—KR1
6. R—KR1	6. Kt—QB3
7. Kt—QB3	7. Kt—KKt1
8. Kt—QKt1	8. Kt—QKt1 (d)
9. Kt—KKt1	9. P—K3
10. P—KKt3 (e)	10. Kt—K2
11. Kt—K2	11. Kt—KKt3
12. P—KKt4	12. B—K2
13. Kt—KKt3	13. P—Q3
14. B—K2	14. Q—Q2
15. P—Q3	15. K—Q1 (f)
16. Q—Q2	16. Q—K1
17. K—Q1	17. Kt—Q2
18. Kt—QB3 (g)	18. R—QKt1
19. R—QKt1	19. Kt—QKt3
20. Kt—QR4	20. B—Q2
21. P—QKt3	21. R—KKt1
22. R—KKt1	22. K—QB1 (h)

Figure 4. "Endon's Affence, or *Zweispringerspott*" (Beckett, *Murphy*, 145).

osophical topics than the former. André Furlani sees a meaningful connection between *Molloy* and Wittgenstein's comments on aspect differentiation. In *Beckett after Wittgenstein* (2015), Furlani suggests that "the bicameral structure of *Molloy* is organized on a principle of change of aspect, its pattern of resemblance, repetition and variation disclosing and enacting the ways that perception blends empirical impressions and normative conceptions" (148). Moving in a different direction, Andrew Gibson sees Beckett in dialogue with the philosopher Alain Badiou—particularly with the latter's thoughts on mathematics and limits. "Molloy's sustained disquiet about himself," Gibson writes in *Beckett and Badiou: The Pathos of Intermittency* (2006), "is a product of the persistent incursion of actual infinity into putatively finite frames" (34). In *Beckett, Modernism and the Material Imagination*

23. B—QKt2	23. Q—KB1
24. K—QB1	24. B—K1
25. B—QB3 (*i*)	25. Kt—KR1
26. P—QKt4	26. B—Q1
27. Q—KR6 (*j*)	27. Kt—QR1 (*k*)
28. Q—KB6	28. Kt—KKt3
29. B—K5	29. B—K2
30. Kt—QB5 (*l*)	30. K—Q1 (*m*)
31. Kt—KR1 (*n*)	31. B—Q2
32. K—QKt2 !!	32. R—KR1
33. K—QKt3	33. B—QB1
34. K—QR4	34. Q—K1 (*o*)
35. K—R5	35. Kt—QKt3
36. B—KB4	36. Kt—Q2
37. Q—QB3	37. R—QR1
38. Kt—QR6 (*p*)	38. B—KB1
39. K—QKt5	39. Kt—K2
40. K—QR5	40. Kt—QKt1
41. Q—QB6	41. Kt—KKt1
42. K—QKt5	42. K—K2 (*q*)
43. K—R5	43. Q—Q1 (*r*)

And White surrenders.

Figure 5. "And White Surrenders" (Beckett, *Murphy*, 146).

(2014), Steven Connor links the novel's sense of finitude and limitation to Martin Heidegger. "Beckett's earth," he writes, "is perhaps also to be seen as closed in Heidegger's sense.... It is never the world as such, but always one or other version of 'my part of the world' (a phrase used twice by Molloy)" (184).[17]

These readings point to some of the most important ideas in Beckett's later fiction. Nonetheless, I think that it's important to see *Molloy* as continuing *Murphy*'s skepticism about the nature and entailments of introspection and the *cogito*. Like *Murphy*, *Molloy* doesn't merely oppose self-knowledge to observation. Instead, it slowly unfolds the logical and causal relations between the two. As it details Molloy's raunchy appeals to empirical knowledge and Moran's faith in reasoning over observation, the novel suggests that these concepts might actually be two sides of the same coin—not unlike the possibility that Molloy and Moran might share a physical body. The novel argues that the notion of introspection as sensory knowledge actually *follows logically* from rationalist doubts about sensory knowledge. Molloy's "sensory"-style introspection and amnesia appear to emerge from his potential alter ego's absolute faith in the *cogito* (assuming, for the moment, that Molloy and Moran could in fact share a physical body). Philosophers such as Ryle and Sellars might have seen themselves in opposition to mentalistic philosophy, but *Molloy* implies that the origins of their behaviorist critiques actually lie in accepting the *cogito* fully and without reservation.

As *Molloy*'s sections are possibly out of order, the novel's account of these concepts and their relations takes a while to emerge clearly. But even as Molloy's memory loss becomes apparent on the first page of the novel, there are hints of its philosophical significance:

> I am in my mother's room. It's I who live there now. I don't know how I got there. Perhaps in an ambulance, certainly a vehicle of some kind. I was helped. I'd never have got there alone. There's this man who comes every week. Perhaps I got here thanks to him. He says not. He gives me money and takes away the pages. So many pages, so much money. Yes, I work now, a little like I used to, except that I don't know how to work any more. That doesn't matter apparently. What I'd like now is to speak of the things that are left, say my goodbyes, finish dying. (*Three Novels*, 3)

Molloy's desire to "speak of the things that are left" is emblematic of his narrative as a whole. He isn't suffering from complete amnesia. But as he knows that his own memory is patchy, he proceeds from the bit of his consciousness that feels most solid: the world around him—that is, sensory data. Indeed, Molloy's "I am" is beyond doubt. But it's not the "I am" of the *cogito*. Instead, it's that of an empiricist subject, with "I" comprising nothing more than what is sensed or perceived at any given moment. The name attached to this "I" will eventually come into question, but for now Molloy is able to use his present perceptions to deduce what must, or must not, be true about his past. As we learn later on, Molloy can't bend either of his legs. Therefore, he reasons that he couldn't have reached his mother's room by himself. His deductions, however, are constrained by his unwillingness to doubt empirical data. When he reasons that "this man" might have helped

Inner Sights

him to his mother's room, he undercuts this speculation immediately: "he says not." It never occurs to Molloy that "this man" might be lying (or that his legs might have worked at some point).

But there is something else peculiar about Molloy's "I am." Molloy isn't an empiricist just in the sense that he relies on a posteriori knowledge. His version of introspection is also empiricist and behavioristic; he knows himself primarily by the same means he knows the world around him. His self-knowledge is predicated on both behavioral observation and mental processes that he perceives as somehow having sensory qualities of their own. Molloy's perception of his mind's operations literalizes Hume's theater of consciousness as "all that inner space one never sees, the brain and heart and other caverns" (6). Molloy knows his own mind by sitting in that "inner space" and watching his "thought and feeling dance their Sabbath." But after Molloy is arrested by the police for leaning on his bicycle in a lecherous manner, we see how poor his self-knowledge really is: "The desire to sit down came upon me from time to time, back upon me from a vanished world. And I did not always resist it, forewarned though I was. Yes, my mind felt it surely, this tiny sediment, incomprehensibly stirring like grit at the bottom of a puddle. . . . And suddenly I remembered my name, Molloy. My name is Molloy, I cried, all of a sudden, now I remember. Nothing compelled me to give this information, but I gave it, hoping to please I suppose" (18). Judging by this episode, Molloy is lucky to access his knowledge of anything at all. In trying to *feel* whether he wants to sit down or not—recalling Murphy's belief that he "felt" his mind—Molloy remembers his own name instead. (Later in the novel we'll learn that this might not be the case either.) Molloy's mental feeling is suspect for other reasons as well. Even though he manages to access some kind of memory, voluntarily or otherwise, the act of remembering is still occluded. What characterizes his memory is its suddenness and its involuntariness (reminiscent, maybe, of Proust's *memoire involontaire*). Molloy can't remember why he said his name out loud or why thinking about sitting down would lead him to say his name. In a manner of speaking, he can't tell the difference between his ass and a proverbial "hole in the ground"—or in this case, the contents of his own head. Without the access he needs to his memories, he tries to reconstruct what he was thinking at the time from a more general sense of his dispositions and conduct. If he said his name, he reasons that he was "hoping to please I suppose." Either way, if the "sediment" in question can't actually be felt, then Molloy must achieve self-knowledge by other means.

And that is why Molloy resorts to behavioral self-observation as a meaningful way of knowing himself. Molloy makes a joke about this after spending a day counting his farts: "Four farts every fifteen minutes. It's nothing. Not even one fart every four minutes. It's unbelievable. Damn it, I hardly fart at all, I should never have mentioned it. Extraordinary how mathematics help you to know yourself" (26). Obviously it's funny that Molloy substitutes observing and counting farts for having any memory of his own life. Here, too, there's an unexpected comparison between knowing one's mind and knowing one's ass. But in a very literal sense Molloy has arrived at a true description of himself and one that, despite his faulty memory, allows for both the evaluation and prediction of future events. The episode where Molloy explains his method for sucking stones extends this reasoning even further—demonstrating the degree to which a kind of self-knowledge can be constructed from observation and counting. Molloy has sixteen stones that he sucks on a regular basis. In order to ensure that he sucks each stone equally, and that he sucks them in a particular order, he distributes them among his four pockets. Then, in a sequence that might remind us of Beckett's *Watt* (1953), he works his way through each pocket:

> Taking a stone from the right pocket of my greatcoat, and putting it in my mouth, I replaced it in the right pocket of my greatcoat by a stone from the right pocket of my trousers, which I replaced by a stone from the left pocket of my trousers, which I replaced by a stone from the left pocket of my greatcoat, which I replaced by the stone which was in my mouth, as soon as I'd finished sucking it. Thus there were still four stones in each of my four pockets, but not quite the same stones. And when the desire to suck took hold of me again, I drew again on the right pocket of my greatcoat, certain of not taking the same stone as the last time. (64)

The contents of Molloy's pockets are emblematic of his struggles with self-knowledge. If he were able to see inside his pockets—if he were actually capable of "being certain of not taking the same stone"—he'd have no need for this elaborate system. But as he lacks such inner sight, so to speak, he attempts to reconstruct the knowledge that such sight would provide. The easiest way to do that is to use his coat's design to diminish the probability of picking the same stone twice. If he keeps all the stones in one pocket, then he can't avoid the 1/16 probability of picking the same stone twice. In dividing the stones among four pockets and then moving individual stones through his pockets clockwise, the odds of picking the same stone twice become 1/256 (1/4 × 1/4 × 1/4 × 1/4). But every time he picks an unsucked stone successfully, he introduces a newly sucked stone to the system. Therefore, with every iteration, his odds get worse. If he avoids picking a sucked stone in the first iteration, then the odds of picking one in the second will be 1/192 (1/3 × 1/4 × 1/4 × 1/4). If he avoids picking a sucked stone that time, his odds in the third iteration will be 1/128 (1/2 × 1/4 × 1/4 × 1/4). His system of rotating pockets will only protect him for so long. He then tries a system where each pocket would have a different number of stones—but the results are the same. Eventually, Molloy concludes that his system would only work if he had sixteen pockets (65)—with a one-to-one correspondence between internal and external phenomena.

It is on this point that *Molloy* recalls some of the behaviorist arguments I raised earlier. In particular, it recalls Wilfrid Sellars's Myth of Jones, which hypothesized how an ancestral people might have derived introspective knowledge from observation. After noticing a correspondence between overt actions and covert thoughts, Sellars explains, "our ancestors begin to speak of the privileged access each of us has to his own thoughts" (*Empiricism*, 107). It's tempting to apply this model to Molloy's sucking stones. But there are crucial differences. If Molloy's concept of introspection is derived from a concept of behavioral observation, then theoretically he should have an easier time deriving introspective data from behavioral data. So why doesn't he? In part it's because Sellars's Myth of Jones still accepts an epistemological distinction between overt and covert actions. It also presupposes the ability to distinguish among different examples within both those categories. And that's because the introspective theory of self-knowledge begins only when Jones notices a correspondence between covert and overt actions. But in order to perceive that correspondence, Jones must already have the ability to distinguish one mental state from another (as well as one behavior from another). Molloy, however, doesn't have those abilities. When he thinks about his desire to sit down, he remembers a name instead; when there's more than one stone in his pocket, he can't tell the stones apart. This means that Molloy can't ever establish the kind of correspondences that the Myth of Jones requires. And without that correspondence, it's impossible to derive self-knowledge from behavioral observation of oneself.

So instead of the Myth of Jones, might we appeal to the Myth of Molloy? We could also call it the Myth of Moran (again, entertaining the possibility that Molloy and Moran share a physical body). As Sellars imagined a behavioristic origin story for introspective knowledge, Beckett imagines a strangely

Cartesian origin for that behaviorism. Empiricism and behaviorism follow from the *cogito*, Beckett suggests, the same way that an utter reliance on empirical evidence (i.e., Molloy) can potentially result from doubting everything but the mind itself (i.e., Moran). At the beginning of the second half of *Molloy*, these philosophical differences are not yet apparent. It will be a while before we realize that the novel's sections aren't necessarily in chronological order and that we can't rule out the possibility that Molloy and Moran might be a single person's dual personalities. Instead, Beckett is keen for us to see Molloy and Moran as mirrored opposites. As the first section began with Molloy sitting at a desk, unsure of who he is or how he got there, the second section begins as follows: "It is midnight. The rain is beating on the windows. I am calm. All is sleeping. Nevertheless I get up and go to my desk. . . . My report will be long. Perhaps I will not finish it. My name is Moran, Jacques. That is the name I am known by" (87). There is none of Molloy's confusion here, nor the logical difficulty posed by Moore's paradox (i.e., the rain is beating on the windows, but I believe it isn't). Beyond the fact that they're both sitting at desks, Moran appears to be everything that Molloy is not. He seems to be some sort of detective, while Molloy doesn't seem to have a job. Moran has no obvious doubts about who he is (or at least "the name I am known by"), where he is, or his own state of mind.

What really separates Moran from Molloy, however, is his faith in his own mental abilities. Whereas Molloy's self-knowledge was so poor that he had to resort to observing his own behaviors, Moran is at the other end of the spectrum. He has such faith in his thinking—in effect, in the Cartesian *cogito*—that he has little faith in empirical knowledge. "My mind," he explains, is "where all I need is to be found" (125). We see evidence of this belief after Gaber hires Moran to find Molloy (or so Moran believes). The real work of finding Molloy, it seems, happens not on the road or in the forest but in bed, where Moran—reminiscent, maybe, of Murphy in his rocking chair—looks inside his own mind to make sense of the external world. "It is lying down, in the warmth, in the gloom," he explains, "that I best pierce the outer turmoil's layer, discern my quarry, sense what course to follow, find peace in another's ludicrous distress. Far from the world, its clamours, frenzies, bitterness and dingy light, I pass judgment on it" (105). Faced with the "clamours . . . and dingy light," Moran perceives only his own thinking to be necessary and beyond doubt. For when Moran gets out of bed, "I drown in the spray of phenomena. It is at the mercy of these sensations, which happily I know to be illusory, that I have to live and work"

(106). If it weren't for his warm, gloomy introspections, we infer, Moran wouldn't be able to see through these "illusory" sensations at all.

The trouble is that Moran's own warm, gloomy introspections are potentially no less illusory—or sensory ("sense what course to follow")—than the empirical knowledge he so distrusts. Subsequently, he loses his ability to distinguish between them. We see why this happens when Moran, unable to recall what he's supposed to do with Molloy (or even if he's supposed to find Molloy at all), looks for guidance by turning inward into his own mind: "I did as when I could not sleep. I wandered in my mind, slowly, noting every detail of the labyrinth, its paths as familiar as those of my garden and yet ever new, as empty as the heart could wish or alive with strange encounters. And I heard the distant cymbals, There is still time, still time. But there was not, for I ceased, all vanished and I tried once more to turn my thoughts to the Molloy affair. Unfathomable mind, now beacon, now sea" (101). Indeed, the external world isn't the only source of doubtable sensations. The very act of looking inward creates them as well. Here it's not clear which aspects of Moran's mind are being *perceived* introspectively (insofar as they existed prior to this inward act) and which aspects of Moran's mind are being *produced* by the occasion of the inward act itself. If the mental "labyrinth" is subject to the desires of the "heart"—or, perhaps, the will—then it stands to reason that everything he perceives must be false. As his consciousness examines itself, it becomes both "beacon" and "sea." It is both the lighthouse and the dark water; it is both the maze and the person walking through the maze. For if everything is subject to the desires of the heart, then any distinctions between Moran and maze, or beacon and sea, could be arbitrary or illusory. Moran's sensory experiences in the maze ("noting every detail," "heard the distant cymbals") generate the same problem. Moran acts as if the cymbals he hears are an objective feature of the mental landscape. But it's also possible that the cymbals are a product of his desire. It's possible that he hasn't reencountered these cymbals through introspection but rather created them through the same process.

This kind of confusion results in Moran being unable to doubt any sensation at all, irrespective of its origins. This includes the voice that Moran hears and listens to despite his knowledge that it's a hallucination. Earlier in the novel Molloy also spoke of hearing voices—"the voice . . . of a world collapsing endlessly" (35) and of "my simple feeling and its voice" (65). The origins of those voices are unclear, though it is telling that "feeling" itself has a "voice." And at the end of his narrative, Molloy describes lying in a ditch and hearing "a voice telling me not to fret.... These words struck it is not too much to say as clearly on my ear, and on my understanding, as the urchin's thanks I suppose when I stopped and picked up his marble" (85). As he invokes "ear" and "understanding" simultaneously, it's impossible to tell if this voice is a hallucination or not. We can't rule out the possibility that this voice tracks onto the external world. The origin of the voice Moran hears, however, is unambiguous. Moran doesn't need to remember Gaber's orders, he reasons, because he gets his orders from a different source:

> The voice I listen to needs no Gaber to make it heard. For it is within me and exhorts me to continue to the end the faithful servant I have always been.... Yes it is rather an ambiguous voice and not always easy to follow, in its reasoning and decrees. But I follow it none the less, more or less, I follow it in this sense, that I know what it means, and in this sense, that I do what it tells me. And I do not think there are many voices of which as much may be said. And I feel I shall follow it from this day forth, no matter what it commands. And when it ceases, leaving me in doubt and darkness, I shall wait for it to come back. (126)

This hallucinated voice stands out for the extent of its sensory qualities, as well as the unquestioning obedience of its audience. Not only does Moran hear the voice, despite knowing that it comes from "within," but his language is filled with reminders of the voice's empirical properties. It is no accident that he specifies the different "senses" by which he knows the voice, or the feeling that he "shall follow it." But what's most important about this voice is the function it assumes for Moran. When the voice "ceases," it leaves him "in doubt and darkness." When he can't hear this hallucinated voice, his very "me"—his *cogito*—is suddenly in "doubt," as if it were inseparable from the sensations it represented.

This becomes even more apparent when Moran uses his hands to perceive himself—recalling Molloy's fart counting and Murphy's panicked reflection in Endon's eye. But what's notable is that even though Moran has ceded control to the hallucinated voice, his new attempts at empirical self-knowledge seem to confirm what he already knew about himself at one point. "Physically speaking," Moran explains,

> it seemed to me I was now becoming rapidly unrecognizable. And when I passed my hands over my face, in a characteristic and now more than ever pardonable gesture, the face my hands felt was not my face any more, and the hands my face felt were my hands no longer. And yet the gist of the sensation was the same as

in the far-off days when I was well-shaven and perfumed and proud of my intellectual's soft white hands. . . . To tell the truth I not only knew who I was, but I had a sharper and clearer sense of my identity than ever before. (164)

If the mark of the intellectual used to be his *cogito*, it's now his "soft white hands." Moran knows himself by quite literally feeling himself. While he doesn't recognize his hands, he recognizes the "gist" of the sensation as if there were no operative distinction between sensory knowledge and rational introspective knowledge. It is in this way that we can see Molloy's behavioristic version of introspection not opposing Moran's but following from it (at least conceptually). And yet insofar as this empirical knowledge seems to confirm Moran's earlier conception of himself—"I had a sharper and clearer sense of my identity than ever before"—we are left with no choice but to wonder whether this "sense" can be trusted. Conceivably, it could very well be accurate. But it could also be akin to the hallucinated voice that Moran refuses to doubt or a product of that voice.

Any optimism we might have, of course, is dashed by the novel's final lines. After his unsuccessful quest to find Molloy, Moran returns to his house and finds it abandoned and derelict. He lives in his overgrown garden for an indeterminate amount of time, where he describes finally understanding the language of the voice that speaks to him. And what it tells him throws into doubt potentially everything Moran has told us—especially those facts about himself he told us early on. The voice, Moran explains, "told me to write the report. . . . Then I went back into the house and wrote, It is midnight. The rain is beating on the windows. It was not midnight. It was not raining" (170). The very separation between introspective and empirical knowledge that anchored Moran's narrative was itself a product of his delusions. The distinctions he asserted between world and mind—between mental representation and nonmental representation—were as illusory as the "spray of phenomena" supposedly falling on his windows. We can only wonder whether the presumed separation of Molloy and Moran is similarly illusory.

All Out

As I discussed in the introduction, one of the defining features of literary minds—whether characters, speakers, or perceived authorial minds (as distinct from the actual minds of authors)—is that they are made of language. This is in contrast to actual minds, which are composed of matter. But insofar as everything in a novel (or a poem) is made of language, there are neither ontological nor epistemological differences between literary minds and literary not-minds—between minds and landscapes, between thoughts and broken bicycles, between rainfall and incorrect beliefs or hallucinations about rainfall. Obviously all of these linguistic objects are differentiated logically, grammatically, conventionally, and formally. But on the whole they are made of the same stuff and we know them by the same means. This is one of the things that makes literary minds so peculiar—particularly as we so often perceive these linguistic objects as if they had mental properties of their own.

And insofar as they dissolve the distinctions between introspection and empirical knowledge, this is a point *Murphy* and *Molloy* make as well. Obviously this chapter works toward other goals too, such as showing the ways in which Beckett encountered behaviorism's critique of introspection and instrumentalized it toward his own philosophical agenda. But within the larger frame of this book, Beckett's novels take on added significance. For even though it would be wrong to label Beckett himself a behaviorist, we might see these novels as offering a behavioristic analysis of their own generic conventions, even as Beckett's fictional characters appear to suffer from the same kinds of empirical problems of mind as actual people. In suggesting that introspection is itself a kind of behavioral observation, Beckett effectively removes one of the things that separates mental language in novels from nonmental language. If everything in *Murphy* or *Molloy* is made of the same stuff and known by the same means, Beckett appears to ask us, then what value do we derive from the assumed differences between a character and an object or setting? What might a novel look like without these mind-body dualisms so firmly embedded?

I think that these questions are at the heart of why *Murphy* so often ceases to look like a novel at all. The text's use of English chess notation is one example of this. But in its final pages *Murphy* rejects its novelistic conventions even more assertively—as if to anticipate Beckett's own turn to other modes and genres in the 1940s. Shortly after Murphy sees himself in Endon's "immunity from seeing himself," he sits in his rocking chair and dies in a gas explosion. In death he finally achieves the escape from sensation he had always sought: "The gas went on in the w.c., excellent gas, superfine chaos. Soon his body was quiet" (151). In a letter found after his death Murphy requests that his "body, mind, and soul be burnt and placed in a paper bag" and flushed down the toilet at the Abbey Theatre—"if possible during

Inner Sights 101

the performance of a piece" (161). Murphy's burial plans foreshadow the novel's closing. Following Murphy's death, his once-girlfriend Celia and her grandfather, Mr. Kelly, go to Regents Park to fly a kite. But the park is closing soon, and the rangers are calling for all visitors to leave: "*All out*" (170). Undeterred, Mr. Kelly flies his kite—until the string drops suddenly and pulls his hat down over his face.

> [He] tossed up his arms high and wide and quavered away down the path that led to the water, a ghastly lamentable figure. The slicker trailed along the ground, the skull gushed from under the cap like a dome from under its lantern, the ravaged face was a cramp of bones, throttled sounds jostled in his throat.
>
> Celia caught him on the margin of the pond. . . . Someone fetched the chair and helped to get him aboard. Celia toiled along the narrow path into the teeth of the wind, then faced north up the wide hill. There was no shorter way home. The yellow hair fell across her face. The yachting-cap clung like a clam to the skull. The levers were the tired heart. She closed her eyes. *All out.* (170)

The two operative phrases here are "the levers were the tired heart" and "*All out.*" Murphy might be dead, but the dissolution between introspection and observation, between internal and external action, still holds. As Celia pushes Mr. Kelly up the hill, her complete exhaustion is figured as a statement of identity between her "heart" and the "levers" of Mr. Kelly's wheelchair. The implication is that Celia's internal mental states and the mechanical movements of the wheelchair are the same kinds of phenomena, knowable in the same kinds of ways and describable in the same kinds of language. And as this happens, the park rangers' repeated call of "all out," which had been diegetic and directed at Kelly and Celia, becomes italicized. In that way the novel's final line doesn't look like a line from a novel at all. Instead, it looks like a stage direction—as if to gesture toward a genre or medium less reliant on, or amenable to, distinctly mental representation.

3 Mental Acts

What kind of existence can mental actions, as distinct from physical actions, have on the dramatic stage?[1] If we go back to Beckett's novels *Murphy* and *Molloy*, we might conclude that the answer to this question is "none." By the end of these novels, mental actions don't really exist anymore—at least not as phenomena unto themselves. For if introspection really is a form of sensation or observation, as these novels suggest, then there can be neither ontological nor epistemological differences between mental actions and physical actions. And it is this lack of distinction between mental and physical actions, this lack of dualism, that *Murphy* identifies with the theater. But even if we don't agree with this reasoning, the conventions of dramatic performance still seem to work against the realization of mental actions onstage. For while written texts (e.g., novels and poems) can distinguish between mental and physical actions easily enough, the theater is constrained by physics and the logical entailments of behavior (including speech). In that way there's an obvious similarity between characters onstage and people offstage. Mental actions can certainly be embodied and represented onstage. But in the same way that I can't extract my mental actions and look at them from across the room, it's hard to imagine how a mental action might happen onstage without some kind of physical embodiment or ownership. Indeed, without embodiment or ownership, it's not clear how we would perceive them or if we would even recognize them as "mental" at all. Therefore, whether for philosophical reasons, formal reasons, or even just folk psychology, it seems unlikely we'd ever conclude that mental actions can exist onstage in their own right.

Ostensibly, the desiccated psychologies we encounter in Beckett's plays would do nothing to change this. Nor would the slightly less desiccated psychologies we find in the early plays of Harold Pinter, whom Ruby Cohn described as both "Beckett's spiritual son" and "at least a cousin of the Angry Young Englishmen."[2] Insofar as the plays of Beckett and Pinter entertain the reduction of psychology to physiology, or either occlude or deny mental states entirely, some have gone as far as describing these plays as "behavioristic." For Theodor Adorno, Beckett's *Endgame* (1957) was an example of drama without meaningful psychology. In "Trying to Understand *Endgame*" (1958), he argued that "the inward element supposedly signified" by dramatic speech and gesture "no longer exists" (128). "Beckett's figures," he wrote, "behave primitively and behavioristically, corresponding to conditions after the catastrophe . . . flies that twitch after the swatter has half smashed them" (128). Unlike Adorno, Hannah Scolnicov doesn't invoke the legacy of "muscle-twitchism," but she asserts the behaviorism of Pinter's plays just the same. In *The Experimental Plays of Harold Pinter* (2012), she notes that "behaviorist psychology treats the individual as a 'black box.' . . . It is this way of thinking about human psychology that Pinter adapted for his plays, representing behavior without providing an inner mechanism" (20).[3] Like Beckett's plays, Pinter's also seem to be evacuated of mental representation, if not evacuated of some mental content as well.[4]

And yet when we turn to moments in some of Beckett's and Pinter's most famous plays—*Waiting for Godot* (1953) and *The Homecoming* (1964)—something else seems to be going on. The mise-en-scènes of these plays, whether *Waiting for Godot*'s emptiness or *The Homecoming*'s unfinished home renovations, bring out the barren, unforgiving physicality of theatrical performance. At the same time, they also insist that mental actions and concepts should somehow be realizable onstage. And they do this despite the logical and practical problems entailed by such realization. In *Waiting for Godot*, Lucky and Pozzo insist that mental actions are in fact the same kind of performable, observable actions as singing and dancing. The grammar of Pozzo's offer to have Lucky "dance, or sing, or recite, or think" reinforces this absurdity. You can watch someone while they think, but you can't watch thinking the same way you'd watch dancing. And yet Lucky makes an earnest attempt to do this kind of public thinking anyway. Part of his performance includes the following commentary on "physical culture": "In spite of the strides of physical culture," he says, "the practice of sports such as tennis football running cycling swimming flying floating riding gliding conating camogie skating tennis of all kinds flying sports of all sorts" (43). "Conating"—the desire to act—sneaks in between "gliding" and "camogie," as if they were all spectator sports. Conating, it would seem, is something you ought to be able to watch at an arena or at the theater, despite the obvious difficulties of doing so.

The Homecoming, too, is invested in drawing the audience's eyes to things that can't be seen onstage. One of Lenny's favorite ways to needle his brother Teddy—who might or might not be a philosophy professor—is to pose logical conundrums. How, he asks, "can the unknown merit reverence?" (52). Teddy doesn't have an answer. But Ruth—who might or might not be Teddy's wife—does: "Look at me. I . . . move my leg. That's all it is. But I wear . . . underwear . . . which moves with me . . . it . . . captures your attention. Perhaps you misinterpret. The action is simple. It's a leg . . . moving. My lips move. Why don't you restrict . . . your observations to that? Perhaps the fact that they move is more significant . . . than the words which come through them. You must bear that . . . possibility . . . in mind" (52-53; ellipses in the original). Ruth's comments seem to pull in two different directions. Ostensibly, Ruth asks for a kind of behaviorism here. Teddy and Lenny—as well as the audience—are directed to "restrict" themselves to observable action. And yet Ruth undercuts this direction by drawing our eyes, so to speak, to things we can't observe—forcing us to conceive of her mental actions as being somehow empirically knowable. To make this point, Ruth draws a parallel between her underwear and her psychological motivation, which she distinguishes from "the words which come through them." Both of these unknown objects, Ruth insinuates, "merit reverence." But Pinter, by way of Ruth, has performed some logical sleight of hand. Ruth's comments here blur the line between objects that *won't* be shown onstage and phenomena that *can't* be staged at all. The implication is that Ruth's motivation is knowable in the same way that her underwear is, even though one is a mental concept and the other is a physical object. Through this parallel, Pinter creates the expectation that Ruth's motives might exist or operate onstage independently of her speech and gestures. He teases us with the possibility that we might get to "see" these motives at some point, although we never do.

My claim here is that, despite what we might infer from the end of *Murphy*, the plays of Beckett and Pinter are not at all the behavioristic enterprises often assumed. Instead, as we see in these moments from *Waiting for Godot* and *The Homecoming*, their plays stipulate that mind-body dualism is a necessary aspect of theatrical performance. Moreover, even as they acknowledge the seeming impossibility of their tasks, these plays try to conceive of mental actions onstage as being somehow epistemologically distinct from physical actions. As I mentioned in the introduction, Gilbert Ryle's *The Concept of Mind* argued that the belief in mind-body dualism manifested itself in several ways. One of these was ontological: the belief that minds and bodies are made of different substances (a point I discussed in the introduction). Another was that minds and bodies are members of the same logical category (a point I have discussed throughout this book). But there was also a third epistemological manifestation, which will be my focus here: a belief in two "collateral histories, one consisting of what happens in and to his body, the other consisting of what happens in and to his mind. The first is public, the second private. The events in the first history are in the physical world, those in the second are in the mental world" (2). Ryle's point, of course, was that this belief in two worlds is a mistake. Beckett and Pinter, however, sought to stage these worlds separately and simultaneously. In their efforts to achieve this, both playwrights ultimately created dualistic mise-en-scènes that could hypothetically accommodate both mental and physical actions while also maintaining an essential epistemological distinction between the two.[5]

To show the ways they did this, as well as the different ways Beckett and Pinter instrumentalized these dualistic spaces, I divide the rest of this chapter into four sections. In the first, I examine behaviorism's logical and epistemological arguments against mind-body dualism. Obviously one of these arguments—Ryle's claim that mind-body dualism comprises a category-mistake—is central to this book as a whole. But in order to analyze the conceptual stakes in Beckett's and Pinter's mise-en-scènes, it's necessary to trace the evolution of behaviorism's critique of dualism, focusing in part on Ryle's distinction between "knowing how" and "knowing that"—and the ways that dualism might nonetheless persist in theatrical performance. In the second section I turn to Beckett's plays *Eleutheria* (1948) and *Krapp's Last Tape* (1957), both of which use a dualistic mise-en-scène to give mental actions a physical reality but do so in a way that doesn't merely turn them into physical actions. In *Eleutheria*, which was Beckett's first play but only published and performed after his death, a split set allows the simultaneous staging of a "main action" and a "marginal action," which comprise different kinds of performances that the audience is encouraged to know in different ways. In *Krapp's Last Tape*, the set's lighting design divides the stage into different epistemological zones corresponding to the different kinds of knowledge that can be accessed there. Additionally, Krapp's memories are stored not in his head but on tape reels, which allow these memories to exist onstage independently of Krapp's body. Pinter's plays *The Birthday Party* (1955) and *The Dumb Waiter* (1957) also make use of a dualistic mise-en-scène—using the main stage to represent "words spoken" and relegating "things known" to an unseen offstage space. And much as Ruth suggested that her motives and underwear were knowable in the same way, *The Birthday Party* and *The Dumb Waiter* let their characters and audiences imagine that the difference between "words spoken" and "things known" is one of degree rather than type. But insofar as Pinter believed that language use necessitated the epistemological separation of mental and physical worlds, he never lets this realization occur. Instead, it's a false promise, and one that his characters, as they exploit the gaps between mental and physical worlds, turn into a weapon. In the chapter's concluding section I argue that even though dramatic minds do have some ontological similarities to actual minds, we must understand them as meaningfully comparable to the written literary minds we encounter in novels and poetry.

Behaviorism and Dualism

In the early days of behaviorism, mind-body dualism wasn't much of a concern. Watson's "Psychology as the Behaviorist Views It" (1913) was largely dismissive of its relevance to psychological study—much as he was dismissive of philosophy more generally. "Those time-honored relics of philosophical speculation," he wrote, "need trouble the student of behavior as little as they trouble the student of physics. The consideration of the mind-body problem affects neither the type of problem selected nor the formulation of the solution to that problem" (166). Insofar as behaviorism was only interested in overt behavior, the Cartesian distinction between being "a thinking, non-extended thing" and "an extended, non-thinking thing" (*Selected Philosophical* Writings, 114-15) was beside the point.

But by the time *Behaviorism* was published in 1924, Watson's attitudes toward dualism had changed. It was also in *Behaviorism* that we see behaviorism's epistemological critique of dualism begin to distinguish itself from materialism's ontological critiques of dualism. In Judeo-Christian religion, Watson explained, believers are taught that

> there is a fearsome God and that every individual has a soul which is separate and distinct from the body. This soul is really a part of the supreme being. This concept has led to the philosophical platform called 'dualism.' All psychology except behaviorism is dualistic. *That is to say we have both a mind (soul) and a body. This*

dogma has been present in human psychology from earliest antiquity. No one has ever touched a soul, or has seen one in a test tube, or has in any way come into relationship with it as he has with the other objects of his daily experience. (4)

There's a lot to be suspicious of in Watson's reasoning here—particularly the claim that "all psychology except behaviorism is dualistic." By the twentieth century, substance dualism—the idea that minds and bodies are made of different substances or materials—had largely disappeared from psychology. The introspective psychologists that Watson attacked in "Psychology as the Behaviorist Views It" were no exception. In *Principles of Physiological Psychology* (1874), Wilhelm Wundt argued against metaphysical conceptions of "mind" and "spirit" explicitly. "Mind, in popular thought," he explained, is "a substance, a real being" (17). In contrast, physiological psychology would understand "mind" as "the logical subject of internal experience . . . freed of all those accretions of crude metaphysics which invariably attach to concepts" (18). Wundt's, of course, were not the only arguments against Cartesian dualism. In *The Principles of Psychology* (1890), William James attacked what he perceived as the substance dualism of Herbert Spencer.[6] And in his later essay "Does 'Consciousness' Exist?" (1904), James made his own version of neutral monism more explicit. "My thesis," he wrote, "is that we start with the supposition that there is only one primal stuff or material in the world, a stuff of which everything is composed, and if we call that stuff 'pure experience,' then knowing can easily be explained as a particular sort of relation . . . into which portions of pure experience may enter" (170).

It would therefore be hard to criticize either James or Wundt for believing in mind-body dualism. But that is precisely what Watson tried to do. Far from establishing a truly "scientific" psychology, he claimed, modern psychology was merely the translation of quasi-religious doctrine into a more technical vocabulary. "All that Wundt and his students really accomplished," Watson suggested, "was to substitute for the word 'soul' the word 'consciousness'" (5). As a concept, "consciousness" was no more scientifically useful or precise than "soul." "To the behaviorist," he wrote, "the two terms are essentially identical, so far as concerns their metaphysical implications" (5). Therefore, when Watson accused Wundt and others of mind-body dualism, he wasn't necessarily criticizing them for believing that mind and body are made of different substances. Instead, he was criticizing them for *conceptual or epistemological dualism*—that is, for having concepts of "mind" or "mental state" at all. When Watson suggested that behaviorism was the only nondualist psychology, what he meant was that behaviorism was the only psychology that dispensed with the myth of consciousness itself.

As I mentioned in earlier chapters, many of Watson's claims provoked controversy. But at the same time, Watson's formulation of mind-body dualism as an epistemological problem set an important precedent for logical behaviorism later on. The phrase "logical behaviorism" first appeared in Carl Hempel's "The Logical Analysis of Psychology" (1935). Hempel's logical behaviorism attempted to synthesize aspects of Watsonsian behaviorism with the epistemology of the Vienna Circle—particularly the sociological behaviorism of Otto Neurath and the translational reductionism of Rudolf Carnap.[7] "We find in [psychological] behaviorism," Hempel explained, "an attempt to construct a scientific psychology which would show by its success that even in psychology we have to do with purely physical processes" (16). But there were key differences between Watson's doctrine and Hempel's. First, logical behaviorism wasn't a psychological theory. Instead, it was a logical theory about the kinds of statements that psychological language could make. Therefore, Hempel abandoned many of psychological behaviorism's methodological claims. From the perspective of the Vienna School, introspection was no less reliable than behavioral observation, such that there was no reason for "psychological research [to] restrict itself methodologically to the study of the responses organisms make to certain stimuli" (20). Second, Hempel dismissed Watson's wholesale rejection of consciousness as a misunderstanding of the concept involved. "Logical behaviorism," Hempel wrote, "claims neither that minds, feelings, inferiority complexes, voluntary actions, etc., do not exist, nor that their existence is in the least doubtful. It insists that the very question as to whether these psychological constructs really exist is already a pseudoproblem" (20).

Nonetheless, what emerged from Hempel's logical behaviorism was a critique of mind-body dualism that converged with Watson's, even as they disagreed on the epistemological value of psychological concepts. For Watson, such concepts were a distorting representation. The term "memory" denoted not a stand-alone mental action but rather the "verbal part of a total habit." Conversely, Hempel claimed that such substitution was precisely the value of psychological language—a way of referring to, and knowing about, more fundamental physical phenomena. But neither psychological language nor psychological phenomena were of any value on their own. Insofar as psychological descriptions are necessarily translatable to physical descriptions, Hempel explained, "the meaning of a psychological statement consists solely in the function of abbreviating the description of certain modes of physical response characteristic of the bodies of men or animals" (19). Hempel's logical behaviorism was the first of many—from Wittgenstein's comments on psychology in *Philosophical Investigations* to Wilfrid Sellars's Myth of Jones, which I discussed in the previous chapter. Few of these philosophers were as committed to physicalist reduction as Hempel. But each advanced the project of logical behaviorism, attempting to strip philosophy of mentalistic assumptions and redefine the epistemological relations between physical and psychological phenomena. For the purpose of analyzing logical behaviorism's critique of mind-body dualism, my focus here will be Ryle's discussion of these topics in *The Concept of Mind*.

As I mentioned earlier, Ryle claimed that one aspect of Cartesian dualism was the belief in two worlds: one physical (which was public) and one mental (which was private). This belief in two counterpart worlds was the product of a category-mistake—of assuming that minds and bodies are comparable and the same types of concept. But that doesn't mean that Ryle believed only in a purely physical world. Instead, he argued that "mind" and "body" couldn't be understood as representing different types of concepts, actions, or worlds. "Mind" and "body" were incorrectly isolated aspects of the same persons, processes, and actions. "When we characterize people by mental predicates," he explained, "we are not making untestable inferences to any ghostly processes occurring in streams of consciousness which we are debarred from visiting; we are describing the ways in which those people conduct parts of their predominantly public behavior" (39). If I say that someone is happy, Ryle's reasoning goes, I am not merely making a statement about that person's mental states; rather, I am making a statement about that person's bearing or comportment as a whole. In effect, mental predicates can't be applied independently of behavioral predicates, particularly if I've used the latter to deduce (or isolate) the former. What we think of as mental phenomena, Ryle claimed, are actually implied logical relations among observed phenomena.

Ryle's most influential proof for this claim was his attack on the distinction between "knowing how" and "knowing that." "Both philosophers and laymen," he explained, "tend to treat intellectual operations as the core of mental conduct; that is to say, they tend to define all other mental-conduct concepts in terms of cognition" (15). As a result, when we talk about intelligent behavior (i.e., doing something intentionally), we tend to separate it into two parts: *knowing how* and *knowing that*. This separation follows, Ryle explained, from the Cartesian separation of body and mind. Let's imagine I want to play chess. In order to play chess, I must first possess factual knowledge about the rules and conventions of chess. I must know which pieces have which names and the different abilities each piece has. That is all factual knowledge that I can acquire before I sit down to play my first game. In short, I think before I move. Ryle called this process "the intellectualist legend": the belief that performing a single intelligent action actually involved two distinct actions (*knowing that* followed by *knowing how*). First, you "consider certain appropriate propositions, or prescriptions"; then, you "put into practice what these propositions or prescriptions enjoin. It is to do a bit of theory and then do a bit of practice" (18). This sounds reasonable enough. But Ryle maintained that the intellectual legend comprises something of a conundrum. "If," he wrote, "for any operation to be intelligently executed, a prior theoretical operation had first to be performed and performed intelligently, it would be a logical impossibility for anyone ever to break into the circle" (19). To return to the example of chess: I want to move my pawn to square K4 (much as Murphy began his final match against Endon). In order to do that, I must first successfully "perform" my factual knowledge in my head. But in order to perform that factual knowledge successfully, I must first perform a different piece of factual knowledge, which must be preceded by another performance, and so on. By this reasoning, the intellectualist myth invariably leads to an infinite logical regress.

Therefore, Ryle concluded, "When I do something intelligently . . . I am doing one thing and not two. My performance has a special procedure or manner, not antecedent" (32). *Knowing how* and *knowing that* comprised not separate consequential activities but, like body and mind, inappropriately separated aspects of the same phenomenon. As an example, Ryle offered the performances of clowns:

> The cleverness of the clown may be exhibited in his tripping and tumbling. He trips and tumbles just as clumsy people do, except that he trips and tumbles on purpose and after much rehearsal and at the golden moment and where the children can see him and so as not to hurt himself. The spectators applaud his skill at seeming clumsy, but what they applaud is not some extra hidden performance executed "in his head." It is his visible performance that they admire, but they admire it not for being an effect of any hidden internal causes but for being an exercise of a skill. . . . The traditional theory of mind has misconstrued the type-

distinction between disposition and exercise into its mythical bifurcation of unwitnessable mental causes and their witnessable physical effects. (22)

When we see someone excel at clowning, Ryle claimed, we don't say they have an encyclopedic knowledge of clowning's rules, techniques, and history. Instead, we praise the clown performance as a whole. But to be fair, clowning is an excellent and convenient example for Ryle's point. It's hard to be a good clown; it takes a lot of effort and practice. However, there are also conventional associations between clowning and performing physical actions stupidly—that is, with an implied lack of thinking, awareness, or planning. In order to make a point about the absence of antecedent mental operations, Ryle has chosen an activity where those kinds of mental predicates are less likely to appear anyway. If we don't generally describe clowns as possessing lots of clowning knowledge "in their heads," it's not just because *knowing that* and *knowing how* are parts of the same process. It's also because we're talking about *clowns*: figures whose humor is precisely that of a person being overwhelmed by physicality. In contrast, if we were to talk about an actor on the stage—someone who assumes a new identity and speaks memorized words likely written by another person—Ryle's arguments against mind-body dualism would not work so well.

A Dualistic Space

This isn't to say that dramatic actors necessarily assume a hard distinction between *knowing how* and *knowing that* when performing. But like pretense and dishonesty, or thinking one thing and saying another, certain theatrical conventions do seem to entail the separation between mental states and physical actions—even though the former are typically visible only through the latter.[8] And we know this from the kind of language we use to describe actors onstage. As audience members we expect that the people onstage are neither making factual statements nor acting like themselves. As Ryle points out, spectators are different from people who have been deceived by liars, as spectators have "paid to see people act who advertise themselves as actors" (154). We realize that an actor's performance onstage is not necessarily the same as their conduct as a person. Indeed, the very concept of "conduct"—which Ryle uses to signify the inherent inseparability of mental and behavioral predicates—doesn't apply during a theatrical performance the way it might before or after the show. There is no apparent contradiction in the following sentence about a hypothetical production of *Waiting for Godot*: "Lucky is unhappy but the actor performing Lucky is not unhappy." (Let's assume for the moment that Lucky and the actor, and their respective mental predicates, are actually comparable in that way—a point I will return to later on.) Even though Lucky and the actor necessarily share the same physical properties—that is, if one has red hair and jumps, then so does the other—the concept of "performing" allows two different sets of mental predicates to be applied to the same individual at the same moment. It does this without indication that these sets are mutually exclusive or that each set has a corresponding phenomenal experience. Instead, these sets of mental predicates have different logical and psychological relations to the behaviors we see onstage. One set, that of Lucky, corresponds to these visible behaviors and is therefore public. The other, that of the actor, is private—submerged beneath the performance. Even if we grant that the offstage separation of mental and physical worlds is a mistake, many actors onstage have little choice but to live "two collateral histories, one consisting of what happens in and to his body, the other consisting of what happens in and to his mind" (2).

This is less of a claim about mind-body dualism generally than it is about dramatic convention. Many performance theorists and critics, however, would disagree with my assertion of these dualistic entailments. For while some modern theater traditions have made a point of separating the actor's mental and physical processes—Brecht's epic theater is an important example[9]—most have rejected any possibility of either complete ontological or epistemological separation. In *An Actor Prepares* (1936), Constantin Stanislavski made the inseparability of mind and body, of mental and physical phenomena, a cornerstone of his method. "The bond between body and soul," he wrote, "is indivisible. . . . Every physical act, except purely mechanical ones, has an inner source of feeling. Consequently we have both an inner and outer plane in every role, inter-laced" (136). In *The Theatre and Its Double* (1938), Antonin Artaud made a parallel point, asserting both physical and mystical unities between mind and body. "The soul," he wrote, "can be physiologically summarized as a maze of vibrations. . . . Belief in the soul's flowing substantiality is essential to the actor's craft. To know that an emotion is substantial, subject to the plastic vicissitudes of matter, gives him control over his passions" (90).

More recent performance theorists, however, have taken even more acutely anti-dualist positions. Some, such as Stanton Garner and William Demastes, have suggested that the theater is itself the space where ontological and epistemological divisions fall away entirely. In *Bodied Spaces: Phenomenology and Performance in Contemporary Drama* (1994), Garner casts the theater as "a non-Cartesian field of habitation which undermines the stance of objectivity and in which the categories of subject and object give way to a stance of mutual implication" (4). Demastes reaches a similar conclusion in *Staging Consciousness: Theater and the Materialization of Mind* (2002). "Theater," he writes, "is phenomenologically complete . . . that place where 'mind-stuff' and 'physical-stuff' intermingle in a manner precisely parallel to our growing sense of material consciousness" (53). And in making the case for the importance of Descartes on seventeenth-century French theater, R. Darren Gobert emphasizes the inseparability, rather than separability, of the Cartesian mind and body. As he writes in *The Mind-Body Stage: Passion and Interaction in the Cartesian Theater* (2013), "Descartes teaches us that the passions united mind and body and that, whatever his commitment to substance dualism, the material and immaterial are inextricable" (6).[10]

Broadly speaking, the critical expectation today is that theater is a thoroughly anti-dualist enterprise. It's presumed that, once onstage, most distinctions between mental and physical concepts dissolve.[11] And this is why it's important to see how a play such as Beckett's *Eleutheria* so explicitly takes epistemological dualism as a principle of its mise-en-scène. During the first two acts, the stage itself is split in half. On one half of the stage we have more traditional theatrical representation, as the Krap family discusses the social withdrawal of their son Victor. On the other half of the stage Beckett compiles silent, repetitive actions into a different kind of theatrical representation —something like a composite picture of private mental life. *Eleutheria* is therefore something of a prototype for a play like *Krapp's Last Tape*, which also features a shut-in named Krap/Krapp and a divided mise-en-scène. Jean-Michel Rabaté sees *Eleutheria* as inheriting material from yet another Beckettian text about a shut-in: *Murphy*. "The central issue" in these texts, Rabaté explains in *Think, Pig!* (2016), "is the dead end created by the insistence on the free possession of one's self—thus Murphy between his mind and body, his sexual desire and his regressive wish to become a psychotic. Victor's autistic refusal leads him to a strange levity, as a sort of levitation over the world of social contracts, which describes his freedom of the void" (108). Indeed, the word "eleutheria" itself means liberty or freedom in ancient Greek. Much as Murphy sought freedom from bodily sensation, we might speculate that Victor seeks freedom from other people.[12]

But I think it would be a mistake to see *Eleutheria* as less concerned with mind-body dualism, or the nature of mental states, than *Murphy*. Victor isn't the student of Descartes or Geulincx that Murphy is. His physician Dr. Piouk, however, has strong feelings about the separation, or lack of separation, between mind and body. Like Lucky and Pozzo in *Waiting for Godot*, Dr. Piouk (pronounced "puke") maintains that nothing is lost when mental phenomena are described in strictly physical terms. For him, mental illness is just a kind of physical illness. When Henri Krap worries that he has become "incapable of reflection myself, it is my organs that have taken over," Dr. Piouk reassures him that this statement is "meaningless":

> M. KRAP. Wait a minute! Meaning what?
> DR. PIOUK. You are your organs, Monsieur, and your organs are you.
> M. KRAP. I am my organs?
> DR. PIOUK. That is so.
> M. KRAP. You are frightening me.
> MME. MECK. [Sniffing out free medical advice] And me, Doctor, am I also my organs?
> DR. PIOUK. Without the least bit left over, Madame. (*Eleutheria: A Play in Three Acts*, 28-29)

Dr. Piouk doesn't distrust "reflection" or introspective knowledge. Instead, what Dr. Piouk identifies as "meaningless" is the conceptual distinction between people and their organs—as if the epistemological distinction between mental and physical phenomena were unnecessary. Similarly, when Dr. Piouk is trying to goad Victor into suicide, physicalism is once again marshaled as an excuse to avoid mentalistic language. The relation Dr. Piouk sees between consciousness and dermatology, however, goes unexplained. "The purest act of consciousness," Piouk explains to Victor, "is howlingly [he takes his head in his hands] physical, howlingly, you know it as well as I do, it's engraved on your comedones" (180). We can only speculate as to what Dr. Piouk finds so philosophically significant about Victor's acne.

As we might infer from his sudden appeal to dermatology, Dr. Piouk shouldn't be taken too seriously. Instead, he is a foil to *Eleutheria*'s own dualistic epistemology and staging. As I mentioned earlier, *Eleutheria* was never staged during Beckett's lifetime—in no small part because its stage directions required "un espace dualiste," or "dualistic space" (3). Moreover, this demand for a dualistic space had an outsized effect on literary history. In 1950, Beckett submitted two French-language manuscripts to the director Roger Blin: *Eleutheria* and *En Attendant Godot*. Blin said he didn't understand *Godot* and that he was inclined toward *Eleutheria*, which was more classically theatrical. Financial considerations, however, prevailed. As Blin explained to Beckett's biographer Deirdre Bair, *Eleutheria* had "seventeen characters, a divided stage, elaborate props, and complicated lighting. I was poor. I didn't have a penny. I couldn't think of anyone who owned a theater suitable for such a complicated production. I thought I'd be better off with *Godot* because there were only four actors and they were bums. They could wear their own clothes if it came to that, and I wouldn't need anything but a spotlight and bare branch for a tree."[13]

Blin's comments, however, give only a limited sense of the technical challenges posed by *Eleutheria*'s mise-en-scène. By itself, the divided stage— split between Victor's bedroom and the Kraps' morning room—wasn't much of a problem. The real difficulty lay in the movement of the stage itself, as the bedroom and morning room switched sides between acts. According to the stage directions, "In each act Victor's room is presented from another angle, with the result that, viewed from the house, it is to the left of the Krap enclave in the first act, to the right of the Krap enclave in the second act, and that from one act to the next the main action remains on the right. This also explains why there is no marginal action in the third act, the Krap side having fallen into the pit following the swing of the scene onstage" (4). These stage directions lack the detail and precision characteristic of Beckett's later plays. It's unclear whether "fallen into the pit" is a figure of speech or not (for the purposes of my discussion here I have chosen to take it literally).[14] Either way, the proposed mise-en-scène could be tough to manage, particularly during performances. Unless the stage itself were built on a rotating platform (which would be expensive, per Blin's concerns), stagehands would have to "rotate" the stage at the end of act 1. In addition to switching stage left and stage right, they would have to rotate props and furniture so the audience perceived them from "another angle." At the end of act 2, Victor's bedroom would be rotated again, while the Kraps' living room would be either removed from the stage or dumped into the orchestra pit. Figures 6-8 are approximate renderings of the stage's appearance in each act of the play.

The point of this dualistic stage was that it allowed two different scenes to be performed at once: the "main action," which was always stage right, and a "marginal action," which was always stage left (or in the pit). But these "main" and "marginal" actions had less in common than their names might

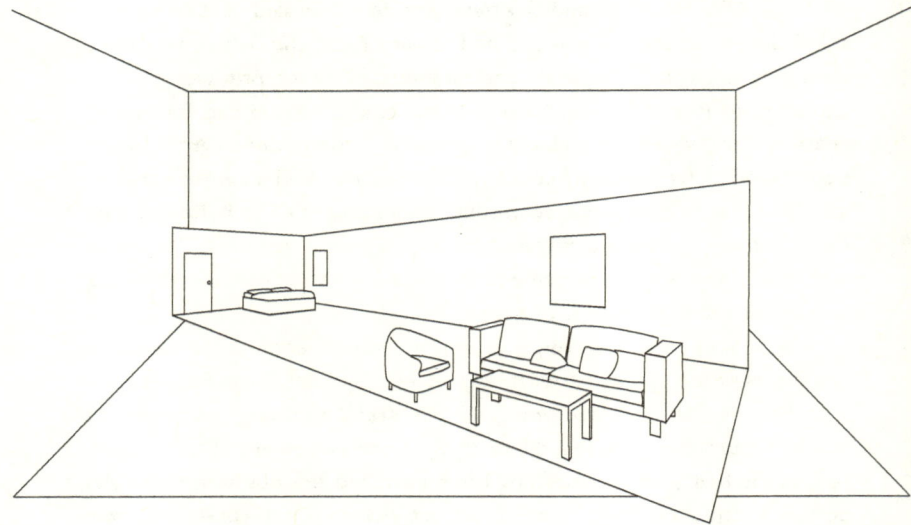

Figure 6. *Eleutheria*, act 1: The morning room (upstage, stage left) is the main action; it faces the audience. The bedroom (downstage, stage right) is the marginal action. Drawing courtesy of Julia Gang.

imply. The main action included all of the play's dialogue, as well as any other observable interactions between characters. The script of *Eleutheria*, we're told, "concerns the main action exclusively" (2). In other words, the main action comprises what we typically expect from plays—monologues, dialogues, choreography, and so on. The marginal action, however, follows a different set of rules. According to the stage directions, the marginal action would be "silent apart from a few short sentences and, as regards non-verbal expression, reduced to a vague attitude and movements of a single character. Strictly speaking less of an action than a site" (4). As the main action drives the play's plot forward, the marginal action behind it is just an endless loop of repeated behaviors. In that way, the marginal action is "less of an action than a site"—a backdrop comprising "vague attitude[s]" and emotions. In act 1, the gathering of Kraps and Piouks in the morning room is set against a backdrop of Victor alternating between motionlessness and listless movement. The stage directions describe "Victor in bed. Motionless. He moves this way and that, sits up in bed, gets up, goes back and forth . . . slowly and vaguely, often stops, looks out the window, toward the audience, goes back to sit on the bed, gets back in bed, becomes motionless,

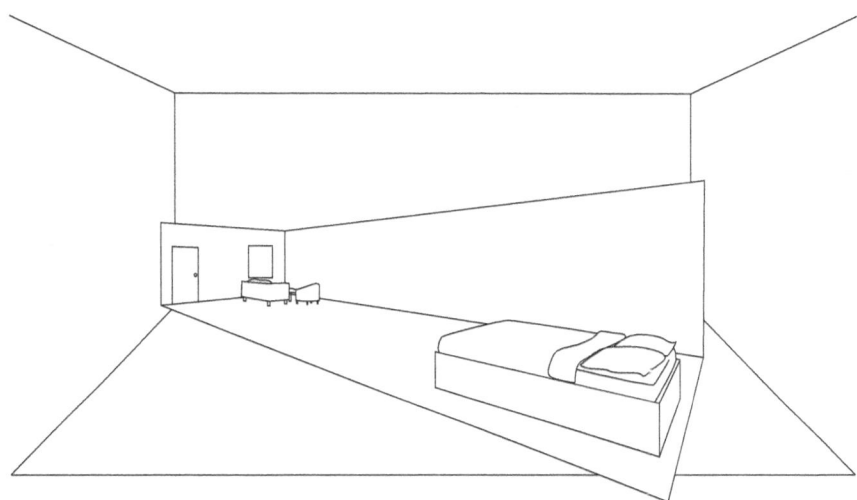

Figure 7. *Eleutheria*, act 2: The bedroom (now downstage, stage left) is the main action; it faces the audience. The morning room (now upstage, stage right) is the marginal action; it now faces away from the audience. Drawing courtesy of Julia Gang.

gets up again, resumes his walk etc." (5). Repeated untold times throughout act 1, these individual observable behaviors blur together as a larger image of Victor's "vague attitude"—which, while composed of physical behaviors, is hardly reducible to them. The picture of this vague attitude serves as the actual backdrop for the conversations happening in the morning room. But while the audience can see this psychological backdrop, the Kraps and the Piouks cannot.

So while Victor's marginal action is still an "action" in the technical sense, it entails a different concept of action than the main event in the morning room, which is why I think Beckett likens it to a "site." Yes, it has a physical presence onstage, but by virtue of its regularity and repetitiveness, the audience learns to know these actions through inference rather than sensation. Indeed, depending on where they happen onstage, given behaviors by a given actor assume different epistemological functions and values. In the main action, the movements and utterances of the characters comprise the play's plot. When Victor rises from his bed in act 2, as Victor's bedroom is the site of the main action, this rising is meaningful as an observable behavior. It is meaningful, in part, because other characters can see it; the Kraps and the Piouks have gathered because of Victor's lethargy, and several other

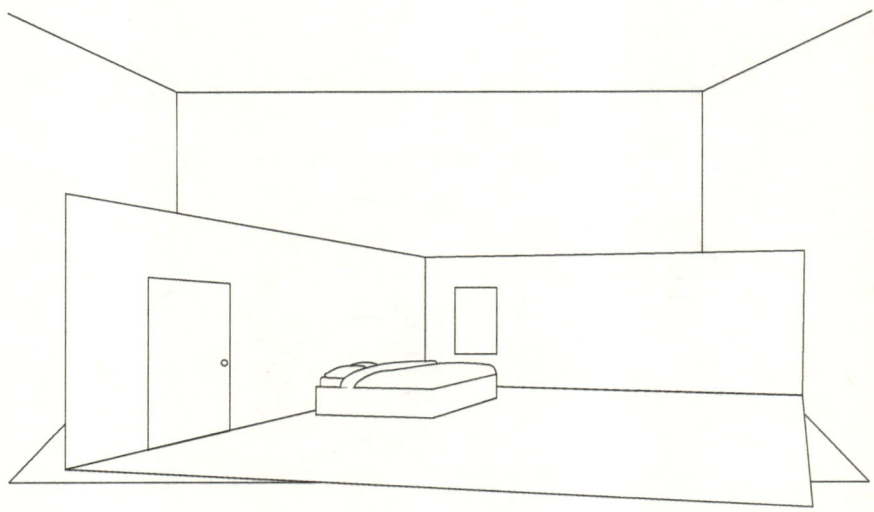

Figure 8. *Eleutheria*, act 3: The bedroom is the main (and only) action. The morning room has fallen into the pit. Drawing courtesy of Julia Gang.

events will occur because Victor has now gotten out of bed. But when Victor gets out of bed in act 1, when his bedroom is the site of the marginal action, this behavior has a different epistemological value. Visible only to the audience and Victor himself, the stage directions tell us that this rising from the bed is separate from the play's plot. And yet we'd be hard-pressed to say that it's not a crucial aspect of Victor's characterization. Repeated throughout act 1, this action is meaningful not because of what it entails physically or narratologically but because it amounts to a composite of mental life.

In act 3, however, the audience loses the ability to view this mental life. Both physical and mental actions occur onstage, but the marginal action has been "swallowed up by the pit" (125).[15] Victor's observable behaviors function to remind us of what we can no longer see, as well as Victor's general inability to function in the physical world. In the play's final moments, Victor tries to minimize his own physical presence onstage:

> (Victor seated on the bed. He looks at the bed, the room, the window, the door. He gets up and undertakes to push his bed to the back of the room, as far from the door and the window as possible, that is, toward the side of the footlights

with the Audience member's stage-box. He has a hard time. He pushes it, pulls it, with pauses for rest, seated on the edge of the bed. It is clear that he is not strong. He finally succeeds. He sits down on the bed, now parallel to the footlights. After a while, he gets up, goes to the switch, turns it off, looks out the window, goes back and sits down on the bed, facing the audience. He looks perseveringly at the audience, the orchestra, the balcony (should there be one), to the right, to the left. Then he gets into bed, his scrawny back turned on mankind.) CURTAIN. (191)

In a certain way, Victor succeeds where Murphy failed. As he turns his back on the audience, he seizes the eleutheria he has sought throughout the play. But even more importantly, Victor's actions here reaffirm the importance—and even necessity—of the prior acts' dualistic mise-en-scènes. In earlier acts, we might have had access to Victor's private mental world. At the end of the play, we have no reason to believe that this mental world has ceased to exist; if anything, Victor's physical weakness implies that he has chosen this mental world over the physical world. But the play's medium for representing that mental world—the divided set—has fallen into the orchestra pit. As a result of this, and of Victor turning away from the proscenium, the audience is left with no means of inferring Victor's mental actions. In effect, *Eleutheria* concludes by forcing the audience to experience the *loss* of Victor's mental life—affirming not only their onstage existence but also the necessity of that which it can no longer represent.

It is tempting to think of *Krapp's Last Tape* as providing us with some of the mental actions obscured at the end of *Eleutheria*. After all, Krapp and Victor Krap differ by only one letter. It's easy to imagine the misanthropic teenager adding another *p* to his name and becoming the misanthropic pensioner. Unfortunately, there's no evidence to support this, similar-sounding names aside. Moreover, we must be careful not to overlook the key logical and epistemological differences between these plays. For all its scenographical complexity, *Eleutheria* only imputes mental properties to human beings. In *Krapp's Last Tape*, however, both mental and physical properties are attributed across logical categories. The issue isn't merely a "tension . . . between the physical immediacy of the live performance (actors and tangible sets) and the cerebral, otherworldly implications of its heightened language," as Sidney Homan suggests (*Beckett's Theaters*, 97). Instead, like so many other literary texts in this book, *Krapp's Last Tape* is grounded in a sequence of category-mistakes—both the attribution of mental properties to objects and the attribution of physical properties to mental concepts. And it is through these category-mistakes, as well as its set and lighting design, that *Krapp's Last Tape* is able to present mental actions as being extractable from the mind—and therefore stageable in their own right.

This investment in the separation of mental actions from physical actions is apparent in the play's opening moments—well before we know that Krapp has recorded (even transferred) his mental states onto audiotapes. Much as *Eleutheria* used its divided stage to distinguish between types of action, *Krapp's Last Tape* uses lighting design to distinguish between different epistemological modes. As the curtain rises, the audience sees Krapp sitting at a small table, which has two drawers facing the proscenium:

> On the table a tape-recorder with microphone and a number of cardboard boxes containing reels of recorded tapes.
>
> Table and immediately adjacent area in strong white light. Rest of stage in darkness.
>
> Krapp remains a moment motionless, heaves a great sigh, looks at his watch, fumbles in his pockets, takes out an envelope, puts it back, fumbles, takes out a small bunch of keys, raises it to his eyes, chooses a key, gets up and moves to front of table. He stoops, unlocks first drawer, peers into it, feels about inside of it, takes out a reel of tape, peers at it, locks drawer, unlocks second drawer, peers into it, feels about inside of it, takes out a large banana, peers at it, locks drawer, puts keys back in his pocket. He turns, advances to edge of stage, halts, strokes banana, peels it, drops skin at his feet, puts end of banana in his mouth and remains motionless, staring vacuously before him. Finally he bites off the end, turns aside and begins pacing to and fro at edge of stage, in the light, i.e., not more than four or five paces either way, meditatively eating banana. (10-11)

In 1969, Beckett was invited to direct *Krapp's Last Tape* (*Das letzte Band*) at Berlin's Schiller-Theater Werkstatt. In his production notes, Beckett offered a distinctly Manichean interpretation of the play's lighting design. The stage's light and dark zones were supposed to correspond to traditional Manichean symbolism, as was the black-and-white imagery in Krapp's monologues. "Note that Krapp [*erasure*] decrees," Beckett wrote, "physical (ethical) incompatibility of light (spiritual) and dark (sensual) only when he intuits possibility of their reconciliation intellectually as rational-irrational" (141). The darkness on stage, it would seem, marks the space of the "sensual"—the space of physicality. The light area onstage, which includes the tape recorder, is "spiritual." But this arrangement is itself contingent on Krapp's realizing the possibility of their "reconciliation," although Beckett neglects to mention when in the play this realization takes place.

In his introduction to the Schiller notebook, James Knowlson warns against taking this interpretation to heart. Following the Schiller production of *Das letzte Band*, he explains, "Beckett showed himself either to be wary of his own Manichaean reading or suspicious at least of being committed to anything as explicit as the [Manichaean portions of the notebook] seems to be" (*Theatrical Notebooks of Samuel Beckett*, xxii). But even without the Manichean specifics, Beckett's notes still identify light and dark as representing different epistemological modes. And this is manifest in the opening scene's stage directions. When Krapp is in the dark, his main activity is the active, *sensuous* (if not quite "sensual") acquisition of information. Here perception and motion are tied together inexorably—fumbling, feeling, peering through the desk's contents. In the light, however, everything slows down. It's too early in the play to know whether the light—including the table, tapes, and tape recorder—is "spiritual." Krapp's conduct, however, is substantially different than it was in the dark. In the dark, his focus is on immediate perception —on empirical knowledge in the present tense. Standing at the edge of the stage, but still in the light, he eats the banana "meditatively," as if his thoughts were elsewhere, so to speak. And as Beckett's production notes show, Krapp moves between light and dark zones methodically. A diagram from Beckett's notes (fig. 9) indicates Krapp's precise movements between light and dark zones while eating the banana, where the drawer (B) and the eating location (3) are at the very edges of the lit area—as if there were carefully placed steps between light and dark.

In that way, the lighting design prepares us for the play's central conceit: that Krapp has transferred his memories to audiotapes and that he accesses these memories by listening to the tapes in the lit area onstage (which he does at location A in the diagram). As a result, much of Krapp's private mental world is now available to the audience. Several layers of category-mistakes make this possible—not only in terms of mental states being imputed to the tape recorder but also in terms of memories having sensory properties. In the previous chapter I discussed the different ways in which introspection was perceived as a kind of empirical knowledge—as if mental states have sensory properties of their own. And that is precisely what has happened to Krapp's memories. Insofar as they only exist on audiotapes, such that remembering cannot happen without hearing, Krapp's mental life has been

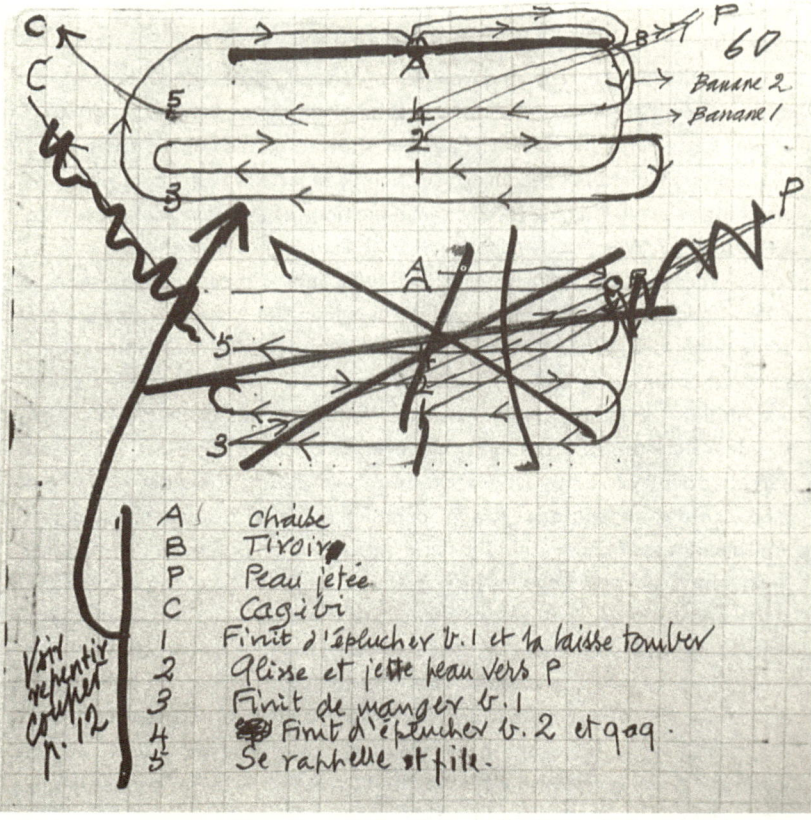

Figure 9. Samuel Beckett's Production Notebook for *Das Letzte Band*, page 60 (Beckett, *Theatrical Notebooks*, 165).

reconfigured epistemologically. Even though we typically think of memory as something private and covert, the audience has the same empirical access to Krapp's memories that Krapp does. Hearing has, somehow, become logically comparable with remembering. The language spoken by the younger Krapp acknowledges this epistemological peculiarity. Box three, spool five begins by announcing that its speaker is "Thirty-nine today, sound as a bell, apart from my old weakness" (14). "Sound" has both literal and idiomatic senses here. He is mentally sound ("sound as a bell")—but he also knows his mind *as sound*. And insofar as these literal and idiomatic meanings are simultaneous, it implies that Krapp's mental actions are both empirically knowable and yet epistemologically distinct types from physical actions. Earlier versions of this line also sought to balance these literal and idiomatic valences. At the same time, these early versions used broken and interrupted idioms to highlight the absurdity of the relations proposed—not unlike Ryle's example of someone arriving in both a flood of tears and a sedan chair. In a 1956 draft of the play, the line read "Thirty-seven today, and sound as a . . . (hesitates) . . . whistle, apart from my old trouble" (ver 5, p2r).[16] Whether fragmented by hesitation or not, "sound as a whistle" could be literally true, although Krapp's hesitation makes the idiom feel less natural. And in the earliest version of the play, which Beckett was still calling the "Magee Monologue," the line was as follows: "This day, being in the third decade of the Ram, I enter upon my 31st year, sound apparently in wind and limb, apart from my old trouble" (segment 86, 01). "Sound and wind" is idiomatic, but it lacks the puns of whistle and bell.[17]

The catachrestic phrase most emblematic of Krapp's mental life, however, is one that the audience never hears at all. We encounter the first instance in the stage directions, as Krapp reads the description of box three, spool five:

> KRAPP. Memorable equinox? . . . [*Pause. He shrugs his shoulders, peers again at ledger, reads.*] Farewell to—[*he turns page*]—love.
> [*He raises his head, broods, bends over machine, switches on and assumes listening posture, i.e. leaning forward, elbows on table, hand cupping ear towards machine, face front.*] (13)

Compared to the other category-mistakes I've discussed, "listening posture" is somewhat unusual. To some it might not seem absurd at all; indeed, assuming a posture while listening presents no obvious logical or physiological difficulties. The trouble is that "listening" is an unusual sort of behavior, not unlike "hoping" or "digesting." While it's very much an action one can perform, it's not typically an overt behavior. From the outside, listening can look like—and happen at the same time as—lots of other activities. Or it can look like doing nothing. This is why Beckett has to define it; the meaning of "listening posture" is initially unclear, as it seems that "listening" has been used improperly. The implication is that Krapp's listening is logically or physiologically impossible without the physical action (i.e., his posture). But as listening is Krapp's primary mode of remembering—recalling the sensory qualities *Murphy* and *Molloy* impute to introspection—this means that Krapp's mental actions are themselves logically or physiologically impossible without demonstrable physical action. Listening therefore serves as something of a gateway for Krapp's mental actions to be extracted from the mental world and given physical reality.

By misattributing physical properties to his own mental actions, Krapp's mental properties themselves become moveable and, even more crucially, attributable to what would otherwise be nonmental objects. As I mentioned earlier, Krapp doesn't merely store his memories on his tapes—he transfers them. As it broadcasts these memories, Krapp's tape recorder suddenly appears as if it had phenomenal consciousness. This was a point that Beckett made in the Schiller notebooks. The "tape-recorder," Beckett explained, is the "companion of [Krapp's] solitude. Masturbatory agent. Tendency to become what is on the tape. . . . Anger and tenderness of Krapp towards an object which through language [becomes] the 'albernen Idioten' [silly idiots] or the girl on the lake" (*Theatrical Notebooks of Samuel Beckett*, 181). Indeed, the tape recorder is so successful at becoming "what is on the tape" that Krapp ceases to recognize his mental states as fully his own. Thus transferred, Krapp greets these mental states as if they originated in the tapes themselves. As he looks up the location of the memories he wants to remember, Krapp attributes a youthful impishness to the missing reel, as if the two of them were playing hide and seek: "Ah! the little rascal . . . ah! The little scoundrel!" (12). The point, of course, is that Krapp is imputing such impishness not to his younger self but rather to the mechanical object where the extracted memory of that younger self has been relocated.

By the end of the play this transference is so complete that it's hard to say where Krapp's mind is actually located. Indeed, insofar as the tape recorder has a "tendency to become what is on the tape," it has the tendency to replace Krapp himself, leaching away not only his memories but his mental properties as well. This is borne out by textual revisions Beckett made to the play for the 1969 production at the Schiller-Theater Werkstatt.[18] The revisions were maintained for the 1973 production at the Royal Court Theatre and the 1975 production at théâtre d'Orsay but are not reflected by most printed editions of the play. In the original text the play ends with "*Krapp motionless staring before him. The tape runs on in silence*" (28), after which the curtain closes. In the revised version, however, Beckett added a stage direction that emphasized the tape recorder's approximation and relocation of Krapp's phenomenal consciousness: "*Slow fade of stage-light and cubby hole light till only light of that 'eye' of tape-recorder*" (*Theatrical Notebooks of Samuel Beckett*, 10). In a 1972 letter to James Knowlson, Beckett referred to this dimming of the lights as "originally an accident—heaven sent."[19] Earlier in the play, of course, darkness is associated with Krapp's physical actions; his mental actions, his memories, are restricted to the light. Now, however, as the entire stage goes dark, there is no longer any light area onstage—as if to suggest that all of Krapp's memories have been moved to the entity with the glowing red "eye." The separation of mental actions and physical actions— the extraction of mental actions from the character's body—would seem complete.

Word Spoken versus Thing Known

As I will show, there are a number of important similarities between the ways Beckett and Pinter register mind-body dualism onstage—from divided mise-en-scènes and voices emanating from objects to broken idioms and catachrestic metaphors. Beckett's influence on Pinter is well known, so these similarities aren't that surprising.[20] At the same time, only so much of this influence can be attributed to Beckett's *drama*. By 1955, Pinter's primary exposure had been through *Murphy*, *Watt*, *Molloy*, and *Malone Dies*.[21] After reading a fragment of *Watt* in the magazine *Poetry Ireland*, Pinter sought out a copy of the novel at the Battersea Reserve Library. He didn't find one. But he did find a copy of *Murphy*, which he borrowed and never returned.[22] *Murphy*, he explained, was like "walking through a mirror to the other side of the world which was, in fact, the real world. What I seemed to be confronted with was a writer inhabiting his innermost self. . . . It was Beckett's own world but had so many references to the world we share."[23] I'm not sure if I would agree with this characterization of *Murphy* allowing Beckett to inhabit his "innermost self" (and we might ask whether this innermost self is known by introspective or sensory means). But it's not hard to imagine how *Murphy*'s fixation with mind-body dualism—with inner selves and private, nonphysical worlds—might have shaped Pinter's first years as a playwright.

There is, however, an important difference between how Beckett's and Pinter's characters experience empirical problems of mind. In Beckett such problems are frequently solitary affairs—Murphy and Victor withdrawing from the physical world, Moran's unchecked *cogito*, Krapp's memory apparatus (even if the tape recorder does become something of a companion). In Pinter, however, problems of mind are frequently the results of interpersonal politics and violence—with characters using psychiatry and even philosophy to hurt and control each other. In Pinter's plays, *The Hothouse* (1958) and *The Caretaker* (1962), electroconvulsive therapy (ECT) ceases to be a treatment for mental illness. Instead, it's a punishment, even a weapon. Pinter's biographer Michael Billington speculates that Pinter himself might have been subjected to ECT in the 1950s, when he volunteered for psychological testing at Maudsley Hospital, Oxford.[24] Set in a psychiatric hospital, *The Hothouse* shows hospital staff using ECT as an instrument of humiliation, interrogation, and torture. After covering up a murder and sexual assault that happened in the hospital, the corrupt administrators Gibbs and Cutts use ECT to silence a young orderly, Lamb, permanently. Early in the play, Lamb describes himself as having "tremendous mental energy. I'm the sort of chap who's always *thinking*—you know what I mean? Then, when I've thought about something, I like to put it into action" (32). As I will show below, it is precisely the disjunction between mental and physical actions that's so central to Pinter's conception of language use and mise-en-scène. Gibbs and Cutts, however, trick Lamb into volunteering for electrical "experiments" (63)—which leave him catatonic. The representations of ECT in *The Caretaker* are no less harrowing. Aston, who is somewhat aloof and erratic, is slowly renovating a home and has invited an unsheltered man, Davies, to be its caretaker. Eventually, Aston explains that he was institutionalized for hallucinations and then given ECT unsafely and without his consent. It's also implied that Davies, whose behavior is even more erratic than Aston's and whose identity can't be confirmed, might also have been institutionalized. At the end of act 2, Aston describes the night when he was subjected to ECT. Some of the patients, he explains, put up a fight:

> But most of them didn't. They just lay there. Well, they were coming round to me, and the night they came I got up and stood against the wall. They told me to get on the bed, and I knew they had to get me on the bed because if they did it while I was standing up they might break my spine. . . . And then suddenly this chief had pincers on my skull and I knew he wasn't supposed to do it while I was standing up, that's why I . . . anyway, he did it. So I did get out. I got out of the place . . . but I couldn't walk very well. I don't think my spine was damaged. That was perfectly alright. The trouble was . . . my thoughts . . . had become very slow . . . I couldn't think at all . . . I couldn't . . . get . . . my thoughts . . . together . . . uuuh . . . I could . . . never quite get it . . . together. (*Caretaker and the Dumb Waiter*, 57; ellipses in the original)

In *The Birthday Party* it's Cartesianism itself that's turned into a weapon, despite the disdain for philosophy we see in *The Homecoming*. As they mock Stanley's assertions of his identity, thereby encouraging the audience to doubt what they know about any of the characters onstage, Goldberg and McCann subject him to a particularly Cartesian style of interrogation:

> GOLDBERG. Do you know your own face?
> MCCANN. Wake him up. Stick a needle in his eye.
> GOLDBERG. You're a plague, Webber. You're an overthrow.
> MCCANN. You're what's left!
> GOLDBERG. But we've got the answer to you. We can sterilize you.
> MCCANN. What about Drogheda?
> GOLDBERG. Your bite is dead. Only your pong is left.
> MCCANN. You betrayed our land.
> GOLDBERG. You betray our breed.
> MCCANN. Who are you, Webber?
> GOLDBERG. What makes you think you exist?
> MCCANN. You're dead.
> GOLDBERG. You're dead. You can't live, you can't think, you can't love. You're dead. You're a plague gone bad. There's no juice in you. You're nothing but an odour! (52)

My point here isn't that this moment from *The Birthday Party* is a precise representation of Descartes's claims (even though by 1955 Pinter had read some of Beckett's most Descartes-haunted titles).[25] Instead, what matters is that Goldberg and McCann are able to beat Stanley into submission by doubting his claims of personal identity and self-knowledge—and in so doing they echo some of the ideas we encounter in the second *Meditation*. There Descartes proved both his own existence and the existence of his soul ("not even some thin vapour which permeates the limbs—a wind, fire, air, breath") through thinking. But what was good enough for Descartes isn't good enough for Goldberg and McCann. Stanley can't be saved through thought alone. Goldberg and McCann are able to doubt his existence to his face (albeit a different sense of "exist" than in *cogito ergo sum*) and insist that nothing of him exists except a foul, ghostly "pong." Even if Stanley knew his identity or could prove it to himself (a point his attackers also dispute), he couldn't prove it to anyone else.

My focus on the separation of mind and body, of mental and physical concepts, amounts to an unconventional approach to Pinter's particular brand of ambiguity and uncertainty. In *The Peopled Wound* (1970), Martin Esslin postulated that such ambiguity and interpretive uncertainty originated in the "solecism and tautology" of Pinter's dialogue, and that Pinter's language could be "likened to nonsense-poetry and the literature of the absurd" (50). More recently, David Z. Saltz has observed that Pinter's dialogue features comparatively little "embedded diegesis"—which would preclude, perhaps, the success of Goldberg and McCann's interrogation. "Pinter," he explains, "reifies drama's generic impulse, untethering drama from its diegetic ties to the past and restoring to it its radical presence" ("Radical Mimesis," 226). The most influential account of Pinter's language, however, remains Austin Quigley's *The Pinter Problem* (1975). Drawing on Wittgenstein's idea of language-games, Quigley suggests that Pinter's plays are an occasion for literary criticism to re-evaluate its assumptions about language use. Reference, he explains, is only one of language's functions—and not every language use is a function of reference. When Goldberg asks Stanley, "What makes you think you exist?" he isn't making a propositional statement about Goldberg's existence. Instead, he's using this peculiar Cartesian language to *do something* to Stanley. As Quigley explains, Pinter hasn't "transcended the boundaries of language. . . . What has been transcended is the limitation of a method of describing how language works" (46-47).

I don't dispute these claims. But I think there's another aspect of Pinter's language use that might explain both the uncertainties we encounter in his plays and what I will show to be the peculiarities of his mise-en-scène. In his essay "Writing for the Theatre" (1962), Pinter explained,

> So often below the word spoken is the thing known and unspoken. My characters tell me so much and no more, with reference to their experience, their aspirations, their motives, their history. Between my lack of biographical data about them and the ambiguity of what they say lies a territory which is not only worthy of explanation but which is compulsory to explore. You and I, the characters which grow on a page, most of the time we're inexpressive, giving little away, unreliable, elusive, obstructive, unwilling. But it's out of these attributes that a language arises. A language, where under what is said, another thing is being said. (*Various Voices*, 22-23)

Like real people, Pinter tells us, characters don't say everything they think. For every "word spoken" there is necessarily some "thing known" that isn't spoken. This has nothing to do with its content or ontological composition. Before we speak, the future "word spoken" and "thing known" might appear interchangeable. But once we start speaking, these actions become differentiated epistemologically and become different types of concepts. The difference between "word spoken" and "things known"—between speech and thought, between text and subtext—is the same type of distinction between physical and mental actions. What were once seemingly interchangeable terms now follow different sets of rules and are known by different means by different individuals and/or sets of people. Pinter's characters find themselves in the position of needing or wanting to discuss "the thing known but unspoken"—and yet find themselves always in possession of thoughts that can't be realized through language. The conclusion of "Writing for the Theatre" speaks to this point precisely, as Pinter quotes from Beckett's *The Unnamable*. "The fact would seem to be," Beckett's narrator tells us, "that I shall have to speak of things which I cannot speak" (*Various Voices*, 25). And yet in a way Beckett and Pinter are referring to different kinds of problems. In Beckett's fiction, the differences between thinking and speaking—or between real voices and hallucinated voices—are often ambiguous. The simultaneous inability and yet compulsion to speak in *The Unnamable* follows from language being both constitutive of and produced by thought. In Pinter's plays, however, there is a strict epistemological distinction between thinking and speaking—between the physical "word spoken" and mental "thing known." The challenge is how to make this "thing known" a force onstage but without sacrificing the epistemological distinction that gave the "thing known" so much mystery and significance.

In *Eleutheria* and *Krapp's Last Tape*, we saw Beckett construct divided mise-en-scènes that allowed him to at least theoretically attribute mental and physical properties across category lines. Pinter's plays demonstrate a similar approach to the stage. But whereas Beckett divided the onstage area into different epistemological zones, Pinter drew a mind-body type-distinction between onstage and offstage.[26] Indeed, both *The Birthday Party* and *The Dumb Waiter* draw attention to the ways they use onstage props to mediate voices or personalities offstage—as if the objects themselves were speaking. Even more importantly, these speaking props mark the difference between onstage and offstage as both a spatial and categorical difference. Different sets of predicates apply to offstage and onstage; different kinds of actions happen, and different rules are followed. At the beginning of *The Birthday Party* this happens so subtly as to be overlooked. In the opening scene, Petey is in the onstage dining room while Meg asks him questions from the offstage kitchen. But Meg's voice doesn't just ring out; instead, the stage directions dictate that "*MEG's voice comes through the kitchen hatch*" (19). Later, their mysterious lodger Stanley hears a conversation through the front door that seems to confirm his fears: a couple of strangers have come to take him away in a wheelbarrow. In reality, it's just Lulu dropping off a package for Meg (which is actually a toy drum for Stanley). But Stanley doesn't know that:

> *A sudden knock on the front.* LULU's *voice: Ooh-ooh!* MEG *edges past* STANLEY *and collects her shopping bag.* MEG *goes out.* STANLEY *sidles to the door and listens.*
> VOICE *(through letter box).* Hullo, Mrs. Boles . . .
> MEG. Oh, has it come?
> VOICE. Yes, it's just come. (24)

If Stanley knew what "it" denoted, then the tension and ambiguity of this scene would be reduced considerably. But I would say that the definition of this "it" matters less than the set of epistemological relations it represents. At the moment when Stanley most evidently projects his paranoid fantasies onto the unseen offstage area, Pinter also draws our attention to how those fantasies are mediated by physical objects onstage—as if to suggest that such fantasies, lacking physical properties, could never be realized on their own. Made available only by vague, disembodied voices speaking through the letter box, Stanley's mental world somehow feels real and yet both indescribable and unstageable.

This becomes clearer in the third act, after Stanley has been interrogated by Goldberg and McCann, and after he has been stopped from attacking Lulu during the blackout. Goldberg and McCann take Stanley upstairs, which is offstage, and torture him for the entire night. It is still not clear who they are, who Stanley is, or what information they extracted from him while upstairs. But they've managed to ensure that Stanley will never speak about any of it:

> GOLDBERG. What's your opinion of such a prospect? Eh, Stanley?
> *Stanley concentrates, his mouth opens, he attempts to speak, fails and emits sounds from his throat.*
> STANLEY. Uh-gug . . . uh-gug . . . eeehhh-gag . . . (*On the breath.*) Caahh . . . caahh . . .
> *They watch him. He draws a long breath which shudders down his body. He concentrates.*
> GOLDBERG. Well, Stanny boy, what do you say, eh?
> *They watch. He concentrates. His head lowers, his chin draws into his chest, he crouches.* (84)

Mental Acts

The key verb here is "concentrates." Typically, concentrating is neither a reflexive verb nor an observable one. Instead, it's often used as a secondary verb that describes or modifies the way a primary verb is performed (i.e., "I concentrated on answering the question"). But in Stanley's case it stands on its own, as he is unable to execute the actions it would otherwise modify. Indeed, from Stanley's noises and shudders, it's not even clear if he's still capable of intelligent or intellectual action at all, or if he's trying to answer the questions posed to him or not. In effect, Pinter hasn't just rendered Stanley mute and still; he has limited, even at the level of grammar, the logical *type* of actions that Stanley can perform as well. "He concentrates" isn't so much a representation of someone thinking as a gesture toward a different universe of actions and concepts—a belated and futile effort to bring the "thing known" onstage and into language.

This division of *The Birthday Party* into mental and physical worlds becomes clearer when we look at "A View of the Party," which Pinter wrote around the time of the play's premiere in 1958. This is not to overlook the ontological and epistemological differences between poems and plays. Nonetheless, the category-mistakes implied by the play's mise-en-scène become more readily accessible through the poem's language. It is worth quoting in its entirety:

> The thought that Goldberg was
> A man she might have known
> Never crossed Meg's words
> That morning in the room.
>
> The thought that Goldberg was
> A man another knew
> Never crossed her eyes
> When, glad, she welcomed him.
>
> The thought that Goldberg was
> A man to dread and know
> Jarred Stanley in the blood
> When, still, he heard his name . . .
>
> The thought that Goldberg was
> Sat in the centre of the room,
> A man of weight and time,
> To supervise the game.

> The thought that was McCann
> Walked in upon this feast,
> A man of skin and bone,
> With a green stain on his chest.[27]

Like Beckett's revisions of "sound as a bell," Pinter uses broken idioms and catachresis to register the difficulty of "thought" moving between mental and physical worlds. But each time "thought" is manifested in the physical action we encounter a category-mistake—as if the category-mistake itself, the impassable boundary between mental and physical categories, were the point. After defining Goldberg as a "thought"—giving him the logical properties of a mental concept—we're told that this thought never "crossed Meg's words." In English idiom, of course, *eyes* cross while *words* do not. Moreover, the cross in "cross-eyed" is not the same as the "cross" in "Why did the chicken cross the road." A doubly broken idiom separates Meg's "words" ("the word spoken") and the thought "she might have known" ("the thing known but unspoken"). And while the second stanza features the crossing of eyes rather than words, it still uses the wrong sense of "cross" as it reasserts Goldberg's identity as "thought." The poem's remaining stanzas are less reliant on idiom and cliché, but perhaps even more explicit in attributing physical properties to mental concepts. After the third stanza suggests that the "thought" of Goldberg "jarred Stanley in the blood"—such that the mental predicate "jarred" now has a precise physical location—the fourth and fifth stanzas attribute physical actions to the "thoughts" of Goldberg and McCann. Even though Goldberg is described as "a man of weight and time," it's still the "thought" of that man that "sat in the centre of the room." Similarly, McCann is a man of "skin and bone," but it's his "thought" that "walked in upon this feast."[28] By calling Goldberg and McCann "thoughts," and yet emphasizing their physical properties, the effect is to make these characters themselves seem like logical absurdities—entities whose appearance and motives defy explanation and whose actions can't quite be put into language.

In many ways, we might expect a similar arrangement from *The Dumb Waiter*. Like *The Birthday Party*, *The Dumb Waiter* aligns physical actions ("word spoken") with the area onstage and aligns mental actions ("thing known") with an unseen upstairs area. Ostensibly these areas are connected by the eponymous prop, which connects the basement onstage with the upstairs area offstage. As hitmen Gus and Ben sit in the basement waiting for their instructions, the dumbwaiter starts delivering food orders from the dining room—even though the rest of the house is supposed to be empty. In that way, the dumbwaiter is not unlike the kitchen hatch or letter box in *The Birthday Party*: in order to register onstage, offstage content must be physicalized and then mediated by a prop. At the same time, the dumbwaiter appears to be an apt metaphor for Gus and Ben themselves. Like the machine in the wall, they can execute physical tasks assigned to them, but they can't choose or refuse any tasks themselves. So while they're in the basement waiting to learn the identity of their target, they nonetheless do their best to fulfill the food orders they receive, including those for "Macaroni Pastitsio" and "Ormitha Macarounada" (*Caretaker and the Dumb Waiter*, 108). They don't know what these dishes are (the first is similar to moussaka; the second appears to be made up), but they send up what they have. As they send the dumbwaiter back upstairs, Gus yells the order up the shaft like a short-order cook ("Three McVittie and Price! One Lyons Red Label! One Smith's Crisps! One Eccles cake! One Fruit and Nut!"). Ben, however, scolds him for doing this (in a moment that I will return to later on): "You shouldn't shout like that. . . . It isn't done" (108). As in *The Birthday Party*, there is the sense that the information Gus and Ben need is beyond reach—a point only reinforced by the inexplicable messages delivered by way of the dumbwaiter. Therefore, despite being a means of coordination between mental and physical worlds, the effect of the dumbwaiter is actually to emphasize the inaccessibility of the offstage person who nonetheless controls the physical action onstage.

In *The Dumb Waiter*, however, Pinter adds a new element to this dualistic arrangement. In *The Birthday Party*, it's implied that many of Stanley's stories might be lies. But no one ever doubts that the house has a second floor. *The Dumb Waiter*, however, asks us to consider that dualistic separation of upstairs and downstairs might actually be a ruse, or at least a malicious instrumentalization of the split between "thing known" and "word spoken." In emphasizing the inaccessibility of the "thing known" offstage, and in making onstage-offstage communications so absurd, the dumbwaiter distracts both Gus and the audience from the possibility that the "thing known"—the knowledge that Gus is the target—might already be onstage and in Ben's possession. For that reason, the issue in *The Dumb Waiter* isn't just one of characters trying to bring the "thing known" onstage—that is, finding out who's upstairs, what they actually want, whom Gus and Ben are supposed to kill, and so on. There is also a concerted effort to convince both characters and the audience that the "thing known" *couldn't* be known by anyone onstage—drawing a categorical distinction between the empirical actions onstage and the covert ones offstage. So while the dumbwaiter offers some coordination between the basement and upstairs, its real function is to make the "thing unknown" appear *less* stageable and to mask the epistemological asymmetry between Gus and Ben.

There are clues to this asymmetry, however, from the very beginning of the play. For while Gus and Ben comprise the "body" in the house's setup, there is an additional mental-physical split in their relationship. This split appears to correspond not only to their dispositions and abilities but also to the power differential between the two. We see this in the opening scene as Gus tries to tie his shoes and Ben reads the morning paper aloud and explains what it means:

> GUS *ties his laces, rises, yawns and begins to walk slowly to the door, left. He stops, looks down, and shakes his foot.*
>
> BEN *lowers his paper and watches him.* GUS *kneels and unties his shoe-lace and slowly takes off the shoe. He looks inside it and brings out a flattened matchbox. He shakes it and examines it. Their eyes meet.* BEN *rattles his paper and reads.* GUS *puts the matchbox in his pocket and bends down to put on his shoe. He ties his lace, with difficulty.* BEN *lowers his paper and watches him.* GUS *walks to the door, left, stops, and shakes the other foot. He kneels, unties his shoe-lace, and slowly takes off the shoe. He looks inside it and brings out a flattened cigarette packet. He shakes it and examines it. Their eyes meet.* BEN *rattles his paper and reads . . .*
>
> BEN. Kaw!
> *He picks up the paper.*
> What about this? Listen to this! (85)

Throughout the play Gus is identified with physical actions while Ben is identified with intellection and judgment. As Quigley remarked in his essay "*The Dumb Waiter:* Undermining the Tacit Dimension" (1978), "What we have here is not just two minor employees getting on each other's nerves, but two sets of complementary and conflicting attitudes toward the necessary correlations between knowing and doing" (4). But the mental-physical split between them is actually far more nuanced and, perhaps, insidious. For while Gus is identified with physical actions, it's also implied that he's not in tune with his body. He fails to remember that he's placed his cigarettes and matches in his shoes. He only realizes this after he has put on each shoe, tied it (with difficulty), and then walked around. Moreover, when "their eyes

Mental Acts

meet," it's implied that Ben knows precisely what Gus has done, and that Ben knows how to avoid such problems himself. Throughout the play Gus demonstrates that he has neither factual nor procedural knowledge—neither "knowing that" nor "knowing how," to return to Ryle's *The Concept of Mind*. Instead, he relies on Ben for both the facts at hand and the practical know-how needed to execute those facts.

This asymmetry is only worsened by the apparatus of the dumbwaiter itself. Attached to the dumbwaiter is a speaking tube. Ostensibly the function of this speaking tube is to let different floors of the house communicate. But insofar as the tube has a single opening that functions as both earpiece and mouthpiece, it doesn't permit users to speak and listen at the same time. So when Ben uses the tube to ask the supposed diners how they liked their food (in this case a collection of old digestive biscuits), neither Gus nor the audience is able to hear the response directly:

> BEN (*speaking with great deference*). Good evening. I'm sorry to—bother you, but we just thought we'd better let you know that we haven't got anything left. We sent up all we had. There's no more food down here.
> *He brings the tube up slowly to his ear.*
> What?
> *To mouth.*
> What?
> *To ear. He listens. To mouth.*
> No, all we had we sent up.
> *To ear. He listens. To mouth.*
> Oh, I'm very sorry to hear that.
> *To ear. He listens. To* GUS.
> The Eccles cake was stale. (112)

On its own this conversation seems innocent enough. If you didn't know how the play ended, you wouldn't necessarily be suspicious of Ben here. But as the speaking tube separates the conversation into its constituent physical and mental (which is to say, sensory) components, it forces Gus to rely on Ben's reporting—widening the epistemological gap between them. And while there's nothing to imply that Ben is misrepresenting what he hears, we also can't rule that possibility out. When Ben mistakenly speaks while the mouthpiece is against his ear, his bumbling could be taken as a sign of his trustworthiness. At the same time, such bumbling could itself be an act to make him appear more trustworthy as he speaks to his conspirators upstairs. Indeed, the best indication of Ben's possible guilt in this moment is from earlier in the play. After Gus yelled the names of several digestive biscuits up the shaft, Ben told him, "It isn't done." Given that Gus and Ben were not in fact working in a restaurant kitchen, and given the logistical complexity and inefficiency of the dumbwaiter speaking tube, you have to wonder why Ben would be so keen to prevent unfettered communication between floors—why he'd be so eager to maintain the separation between onstage and offstage.

But *The Dumb Waiter* is structured to ensure that neither Gus nor the audience can ever confirm what Ben knows or when he knows it. So even if he isn't aware of the conspiracy to kill Gus, either way his knowledge remains parallel to that of whoever is offstage. Irrespective of Ben's knowledge, and whether or not the division of the house was a ruse, *The Dumb Waiter* still manages to uphold the epistemological type-distinction between "word spoken" and "thing known." And for that reason the play's conclusion comes as a real shock to the audience—and, of course, to Gus. When Gus goes to the washroom offstage, Ben has a final conversation through the dumbwaiter—but without any of the discussion about food from before. After receiving his instructions, Ben responds, "Understood. Repeat. He has arrived and will be coming in straight away. The normal method to be employed. Understood" (120). From these words alone, in particular the unspecified "he," we still don't know what Ben knows. It's possible that all Ben knows is that he will kill whomever "he" is; it's also possible that he knows that Gus is the target and is using the pronoun "he" to refer to him. Pinter never resolves this ambiguity for us. And, as Ben's knowledge remains undefined whether he's guilty or not, it's ultimately irrelevant. Instead, Ben's statement of "Understood. Repeat" is far more telling—anticipating, perhaps, Ruth's epistemological equivocation between underwear and the metaphysical unknown in *The Homecoming*. For while Ben's ability to "repeat" what he has "understood" implies that he's reporting his conversation truthfully, it's also Pinter's dishonest promise to the audience that "word spoken" and "thing known" are epistemologically comparable and knowable by the same means. We only realize the extent of Pinter's dishonesty when Gus enters the stage *"stripped of his jacket, waistcoat, tie, holster and revolver"* (121). But as if to uphold the mystery of the offstage "thing known," the curtain comes down before we get any explanation of what's happened.

"The rest is Ibsen"

At the beginning of this chapter I noted a key difference between types of literary minds—those constituted by language exclusively (those found in poems and novels) and those that occur onstage. By virtue of their physicality and reliance on action, plays constrain mental representation in a way that novels and poems do not. My goal here has been to show the ways Beckett and Pinter use mise-en-scène to work around such constraints—drawing an epistemological distinction between mental and physical actions and insisting that "drama" comprises not one concept of action but two. In that way, dramatic minds would seem comparable to actual minds in a way that written literary minds are not—implying, maybe, that Stanley's mind is "real" in a way that Murphy's is not. After all, people onstage and offstage are made of the same physical materials and often operate by similar means. Pinter's distinction between "word spoken" and "thing known" isn't specific to the theater—it follows from ordinary language use more generally. And as it makes sense to talk about both physical and mental actions occurring onstage, it also makes sense to distinguish between the physical and mental actions of people who aren't acting.

Ryle makes a version of this point in *The Concept of Mind*—not about the necessity of epistemological dualism, of course, but rather about the comparability of minds onstage and offstage. As he explained, the theater is more than just a source of entertainment. It's also a source of information; audiences, he claimed, imitate what they see onstage and in that way learn to behave and talk about behavior themselves. In the case of avowal statements ("I am," "I believe," etc.), "people have to learn how to use avowal expressions appropriately and they may not learn these lessons very well. They learn them from ordinary discussions of the moods of others and from such more fruitful sources as novels and the theatre. They learn from the same sources how to cheat both other people and themselves by making sham avowals in the proper tones of voice and with the other proper histrionic accompaniments" (87). Even if you share Ryle's claim that theatrical performance is nondualistic (i.e., clowning), this analysis still raises some red flags—and even maybe some category-mistakes. Given the epistemological and formal differences between plays, novels, and "ordinary discussions of the moods of others," it seems unlikely they would all provide the same information about behavior. You can't imitate a novel the same way you can a play. But it is conceivable that you might imitate a play the same way you imitate a conversation among friends. So might it be possible that Ryle's implicit comparison between dramatic minds and actual minds holds up logically? Given the properties they share, might it make sense to think of dramatic minds and actual minds as the same kind of concept?

I don't believe so, no—and I don't think Beckett would have either. Insofar as they involve brains and bodies, it is tempting to say that dramatic minds are more realistic than novelistic or poetic minds. On the point of physical composition alone, dramatic minds might be comparable to actual minds—actors are, after all, people. But as dramatic minds and actual minds still follow different kinds of rules (i.e., conventional and formal rules vs. psychological ones), they would still constitute different kinds of concepts most of the time with different sorts of entailments. Beckett spoke to this point in a 1972 letter to the director Alan Schneider, who was directing the premier of Beckett's play *Not I* (1972). In the play, a disembodied "Mouth" hangs in the middle of the stage, giving what appears to be real-time verbalization of disembodied consciousness: " . . . all over in a second . . . or grabbing at straw . . . the brain . . . flickering away on its own . . . quick grab and on . . . nothing there . . . on to the next . . . bad as the voice . . . worse . . . as little sense . . . all that together . . . can't— . . . what? . . . the buzzing? . . . yes . . . all the time the buzzing" (*Ends and Odds*, 20). Schneider said he assumed that Mouth was "in some sort of limbo. Death? After-life?" In an October 16, 1972, letter to Schneider, Beckett made it clear he didn't know—and, even more importantly, insisted on the nonmental objects and conventions from which her mind emerged: "This is the old business of the author's supposed privileged information as when [Ralph] Richardson wanted the lowdown on Pozzo's background before he could consider the part. I no more know where she is or why thus than she does. All I know is in the texts. 'She' is purely a stage entity, part of a stage image and a purveyor of a stage text. The rest is Ibsen" (283).

4 The Form of Thought

This book has examined the ways in which category-mistakes allow representations of mental states—whether in novels, in poems, or in the theater—to appear as if they are comparable to actual mental states. This apparent comparability is a crucial aspect of literary experience. And as I have shown, it's a crucial aspect of how critics talk about literary form as well. We routinely project the apparent properties of these "literary minds" onto the linguistic objects they seem to emerge from. This, I have argued, is why it's important for us to read with a behavioristic awareness or sensibility: to remember the fundamentally nonmental origins of the mental representations we encounter in literature and, in that way, discover the mentalistic assumptions embedded in our practices as readers and critics. My aim hasn't been to discourage, or diminish the pleasures of, identifying with fictional characters. Nor has it been to deny the apparent intuitiveness of perceiving a writer's style as an extension of their consciousness. Instead, it's been to reveal the logical structures that make such pleasures and intuitions possible—to uncover the concepts and relations that enable mental representations to feel like more than just representations.

To that end, each of the preceding chapters has made a key assumption: that language can in fact represent mental states at all. This ought to be an uncontroversial assumption. We use language to express ourselves all the time, and generally these expressions are understood. Moreover, we don't typically experience these expressions as producing logical absurdity—as if we were trying to misattribute properties to consciousness or force our thoughts into following the wrong kind of rules. Obviously, language and thinking do indeed have different properties and follow different kinds of rules. But it feels like there's just enough correspondence or overlap between the domains of language and thought to let us express ourselves effectively.

And yet, in his novels and academic writing, it was precisely this reasoning that John Maxwell (J. M.) Coetzee rejected. Instead, he showed that *all linguistic representation of mental states* must depend partly on a kind of category-mistake. This is a fairly counterintuitive claim. Insofar as mental states are most accessible through language (whether we're talking about our own minds or those of other people), the pairing of linguistic form and mental content feels natural enough. And yet this pairing, Coetzee maintained, belied the necessary logical differences between language and thinking. This was a key component of his linguistics dissertation, "The English Fiction of Samuel Beckett," which he completed at the University of Texas at Austin in 1969.[1] Part of this dissertation comprised a computational analysis of the style of Beckett's English-language fiction (building on Coetzee's work as a computer programmer earlier in the decade). At the same time, "The English Fiction of Samuel Beckett" was also a part of behaviorism's literary history—a rejoinder to a rising generation of cognitive literary critics bringing Chomskyan linguistics to bear on stylistic analysis. In texts such as *Syntactic Structures* (1957) and his infamous review of B. F. Skinner's *Verbal Behavior* (1959), Chomsky argued for the necessity of innate linguistic content and for a transformational relationship between grammatical surface structures (forms and rules specific to particular languages) and deep structures (forms and rules common to all languages). This transformational grammar inspired critics such as Richard Ohmann and Donald Freeman to use written style (i.e., surface structures) to reconstruct the deep structures, or "epistemic stances," of authors. As Ohmann wrote in *Shaw: The Style and the Man* (1962), Shaw's style "offers strong evidence of a cognitive system whose crux is similarity and neat, lawful categories" (23). Well-ordered sentences, the reasoning goes, come from not only a well-ordered mind but also a mind that is well ordered in precisely the same ways.

According to Coetzee, however, this conclusion rested on what was effectively a category-mistake: the mistaken belief that language and thinking follow the same kinds of rules and act in the same kinds of ways. "There are no grounds for believing," he wrote, that "the order of operations in the grammar, a logical order, corresponds to the order of operations in the mind, presumably a temporal order. The best we can hope for is an isomorphy between grammatical operations and mental operations" ("English Fiction of Samuel Beckett," 245-46n48). Such "isomorphy" could indeed look like a resemblance between grammatical operations and mental operations. But what this resemblance reflected was not a history of causation but one of association, with grammatical rules projected onto psychological phenomena.[2] In that way, "The English Fiction of Samuel Beckett" echoed some of the behavioristic psychology and linguistics that Chomsky's work had superseded. As Watson wrote in *Psychology from the Standpoint of a Behaviorist* (1919), there is no necessary relation between grammatical form and "the forms of thought" —only the speaker's individual history of association. "Whether the individual actually thinks in syllogistic forms or in accordance with the laws of syntax," he wrote, "is extremely doubtful. Probably if he has been brought up in a family where careful diction and logical presentation are insisted upon from the start his thoughts will take the same orderly form" (329).[3]

This associative, and logically disjunctive, relation between grammar and thought appears not only in Coetzee's other academic writings but in his fiction as well.[4] In the latter it serves to highlight the kinds of linguistic, psychological, and political damage entailed by colonialism and apartheid. In *In the Heart of the Country* (1977), Magda finds her native language distorted by generations of violence in the Western Cape. While Magda wishes to speak against that violence, she finds that the grammar of her language won't allow her to express that idea. Instead, she explains, this language "was subverted by my father and cannot be recovered. . . . I was born into a language of hierarchy, of distance and perspective. It was my father-tongue. I do not say it is the language my heart wants to speak" (97). Instead of actually being able to say what she wants directly (i.e., "I want to speak a different language"), she is forced to express her thoughts through negation and through a syntax that redirects both agency and intention (whereby it's her "heart" that wants and speaks rather than Magda herself). Conversely, in *Disgrace* (1999), David Lurie believes that some thoughts and experiences —like those of apartheid's victims—could not be expressed in English at all. He reaches this conclusion as he considers the perspective of a local landowner, Petrus: "More and more [Lurie] is convinced that English is an unfit medium for the truth of South Africa. Stretches of English code whole sentences long have thickened, lost their articulations, their articulateness, their articulatedness. Like a dinosaur expiring in the mud, the language has stiffened. Pressed into the mold of English, Petrus's own story would come out arthritic, bygone" (117). As Magda could not press her intentions into the "mold" of her father's language, Petrus's thoughts and feelings cannot be expressed through the language of the colonizer.[5]

In some of Coetzee's novels, however, the discussion of the disjunction between grammar and thought goes even further—particularly with respect to the legacies of colonialism and apartheid.[6] In novels such as *Waiting for the Barbarians* (1980) and *Foe* (1986), the lags and mismatches between grammatical and mental operations continue. But whereas *In the Heart of the Country* and *Disgrace* attribute this to specific histories of racist oppression, *Waiting for the Barbarians* and *Foe* identify a potentially broader origin—returning to the logical arguments made by "The English Fiction of Samuel Beckett."[7] Initially, when the narrators in these novels perceive the colonized subject's mind as being inaccessible, they attribute this inaccessibility to racial difference and to the violence of colonialism. As these novels progress, however, these narrators realize that racism and colonialism have not created but rather exacerbated logical mismatches between language and thought. They learn that their own minds are no more accessible than those of colonized subjects and that their efforts at self-expression are no less weighed down by the gaps between grammar and cognition. The only way to express mental content, they conclude, is to make it effectively nonmental—to foist linguistic properties and rules upon it. In other words, what *Waiting for the Barbarians* and *Foe* first present as the problem of other minds, and the problem of Other minds, is then portrayed as the problem of mental expressivity more generally.[8]

To show the ways Coetzee's novels arrive at these conclusions, as well as the relations between Coetzee's writings and the histories of behaviorism and cognitive science, I divide the rest of this chapter into four sections. In the first section I show the ways that behaviorism's theories of language acquisition, as exemplified by Watson and Skinner, gave way to Chomsky's hypothesis of an innate generative-transformational language apparatus—and to theories by philosophers such as Jerry Fodor and Jerrold Katz, who worked to deduce this apparatus's properties and functions. As I show, what was at stake in these debates about language acquisition was not only the existence of a priori linguistic knowledge but also the broader conceptual relations and differences between grammatical operations and cognitive ones. In the second section I offer an in-depth account of "The English Fiction of Samuel Beckett" and its criticisms of how Ohmann instrumentalized Chomskyan linguistics in his attempt to revitalize the stylistic project of Leo Spitzer. Insofar as there cannot be a determinate relation between cognitive operations and grammatical operations, Coetzee argued, it was impossible to deduce a "psychological etymon" from the details of style. Instead, the

The Form of Thought

generative properties of style, he claimed, were not mental but linguistic—such that one could account for Beckett's style without appealing to any inferences about Beckett's mind. In the third section I turn to *Waiting for the Barbarians* and *Foe* and examine the ways their colonizing characters attempt to impose linguistic forms on the minds of colonized subjects and the logical reasons these attempts fail. In *Waiting for the Barbarians*, the Magistrate's encounter with an indigenous woman—who appears to him to have "no interior" (43)—forces him to reconceive not only the language politics of colonialism but also his own ability to put words to thought. In *Foe*, Susan Barton conceives of language as not mirroring thought but actually realizing it. But when she tries to teach Friday to speak, such that he might share his story of imprisonment and slavery, she finds herself unable to affix language to thought without the aid of fiction—a point the novel then extends to all of its characters. Building on the conclusion of *Foe*, in the final section I turn to W. V. O. Quine's concept of the indeterminacy of translation and its relevance for Coetzee's warnings about mental representation.

Language, Behavior, and Mind

By the time he published *Behaviorism* in 1924, Watson had abandoned the notions about grammatical and cognitive structure that I mentioned earlier. Whereas in 1919 he proclaimed an associative relation between word order and the orders of thoughts, in 1924 he asserted nothing short of physiological identity between language and cognition. Thinking, he wrote, is just "talking to ourselves" (*Behaviorism*, 237). Nonetheless, the assertion of an associative relationship between language and cognition remained part of behaviorist discourse about language acquisition. Skinner's *Verbal Behavior*, which was methodologically behaviorist but did not share Watson's rejection of consciousness, was no exception. Skinner claimed that word order was caused by nonmental phenomena (a point Coetzee would later echo in "The English Fiction of Samuel Beckett"). First, Skinner argued, word order could be influenced by speech sounds, as similar sounds often gravitate toward each other (as in the case of alliteration, assonance, consonance, etc.). Second, a sentence's word order could be determined by the temporal order of the phenomena it sought to represent. As Skinner wrote, "The responses of an announcer in describing a boxing match stand in fairly simple temporal relation to the events described. The three responses *Veni, vidi, vici* occur in that order for good reason" (333). Third, word order could be shaped by the speaker's own previous utterances, with speakers effectively producing verbal stimuli in response to their own speech. A "train of thought," he explained, "in free association follows the order in which verbal stimuli evoke other verbal responses. In the recitation of a long passage the order is due to a similar intraverbal linkage" (333). Fourth, word order could be determined by the strength and frequency of certain words in the speaker's repertory, with some words and word combinations appearing more frequently than others. The fifth and final determining factor, Skinner suggested, was "rhetoric"—the anticipated effects a particular word order might have on a listener. These anticipated effects, he noted, could work either in concert with the other functions that determined word order or in a contrary motion. "In the response *Him I despise*," Skinner wrote, "the position of *him* may be in part a function of relative strength, but the rhetorical pattern has been designed for a special effect upon the listener. The periodic sentence is a well-known device in which an important word is held until the listener or reader is thoroughly prepared for it" (333).

But Skinner did distinguish his work on language from Watson's in key ways, many of which are vital for understanding the stakes of Chomsky's critique and Coetzee's critique of Chomsky's acolytes. In contrast to Watson's experiments on involuntary reflex actions, Skinner's research focused on the conditioning of voluntary behaviors. As he explained in *The Behavior of Organisms* (1938), "The attempt to force behavior into the simple stimulus-response formula has delayed the adequate treatment of that large part of behavior which cannot be shown to be under the control of eliciting stimuli. . . . The kind of behavior that is correlated with specific eliciting stimuli may be called *respondent* behavior and a given correlation a *respondent*. The term is intended to carry the sense of a relation to a prior event. Such behavior as is not under this kind of control I shall call *operant* and any specific example an *operant*. The term refers to a posterior event" (20). In respondent conditioning (i.e., Watsonian conditioning), there is one defined stimulus and one defined response. As a result of conditioning, a causative relation between these terms is established. The presence of the stimulus causes the organism in question to perform the respondent. In operant conditioning, however, there is no one-to-one correspondence between stimulus and response. Instead, the organism is understood to exist in a dynamic environment that comprises multiple stimuli and that allows multiple possible operants. Using environmental engineering and behavioral reinforcement (not unlike Thorndike's laws of exercise and effect), the goal of operant conditioning is for the organism to choose one particular operant as opposed to another. For example, if we want a pigeon to request food by tapping on a particular button (i.e., the operant), then we add a number of positive stimuli to the pigeon's environment to make the operant more appealing and more likely. This might involve placing a small amount of food on the button itself. Or it might involve waiting for the pigeon to press the button randomly and rewarding it for doing so—while pressing the wrong button would not be rewarded (unlike Watson, Skinner felt that aversive stimuli were less effective than positive stimuli). Over time the pigeon will come to press the correct lever on its own without stimulation, so long as the association between the button and positive stimuli isn't extinguished.

Broadly speaking, Skinner claimed in *Verbal Behavior*, this was how children acquired language: "A child acquires verbal behavior when relatively unpatterned vocalizations, selectively reinforced, gradually assume forms which produce appropriate consequences in a given verbal community" (31). No assumption of a priori linguistic knowledge was necessary to explain such acquisition—in the same way, we might infer, that no a priori lever knowledge was necessary to explain the pigeon's behaviors. Every verbal behavior, whether written or spoken, active or passive, was necessarily the result of an extended process of conditioning and association building. However, Skinner did not assume a one-to-one correspondence between stimuli and responses: "There is no stimulus which makes a child say *b* or *ă* or *ē*, as one may make him salivate by placing a lemon drop in his mouth or make his pupils contract by shining a light into his eyes. The raw responses from which verbal behavior is constructed are not 'elicited'" (31). Verbal behaviors, Skinner insisted, were both voluntary and multiple; any given stimulus could lead to (but not "elicit") a range of possible responses. When humans speak, he suggested, they do so not only with intention but also with discernment. When we perceive either an opportunity or a need for verbal behavior, we sort through the range of verbal behaviors we've encountered before and select the one that makes the most sense.

In his infamous 1959 review of *Verbal Behavior*, however, Chomsky argued that Skinner was wrong for several reasons. First, Chomsky argued that Skinner's use of operant conditioning was unscientific and illogical. If there was no one-to-one correspondence between stimulus and response, he claimed, you could only ever identify the operative stimulus retroactively. When testing something like language acquisition, this meant that the experimenter had no choice but to construct hypotheses about the organism's subjective experience. But this was exactly the kind of mentalistic speculation behaviorism was supposed to avoid. In Skinner's experimental setup, Chomsky explained, "stimuli are no longer part of the outside physical world; they are driven back into the organism. . . . It is clear from such examples, which abound, that the talk of 'stimulus control' simply disguises a complete retreat to mentalistic psychology. We cannot predict verbal behavior in terms of the stimuli in the speaker's environment, since we do not know what the current stimuli are until he responds" (32). Second, Chomsky argued that the objective features of childhood language acquisition couldn't be explained through empirical or a posteriori data alone. Children aren't limited to understanding or imitating those verbal behaviors they've encountered before. Instead, they're able both to comprehend and produce entirely new utterances that nonetheless follow the rules of grammar. In *Rules and Representations* (1980), Chomsky suggested this was evidence of the "poverty of the stimulus" (37)—the relative impoverishment of the stimulus as compared to the verbal responses that follow it. When we encounter a new linguistic utterance, Chomsky wrote in his review of Skinner, "we recognize a new item as a sentence not because it matches some familiar item in any simple way, but because it is generated by the grammar that each individual has somehow and in some form internalized. And we understand a new sentence, in part, because we are somehow capable of determining the process by which this sentence is derived in this grammar" (56). Chomsky had also posited the existence of such a generative grammar in *Syntactic Structures* (1957).[9] Given the ability of children to produce new grammar-abiding sentences, as well as the speed by which they acquire this ability, Chomsky concluded that there had to be a "built-in . . . information processing (hypothesis forming) system"—an innate generative rule-based apparatus that could "arrive at the grammar of a language from the available data in the available time" (review of *Verbal Behavior*, 58). And this was why it was so crucial for scientists to turn away from things like operant conditioning and instead toward the cognitive architecture of language.

Even so, Chomsky claimed that research into this apparatus would present both empirical and conceptual challenges. For while it was possible to infer information about deep structures from surface structures, the innate foundations of those deep structures presented a different sort of problem. As he explained in *Aspects of the Theory of Syntax* (1965), the trouble was that any hypothesis about this innate foundation would need to satisfy different (and not always compatible) requirements. First, it would need to be

The Form of Thought

general enough to allow for variations among different languages. But at the same time, a hypothesis would only be meaningful if it could account for the grammatical details of those different languages. Otherwise, the hypothesis would be so general as to be useless. Moreover, any hypothesis of the innate content would also need to explain the mind's ability to deduce broader grammatical rules from isolated verbal stimuli—the aforementioned "information processing (hypothesis forming) system." Given those requirements, Chomsky concluded that it wasn't yet possible to "formulate an assumption about initial, innate structure rich enough to account for the fact that grammatical knowledge is attained on the basis of evidence available to the learner. . . . The real problem is that of developing a hypothesis about initial structure that is sufficiently rich enough to account for the acquisition of language, yet not so rich as to be inconsistent with the known diversity of language" (60).

Not everyone was as skeptical as Chomsky. During the 1960s and 1970s, there were several noteworthy attempts to deduce innate structure and content from instances of language use—and in that way reconceive of the empirical and conceptual relations between language and mind. One of the most successful—both rich and general—was Jerry Fodor's *The Language of Thought* (1975). But insofar as it made a hypothesis about cognitive processing, attempting to describe aspects of cognition that are both hidden and innate, it, too, was somewhat limited in detail. In contrast to the models of mind that I have discussed elsewhere in this book, Fodor's "language of thought" (LOT) hypothesis was fundamentally computationalist. Much as machines process input data and output transformations of that data, the theory goes, the human mind processes and transforms sensory information into mental representations.[10] If this were indeed the case, Fodor argued, then certain things could be deduced about thinking more generally. First, if consciousness was computational, then there had to be a "medium of computation" (27): a representational system capable of transforming input data. Second, as this system necessarily preceded the processing of any empirical data, it had to be innate. Third, by virtue of the logical and biological constraints on language acquisition, certain aspects of this computational system had to be *language-like*, even though this system couldn't be a natural language itself (as it preceded experience). This was Fodor's explanation: "Learning a language . . . involves learning what the predicates of the language mean. Learning what the predicates of a language mean involves learning a determination of the extension of those predicates. Learning a determination of the extension of predicates involves learning that they fall under certain rules (i.e., truth rules). But one cannot learn that *P* falls under *R* unless one has a language in which *P* and *R* can be represented. . . . My view is that you can't learn a language unless you already know one. It isn't that you can't learn a language unless you've already *learned* one" (63-65). In effect, Fodor's LOT hypothesis potentially explains the phenomenon I referred to earlier: language and thought aren't identical, but they share enough features for the former to effectively express the latter. If thought is necessarily language-like, then phenomena such as grammatical structure and cognitive structure—relying on the same kinds of symbolic, extensional, and computational processes—are potentially more comparable than they appear. Where the LOT hypothesis falls short, however, is the amount of detail it can offer, particularly with respect to language acquisition. Fodor's is a hypothesis about the kinds of things that must be true about the a priori structure of the mind. But it is not an empirical examination of that structure itself—and is therefore unable to map some of the more specific relations between cognitive processes and grammar that might interest us.

Nonetheless, Fodor's model was still more detailed and successful than the one offered by Jerrold Katz in *The Philosophy of Language* (1966). It was indeed possible, Katz claimed, to deduce information about the innate language acquisition device (LAD) "on the basis of definite empirical evidence from the analysis of natural languages" (270). This was Katz's description of the LAD's content:

(i) the linguistic universals which define the form of a linguistic description,
(ii) the form of the phonological, syntactic, and semantic components of a linguistic description,
(iii) the formal character of the rules in each of these components,
(iv) the set of universal phonological, syntactic, and semantic constructs out of which particular rules in particular descriptions are formulated,
(v) a methodology for choosing optimal linguistic descriptions. (269)

Katz's hypothesis does seem to satisfy at least one of Chomsky's requirements: it is so general as to be limited in its richness. Nothing about the hypothesized LAD would obviously preclude the diversity of languages. Instead, the issue is whether this LAD would be "rich enough." As Chomsky warned, the generality of Katz's LAD comes at the expense of useful detail. Rather than specifying the actual innate content of the LAD, Katz emphasizes the functions the LAD must perform. In that way he doesn't offer much more information about the nature of the LAD than Chomsky does in his review of Skinner. For while Katz's hypothesis claims that the LAD contains the "formal character" of any and all phonological, syntactic, and semantic operations, it doesn't tell us what that formal character is—even though knowing that formal character would be required for any claim that phonological, syntactic, and semantic operations all share this same property. Similarly, while Katz claims that the LAD possesses a "methodology for choosing optimal linguistic descriptions," it tells us nothing about this methodology or what it comprises. It also doesn't say whether individual languages would have their own standards for optimization, or if a universal "methodology" entails that all languages share the same standards for signal clarity and ease of parsing and articulation. In short, Katz's model takes an enormous leap by suggesting that the analysis of natural language can provide significant information about the LAD. But the information it provides doesn't get us very far.

From Style to Soul

In "The English Fiction of Samuel Beckett," Coetzee subjected Katz's *The Philosophy of Language* to substantial criticism, along with those literary critics he perceived as operating along similar lines. For even as Coetzee acknowledged the value of Katz's "discussion of the issues between the generative school on the one hand and the logical empiricists (Hilbert, Carnap et al.) and ordinary language philosophers (Wittgenstein, Ryle, et al.)" (295n16) on the other, he had two major concerns about Katz's model. First, even though Katz claimed that his model had been derived from instances of "linguistic performance" (*Philosophy of Language*, 270), Coetzee suggested that these claims were not thus derivable. Second, Katz's assumption of a one-to-one correspondence between language and mind—which seemed to conflate "mental experience" with cognition's overall architecture—amounted to the misattribution of grammatical rules onto thought. It assumed that language and thought were in fact both logically and physiologically comparable —if not identical. As Coetzee explained, "Insofar as Katz uses phenomena of language learning as a basis for statements about an innate system for organizing linguistic experience into a linguistic system of lower order, and insofar as he identifies mental experience with the operations of the latter system, I am therefore reluctant to accept his identification of thought and syntax" ("English Fiction," 297-98n19).

Fundamentally, this "identification of thought and syntax" was the same problem that Coetzee would identify in the Chomsky-inflected work of Richard Ohmann. But Coetzee also cautioned that versions of this problem existed in literary criticism well before Chomskyan linguistics—in particular in the work of Leo Spitzer. In *Linguistics and Literary History* (1948), Spitzer had modeled a "philological circle" by which psychological data could be extrapolated from linguistic data. As Spitzer wrote of Charles-Louis Philippe's novel *Bubu de Montparnasse* (1905), the analysis of style and syntax leads "toward a psychological etymon, which is at the bottom of the linguistic as well as of the literary inspiration of Philippe. Thus we have made the trip from language or style to the soul" (13-14). This "etymon" was the origin of those qualities that made an author's writing unique—not only their conscious choices but their unconscious choices as well, with written style reflecting things outside the author's self-knowledge. But this psychological "etymon" wasn't merely a guide to that author's individual style; it could also be a tool for articulating the progress of literary history. "The individual stylistic deviation from the general norm must represent a historical step taken by the writer . . . it must reveal a shift of the soul of the epoch, a shift of which the writer has become conscious and which he would translate into a necessarily new linguistic form" (11). But according to Coetzee, Spitzer had no proof for these assertions beyond intuition and common sense. Moreover, Spitzer's proclamation of a rule-like correspondence between an author's new ideas and "new linguistic form" wasn't just lacking evidence—it also couldn't function as a rule. For if we "regard language as the graph of thought," Coetzee explained, "we cannot regard certain features or kinds of language as graphs of thought while others are not" ("English Fiction of Samuel Beckett," 88). If "grammar mirrors thought" is a rule, then it should be the case that *every* word and grammatical relation on the page have a similar-looking psychological determinant. Otherwise, "grammar mirrors thought" isn't a rule at all, but rather a few instances of perceived correlation that have been misinterpreted as causation.

Spitzer himself died in 1960—but Coetzee reckoned that Chomskyan linguistics had breathed new life into Spitzer's work. As Donald Freeman wrote in *Linguistics and Literary Style* (1970)—the title alone revealing the volume's indebtedness to Spitzer—"the study of style . . . is in essence inspired mind-reading" (15). By Freeman's reasoning, such mind reading wasn't necessarily the purpose of literary criticism. But he nonetheless asserted that "modern linguistics, with its increasing interest in those characteristics of mind which underlie aspects of natural language, can make substantive theoretical and factual contributions to our understanding of the poetic process" (15-16). Ohmann's claims, however, went considerably farther than Freeman's—not only in terms of literary criticism's indebtedness to Chomskyan linguistics but also in terms of what such Chomsky-inspired criticism might achieve. "It is my contention," Ohmann wrote in "Generative Grammars and the Concept of Literary Style" (1964), "that recent developments in generative grammar, particularly on the transformational model, promise, first, to clear away a good deal of mist from stylistic theory, and, second, to make possible corresponding refinements in the practice of stylistic analysis" (426). The core of Ohmann's approach was treating an author's style not as the sole object of analysis but as one possible stylistic, or grammatical, transformation of a single deep, underlying structure. Given a sentence in a particular author's style, Ohmann maintained that it was possible to "undo" that sentence's stylistic transformations—thereby separating the deep "kernel" sentence from the "epistemic choices" made at the surface. From this kernel sentence new stylistic transformations could be deduced. By comparing these new transformations to the original sentence, Ohmann argued that it was possible to isolate the author's principles of stylistic selection and more general psychological dispositions.

As an example, Ohmann analyzed what he described as a "quite typically Faulknerian" sentence from Faulkner's "The Bear," from *Go Down, Moses* (1942). The sentence, which I will only quote from briefly, as it is hundreds of words long, includes "the desk and the shelf above it on which rested the letters in which McCaslin recorded the slow outward trickle of food and supplies and equipment which returned each fall as cotton made and ginned and sold."[11] To extract the kernel sentence, Ohmann removed a range of common grammatical transformations, including relative clauses, conjunctive transformations, and comparative transformations. The resulting kernel "sentence" was as follows: "The desk. The shelf was above it. The ledgers rested on the shelf. The ledgers were old. McCaslin recorded the trickle of food in the ledgers. McCaslin recorded the trickle of equipment in the ledgers. The trickle was slow. The trickle was outward. The trickle returned each fall as cotton. The cotton was made. The cotton was ginned. The cotton was sold" (432-33). As Ohmann noted, the process of de-transforming the sentence was somewhat arbitrary. But in separating this kernel sentence from Faulkner's original, it became clear how foundational these transformations were to Faulkner's style. Moreover, Ohmann claimed that "it seems reasonable to suppose that a writer whose style is so largely based on just these three semantically related transformations demonstrates in that style a certain conceptual orientation, a preferred way of organizing experience" (434). This would happen despite, we assume, the fictionality of Faulkner's text and the writer's ability to create characters and narrators with different linguistic dispositions.

"The English Fiction of Samuel Beckett," however, wasn't merely the analysis and subsequent rejection of this kind of determinative reasoning. Instead, Coetzee offered a computational analysis of Beckett's English-language fiction to show why theories like Ohmann's couldn't be correct and why it was necessary to explain a writer's style without appeals to authorial psychology. (This, of course, recalls many of the arguments I discussed in chap. 1.) As Coetzee explained, "I too am looking for an etymon, but I see no need to introduce the writer's psyche into the investigation" (76). In a novel such as Beckett's *Watt*, he wrote, the character of Watt shows that language is not "a magic correlative of logical thought, but rather the kind of language, particularly in its syntactic patterns, which we most often associate with logical thought" (88).[12] Instead, the causes of Watt's seemingly hyperlogical style weren't logical or "mental" but rather properties of language itself. As an example, we can turn to Coetzee's analysis of a moment from *Watt* where the title character goes through a number of possible reasons to explain why Erskine keeps running up and down the stairs. As is true of so many of Beckett's narrators, including Molloy and Moran, there seems to be little daylight between Watt's thinking and the language that represents such thinking:

> Watt did not care to enquire in so many words into the meaning of all this, for he said, All this will be revealed to Watt, in due time, meaning of course when Erskine went, and another came. But he was not easy until he had said, in short and isolated phrases, or fragments of phrases, separated by considerable periods of time from one another, Perhaps Mr Knott sends him now upstairs, and now downstairs, on this errand and on that, saying, but hasten back to me, Erskine, don't delay, But hasten back to me. But what kind of errand? Perhaps to fetch him something that he has forgotten, and that suddenly he feels the need of, such as a nice book, or piece of cotton wool or tissue paper. Or perhaps to look out of a top window, to make sure that nobody is coming, or to have a quick look round below stairs, to make sure no danger threatens the foundations.[13]

This moment is fairly typical of *Watt*—both in terms of its complexity and in terms of its grammatical and logical permutations. Moreover, as Co-

The Form of Thought

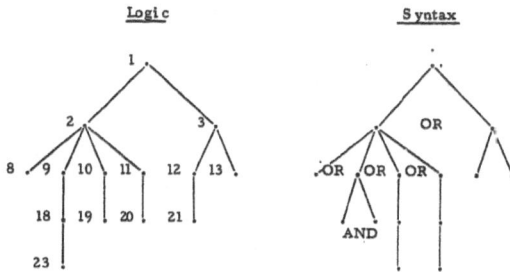

Figure 10. Logical and grammatical diagram of sentence from Samuel Beckett's *Watt* (Coetzee, "English Fiction," 83).

etzee's diagram shows (fig. 10), the logical and grammatical structures of this excerpt are incredibly similar. According to Coetzee, the syntax and logic of Beckett's sentence are "nearly isomorphic." Their structures are similar enough that one can infer that "the logic and the syntax of the paragraph have at least the same basis, if one is not the basis of the other" (84). The temptation, he acknowledged, was to assume that this is an example of "imitative form ... a 'dramatic syntax' which follows the 'form of thought'" (84). But Coetzee's point was that even if grammar and thought did in fact follow the same rules, not even this near-perfect mirroring would be enough to establish a one-to-one determinative relation between the two. And in that way Coetzee's conclusions about *Watt* take us back to the accounts of style offered by Watson and Skinner and their appeals to individual histories of conditioning. Any perceived correspondence between grammatical structure and the "form of thought" had to be a product of the author's own history of associations, as well as any associations that might be entailed by genre. "The relation between syntax and what we understand to be the thought that produces it," Coetzee wrote, "depends on our experience of the kinds of syntax and the kinds of meaning that usually occur together, as well as on literary convention" (89). And insofar as mind and language are different kinds of phenomena following different kinds of rules, Coetzee would therefore have us doubt that language could ever faithfully represent the "form of thought" at all.

"It is as if there is no interior"

In many ways, this is precisely the problem tackled by *Waiting for the Barbarians* and *Foe*. In order to access the minds of colonized subjects, both the Magistrate and Susan Barton treat these minds as if they were *language-like*—as if they had linguistic properties and as if they were somehow less interiorized than their own minds. Ultimately the Magistrate and Susan Barton are unsuccessful in their efforts, with each novel emphasizing how they have misconstrued not only the interiority of the colonized subject but their own as well. In that way, *Waiting for the Barbarians* and *Foe* build on a long history of anti-colonial critique, particularly with respect to the ways European colonizers have distorted, or denied entirely, the psychological interiority of colonized subjects. One of the most forceful of these critiques was that of Frantz Fanon's *Black Skin, White Masks* (1952). Responding to Sartre's claim in *Anti-Semite and Jew* (1944) that Jewish conduct "is perpetually over-determined from the inside" (95), Fanon explained that his experience as a Black man was the opposite: "I am overdetermined from the outside. I am a slave not to the 'idea' others have of me, but to my appearance. . . . I see in this white gaze that it's the arrival not of a new man, but of a new type of man, a new species. A Negro, in fact!" (95). This white gaze, Fanon argued, understood the Black subject's interiority as merely an extension of their overt behaviors—as if mind and body, or thinking and behaving, were logically comparable concepts, and as if there were no interiority at all. The result of this projection was a dehumanized and soulless "Other" whose inner life was purely physiological or driven by instinct. "To have a phobia about black men," Fanon explained, "is to be afraid of the biological, for the black man is nothing but biological. Black men are animals. They live naked. And God only knows what else" (143). In "An Image of Africa" (1977) Chinua Achebe described a related problem in Conrad's *Heart of Darkness*, where the European mind and the African mind almost seem as if they are different concept types. Conrad's sense of the European mind, as exemplified by Colonel Kurtz, is of seemingly infinite psychological depth (and problematically so). But as Achebe points out, the African characters in *Heart of Darkness* are given no such psychological depth. Instead, they are dehumanized, and their "rudimentary souls" cease to seem like souls at all. They become part of the scenery, the backdrop for what are presented as the properly psychological struggles of Marlow and Kurtz. Conrad's Africa, Achebe wrote, is "a metaphysical battlefield devoid of all recognizable humanity, into which the wandering European enters at his peril. Of course, there is a preposterous and perverse kind of arrogance in thus reducing Africa to the role of props for the breakup of one petty European mind" (9).[14]

Fanon and Achebe are incredibly useful in their assessments of some of the relations among the colonization of Africa, racism, and problems of mind. Their comments also resonate with many of the critiques leveled by anti-apartheid writers and activists in South Africa, many of whom seized on the literary and political necessity of expressing psychological interiority. Drawing on Fanon, as well as Aimé Cesaire and W. E. B. Du Bois, members of the Black Consciousness Movement argued that such expressions were essential for South Africa's future. As writer and activist Steve Biko wrote in "Black Consciousness and the Quest for a True Humanity" (1972), Black Consciousness is based on the "self-examination which has ultimately led [Black citizens of South Africa] to believe that by seeking to run away from themselves and emulate the white man, they are insulting the intelligence of whoever created them black. The philosophy of Black Consciousness therefore expresses group pride and the determination of the black to rise and attain the envisaged self" (*I Write What I Like*, 92). In his discussions of the contemporary South African novel, the writer Njabulo S. Ndebele extended this reasoning and rejected the claim that "a writer's concern with subjectivity in character development may amount to a bourgeois or liberal escapism into an ethos of individualism" (33). Instead, Ndebele argued that a new generation of South African writers were rightly focusing on interiority and leaving the "spectacle" of earlier fiction behind. As he wrote in "The Rediscovery of the Ordinary: Some New Writings in South Africa" (1984), "Judging from some of the writing that has emerged from the South African townships, one can come to the conclusion that the convention of the spectacular has run its course. Its tendency either to devalue or to ignore interiority has placed it firmly in that aspect of South African society that constitutes its fundamental weakness" (49). A novel such as Zoë Wicomb's *Playing in the Light* (2006) makes a related point—showing the continuing importance, but also precariousness, of such interiority even after the end of apartheid. After learning that her family started passing as white in the 1960s, Marion speculates about how this public performance of race and culture occluded any kind of thinking about identity or morality. "The public selves," Wicomb writes, "required all their energies. Playing—as others would call it—in the light left no space, no time for interiority, for reflecting on what they had done. . . . The past, and with it conscience, shrunk to a black dot in the distance" (123). The interiority of Marion's family members isn't quite "overdetermined from the outside," to return to Fanon's *Black Skin, White Masks*. Nonetheless, public life—that is, overt behavior—has somehow displaced the private life of the mind.

This kind of external displacement and distortion of interiority, particularly that of the colonized or racialized subject, appears throughout *Waiting for the Barbarians*. In the novel's opening pages we encounter Colonel Joll, who is visiting the colonial outpost overseen by the novel's narrator, the Magistrate. Joll is torturing members of the colonized population to extract information about threats to the empire. When the Magistrate questions the effectiveness of torture, Joll asserts that it is possible to assess the veracity of his victim's confessions from linguistic properties alone.

> "There is a certain tone," Joll says. "A certain tone enters the voice of a man who is telling the truth. Training and experience teach us to recognize that tone."
>
> "The tone of truth! Can you pick up this tone in everyday speech? Can you hear whether I am telling the truth?" . . .
>
> "No you misunderstand me. I am speaking only of a special situation now, I am speaking of a situation in which I am probing for the truth, in which I have to exert pressure to find it. First I get lies, you see—this is what happens—first lies, then pressure, then more lies, then more pressure, then the break, then more pressure, then the truth. That is how you get the truth." (5)

This is a crucial scene in the novel. As Anthony Uhlmann notes, Joll's interrogation speaks to the novel's broader interest in what "truth" is, how it's known, and what it comprises.[15] Moreover, as Kelly Adams suggests, this concept of "truth" is inseparable from Coetzee's use of the passive voice here and is valuably contextualized by the aforementioned "The Rhetoric of the Passive in English."[16] But as evidenced by the stylistic criticism discussed in "The English Fiction of Samuel Beckett," there is another overarching philosophical concern here: the misattribution of properties across category lines and the comparability assumed between different types of concepts. Joll believes that torture effectively eliminates the possibility of lying. Insofar as "truth" is actually a figure for his victims' honesty, the tone of truth is supposed to indicate a perfect correspondence between linguistic properties and mental state. But while the phrase "tone of truth" isn't immediately absurd to our ears, it is nonetheless an example of a category-mistake. As both truth and honesty are abstract concepts, neither of them has empirical properties. So if Joll perceives a "tone of truth," then what he must be perceiving is a sound that he has come to associate with truth—that is, the tone of pain. But while pain might conceivably motivate people to tell the truth, there is no necessary connection between them. Accordingly, Joll tortures his prisoners not until they actually offer honest confessions

The Form of Thought

but until they make a particular kind of noise—which might or might not have any connection to the content of their speech or mental states.

In many ways, the Magistrate is presented as a foil to Colonel Joll. Generally, he appears benevolent and even sympathetic to many of the colonized subjects under his control. When an old man is killed during an interrogation by Joll's soldiers, the Magistrate arranges for his burial and ensures that the man's grandson receives food (although he also confesses "that an interrogator can wear two masks, speak with two voices, one harsh, one seductive"; 7). But despite his relative compassion for the colonized population, his sense of their "interior"—of meanings or mental states hidden from view—is no less distorted than Colonel Joll's. Indeed, when he finds indigenous relics he can't decipher—including ancient ruins and "a cache of wooden slips on which are painted characters in a script I have not seen the like of" (15)—we see the Magistrate rely on the same kind of bad logic and equivocation between unlike terms.[17] As he stands in the ruins, he imagines that

> perhaps when I stand on the floor of the courthouse, if that is what it is, I stand over the head of a Magistrate like myself, another grey-haired servant of Empire. . . . I cleared the floor of my office and laid [the wooden slips] out, first in one great square, then in sixteen smaller squares, then in other combinations, thinking that what I had hitherto taken to be characters in a syllabary might in fact be elements of a picture whose outline would leap at me if I struck on the right arrangement: a map of the land of the barbarians in olden times, or a representation of a lost pantheon. I have even found myself reading the slips in a mirror, or tracing one on top of another, or conflating half of one with half of another. (16)

Again, what marks the Magistrate's efforts here is sympathy for colonized and indigenous peoples—so much so that he imagines them in lives analogous and comparable to his own. But the logic beneath the Magistrate's efforts to interpret the wooden slips is not unlike the logic beneath Colonel Joll's belief in the "tone of truth." Even though the Magistrate confesses he does not know what kind of concepts the slips represent—if they are part of a "syllabary" or a visual image—he ultimately imposes onto the them the structure of his own life and his fantasies about indigenous cultures. Coetzee actually implies that these two activities—the good faith effort to interpret the slips and the colonizer's insidious projection of himself onto the colonial object—are inseparable. As the Magistrate holds the slips up in the mirror, the phrase "conflating half of one with half of another" works at multiple levels. First, it describes the Magistrate's use of the mirror image to mix and match the different ends of the slips—reaffirming his ignorance of what they do, how they come together, or even if they're upside down. At the same time, it is the Magistrate's own reflection in the mirror that he is "conflating" with the people he imagines having used the wooden slips. However he tries to interpret the slips, the implication is that his efforts will always yield more information about *his* thoughts and desires than they will about the slips' original users.

The Magistrate only realizes his errors when he begins a sexual relationship with a blinded woman from the colonized population. As he becomes aware of the parallels between their relationship and the torture that blinded her, he begins to doubt that he ever knew the minds of colonized subjects at all. Indeed, where there were once thoughts to be mapped and depths to be explored, he finds now only the exterior of her body:

> I prowl about her, touching her face, caressing her body, without entering her or finding the urge to do so. I have just come from the bed of a woman for whom, in the year that I have known her, I have not for a moment had to interrogate my desire: to desire her has meant to enfold and enter her, to pierce her surface and stir the quiet of her interior into an ecstatic storm; then to retreat, to subside, to wait for desire to reconstitute itself. But with this woman it is as if there is no interior, only a surface across which I hunt back and forth seeking entry. Is this how her torturers felt hunting their secret, whatever they thought it was? For the first time I feel a dry pity for them: how natural a mistake to believe that you can burn or tear or hack your way into the secret body of the other! (43)

This description of the woman's mind as "the secret body of the other" recalls many of the mind-body category-mistakes I've discussed throughout this book—particularly those where minds and bodies appear as if they are known by the same means. If Colonel Joll and the Magistrate thought that the mind of the colonized subject was in fact knowable—whether through torture or through moving around wooden slips—it is only because they treated this mind as if it were something that operated in the external world. It was only a category-mistake that enabled the "natural mistake" of believing they could access the interiority of colonized persons. As the Magistrate realizes this, he also finds that the external signs that he once took as evidence of interiority no longer have that meaning. Instead, "with this woman it is as if there is no interior, only a surface"—such that there is no way to deduce the contents, or even existence, of one from the other.

And as the logical relations among mind, body, and language become clearer to the Magistrate, his desires to "enfold and enter" and "pierce and stir" dissipate as well.

In this encounter with the blind woman, however, it's not only the Magistrate's attitude about the minds of colonized and indigenous peoples that changes. Indeed, as he perceives the blind woman's body as having "no interior," he also begins to perceive disjunctions between his own body and mind—as if he had been making the same "natural mistake" about his own ability to express his thoughts through language. As he lies next to the blind woman in bed, he experiences a new distance between his thoughts and speech: "My lips move, silently composing and recomposing the words. 'Or perhaps it is the case that only that which has not been articulated has to be lived through.' I stare at this proposition. . . . The words grow more and more opaque before me; soon they have lost all meaning" (64). By figuring his lips as the origin of language, rather than something in his mind, the Magistrate emphasizes the degree to which this language is physically and epistemologically disconnected from his phenomenal consciousness. Moreover, by figuring this proposition as if it had visual properties ("I stare at this proposition"), the Magistrate emphasizes the degree to which it feels like it is outside his head—as if it were something he could see rather than merely know through reflection. As these "words grow more and more opaque," the Magistrate conceives of the opacity of *all* language and behavior insofar as they fail to correspond to mental phenomena. The Magistrate's reasoning here also recalls my discussion in chapter 2 of Beckett's *Murphy* and *Molloy* and the ways they attribute sensory properties to introspective knowledge—although, unlike Beckett, Coetzee seems to find value in maintaining the conventional differences between psychological and nonpsychological language.

The Magistrate also sees the wooden slips as exhibiting this kind of opacity. If he once interpreted the slips by way of his mirror image, he now concedes he has no way of knowing what kind of thing they refer to—or if they refer to anything at all. "Does each sign," he asks, "represent a different state of the tongue, the lips, the throat, the lungs, as they combine in the uttering of some multifarious unimaginable extinct barbarian language? Or are my four hundred characters nothing but scribal embellishments of an underlying repertory of twenty or thirty whose primitive forms I am too stupid to see?" (110-11). However, when Colonel Joll interrogates him about the meaning of the slips, the Magistrate tries to scare the colonel away from further attacks against the indigenous population by suggesting that the slips' indecipherability is in fact part of the enemy's strategy. "Now let us see what the next one says," he tells Colonel Joll. "See, there is only a single character. It is the barbarian character *war*, but it has other senses too. It can stand for vengeance, and, if you turn it upside down like this, it can be made to read *justice*. There is no knowing which sense is intended. That is part of the barbarian cunning" (112). He cannot convince Colonel Joll that these slips are beyond interpretation or that there is no "tone of truth." But he can try to use the colonel's own distorted notions of interiority against him and convince him that the colonized subject's mind is well beyond his reach.

This marks an important parallel with *Foe*, which also stipulates the difficulties—and political implications—of European male writers representing the mental lives of colonized subjects, as well as those of European women. The novel is framed as a rewriting of Daniel Defoe's *Robinson Crusoe* (1719) and *Roxana* (1723). An English woman named Susan Barton, looking for her lost daughter off the coast of Bahia, is shipwrecked on a Caribbean island. There she meets a shipwrecked Portuguese trader, Cruso, and his mute servant, Friday, whose tongue has been removed (possibly by Cruso). Much of *Foe* concerns Barton's efforts to learn Friday's "story" and to tell her own, despite the challenges of communicating with Friday and the interferences of the eponymous author figure. The relations among narration, sex, and colonialism are therefore mainstays of *Foe* scholarship. In *A Critique of Postcolonial Reason* (1999), Gayatri Spivak argues that *Foe* upends male narratives of imperialism by employing a female narrator—even as that female narrator is largely unsympathetic to the story she is required to tell. Moreover, Spivak claims that *Foe* does nothing to repair these damaged imperial narratives, or to "defend itself against the undecidability and discomfort of imagining a woman" (179). In *J. M. Coetzee and the Ethics of Reading* (2004), Derek Attridge makes a corollary point. *Foe*, he writes, "focuses on what might be considered the most fundamental narrative of bourgeois culture not only to examine the processes of canonization and legitimation ... but also to bring forcefully to its readers' attention the silences which those processes generate and upon which they depend: in particular, a gender silence and a race silence" (85).[18]

However, there's something else at stake in narration in *Foe* as well. By Barton's reasoning, language isn't merely a representation of thinking but an extension of it. To read another person's writing, she believes, is to encounter some aspect of that person directly. This is an idea Barton raises early in her time on the island, expressing surprise that Cruso has "no record of years as a shipwreck" (17). It's not merely the content of Cruso's writing that interests Barton; it's also the possibility that if she were to write a similar record, her own experiences might somehow survive her death. "Is it not possible," she asks Cruso, "to manufacture paper and ink and set down what traces remain of these memories, so they will outlive you?" (17). For Barton this idea that memories might "outlive" her is not a figure of speech. Throughout *Foe*, she describes language either as being alive or as somehow capturing her own phenomenal experiences—possessing the sorts of properties that people have but that language does not. As she prepares to send Daniel Foe an account of her time on the island, she suggests that the letter itself will carry her experiences: "Closing my eyes," she writes, "I gather my strength and send out a vision of the island to hang before you like a substantial body, with birds and fleas and fish of all hues . . . and rain drumming on the roof-fronds, and wind, unceasing wind: so that it will be there for you to draw on whenever you have need" (53). She puts even greater faith, perhaps, in Foe's own writing (or at least his ink), going so far as to imagine his words as having phenomenal experiences of their own. While she and Friday occupy Foe's house, waiting for the absent author, she sends him letters on his own stationary. As she describes Friday's dancing, Barton explains that "it is as though animalcules of words lie dissolved in your inkwell, ready to be dipped up and flow from the pen and take form on paper. . . . After that the words of themselves do the journeying" (93). To briefly recall Beckett's "Dante . . . Bruno," as Barton sees Friday dancing, so the words also dance—with body, thought, and language all appearing to move in unison.

Barton's attribution of nonlinguistic properties to language is important for several reasons. First, as I mentioned, it's how Barton conceives of her memories taking a durable and public form. The implication is that these nonlinguistic properties are essential for expressing her memories properly and permanently. Second, it is through her own misattribution of mental properties to language that Barton can conceive of language permitting direct knowledge of other minds. As made possible by the "animacules of words," the tiny living organisms Barton imagines in the ink, Barton conceives of the relation between language and thought as one of not only correspondence but also identity. But like *Waiting for the Barbarians*, which asked us to understand the disjunctions between language and thought as necessary and a priori, this is a point that *Foe* rejects with some force. Indeed, it is not merely the removal of Friday's tongue that renders his mind inaccessible to Barton. Instead, Barton—who so readily believed that her words could sustain sensory predicates and transmit her thoughts "like a substantial body"—finds insurmountable disconnections between Friday's actions and what she believes to know about his mind. Moreover, as the novel decries the ways that Barton distorts and violates Friday's interiority and her attempts to turn him into a vessel for her story, it ultimately concludes that Barton's sense of her own interiority and language is no less distorted.

The novel establishes these disjunctions, and ultimately its critique of Barton's interiority, through its representations of language acquisition—returning us to many of the empirical and logical problems I discussed at the beginning of this chapter. Indeed, one of the biggest difficulties facing Barton is not only how to teach Friday language but also how to determine whether he has ever acquired language before (specifically, English or Portuguese). But even determining the existence of linguistic knowledge in Friday's mind—a task far less difficult than, say, determining the content of specific beliefs or attitudes—proves impossible. Even though some of Friday's actions seem to be in response to verbal stimuli, Barton finds it impossible to reconstruct anything about his knowledge or thinking from these behaviors. When Barton says, "Bring more wood, Friday," she claims that "Friday heard me, I could have sworn, but he did not stir. So I said the word 'Wood' again, indicating the fire; upon which he stood up, but did no more" (21). In response, Cruso explains, "*Firewood* is the word I have taught him . . . *Wood* he does not know" (21). If Friday actually understood the semantic meaning of "firewood," she reasons, he would "understand that firewood was a kind of wood." This, of course, recalls Chomsky's critique of Skinner. Presumably, if Friday understood the meaning and grammatical uses of "firewood," he would be able to extrapolate the meaning of "wood." He would demonstrate that such extrapolation had occurred by acting in response to "wood," and this action would constitute proof of Friday's linguistic competence, as well as his possession of some kind of generative-transformational apparatus in his brain. But at the same time, Friday's failure to respond to "wood" is not dispositive. It raises questions about how much he understands, but it can't rule out the possibility that he understood "wood" and chose to ignore it. Friday's standing up only adds to this ambiguity, as it makes it even more difficult to imagine a correspondence between language and thought. Additionally, Cruso, who claims to speak for Friday, adds another variable. Echoing the conditioning-based theories of language acquisition advanced by Watson and Skinner, Cruso maintains that Friday only understands those specific words (i.e., stimuli) that he has been exposed to. This explanation is perhaps borne out by Friday's actions. Then again, it could also be the case that Friday responded to Cruso's command not because he failed to understand Barton's but rather because he fears, and has been conditioned by, Cruso's brutality. Later in the novel, Barton encounters a similar set of ambiguities when she tries to teach Friday writing. "On the slate," Barton explains, "I drew a house with a door and windows and a chimney, and beneath it wrote the letters h-o-u-s . . . and Friday wrote the four letters h-o-u-s, or four shapes passably like them: whether they were truly the four letters, and stood truly for the word *house*, and the picture I had drawn, and the thing itself, only he knew" (145). A writer's style, Freeman claimed, "is in essence inspired mind-reading"—but what if you can't be sure you're looking at written language at all?

In many ways, Cruso appears to be a foil for Barton—just as Colonel Joll was for the Magistrate in *Waiting for the Barbarians*. Where Cruso is cruel and uses these verbal stimuli to control and speak for Friday, Barton appears more generous and genuinely interested in Friday's mind and personal history. Her motivations for teaching him the word "spoon" appear pure: "I hold up a spoon and say 'Spoon, Friday!' and give the spoon into his hand. Then I say 'Spoon!' and hold out my hand to receive the spoon; hoping thus that in time the word Spoon will echo in his mind willy nilly whenever his eye falls on a spoon" (43). But even though Cruso seems to have conditioned Friday to respond to "firewood," Barton is unable to teach him "spoon" and therefore wonders, "how can I be sure he does not think I am chattering to myself as a magpie or an ape does?" (43). In many ways, however, Barton's motivations are no less nefarious than Cruso's. After she fails to teach Friday "spoon," her approach changes: she reasons that *her* language, her voice, will become Friday's new "tongue." And where her earlier method of teaching language relied on a one-to-one correspondence between word and mental "echo," Barton now seeks to immerse Friday in an environment saturated with her own "chatter":

> Throughout all my chatter Friday labours away at a washing board. I expect no sign that he has understood. It is enough to hope that if I make the air around him thick with words, memories will be reborn in him which died under Cruso's rule. . . . Friday may have lost his tongue but he has not lost his ears—that is what I say to myself. Through his ears Friday may yet take in the wealth stored in stories and

so learn that the world is not, as the island seemed to teach him, a barren and a silent place (is that the secret meaning of the word story, do you think: a storing place of memories?). (59)

In saying that her "chatter" might allow some of Friday's memories to be "reborn," Barton reveals that she is looking to do far more than give him language. Instead, she believes that her own speech will give Friday access to his own mind—as if he didn't have access to it before her arrival. In effect, Barton envisions her language becoming the medium of Friday's thoughts. But because Barton also believes that language can transmit mental properties, whereby a story becomes a "storing place of memories," this process would also recast Friday's subjectivity in the image of her own. Instead of her language allowing his story to be told, it would in fact supplant his experiences and memories with hers. This is why she feels able to speak *for* Friday to Foe: "Friday's desires are not dark to me. He desires to be liberated, as I do too. Our desires are plain, his and mine" (148).

And yet "Friday's desires" are in fact dark to Barton. Unable to draw out Friday's thoughts through language, Barton decides that the only way to give Friday a voice is through fiction—as if actual minds and literary minds were in fact interchangeable. "The story of Friday's tongue," she tells Foe, "is a story unable to be told, or unable to be told by me. That is to say, many stories can be told of Friday's tongue, but the true story is buried within Friday, who is mute. The true story will not be heard till by art we have found a means of giving voice to Friday" (118). Recalling Fanon's comment that the Black subject is "overdetermined from the outside," Barton's decision amounts to remaking Friday's interiority through fiction—not finding, but forcing, a correspondence between internal and external phenomena. The irony of this, of course, is that Barton presents this as a measure that might prevent others from victimizing Friday in the same way. "Friday has no command of words and therefore no defence against being re-shaped day by day in conformity with the desires of others. I say he is a cannibal and he becomes a cannibal; I say he is a laundryman and he becomes a laundryman" (121). Whereas Barton presented her own language as carrying her experiences and sensations out into the world, her language now moves in the opposite direction. It overwrites Friday's interiority and phenomenal consciousness with the semantic meaning of her utterances.

This overwriting of Friday's mind is a gesture that *Foe* eventually places at the historical origins of the English novel. And yet, parallel to this literary historical claim, I think that *Foe* concedes a somewhat surprising point. If we do want to express the mind through language, the novel suggests, and in that way want to circumvent the disjunctions between language and thought, then we might have no choice but to emulate Barton's approach. It is only through the category-mistake, we infer from Coetzee, that mental representation is possible at all. So at the novel's end, when a new nameless narrator—a stand-in for Coetzee, perhaps—refuses to engage in this kind of logical sleight of hand, we lose mental representation entirely. In an underwater dreamscape, aboard a sunken ship, this narrator encounters the floating bodies of Friday, Barton, and Cruso. And like those who came before, the narrator tries to get Friday to talk. But here, where the narrator explains "bodies are their own signs," something else happens:

> I tug his woolly hair, finger the chain about his throat. "Friday," I say, I try to say, kneeling over him, sinking hands and knees into the ooze, "what is this ship?" . . .
>
> His mouth opens. From inside him comes a slow stream, without breath, without interruption. It flows up through his body and out upon me; it passes through the cabin, through the wreck; washing the cliffs and shores of the island, it runs northward and southward to the ends of the earth. Soft and cold, dark and unending, it beats against my eyelids, against the skin of my face. (157)

The political significance of the narrator's attempt to get Friday to speak is unmistakable. Juxtaposing his question with tugging on Friday's hair and holding "the chain about his throat," the narrator presents their actions as being no less pernicious than Barton's or Cruso's. But the material—the nonlinguistic material—that comes out of Friday's mouth is important too. For in a place "not of words" but "where bodies are their own signs" (157), there is only physicality. There is only behavior and the body itself, with no language for denoting or describing anything psychological. Instead of forcing new signs and rules onto Friday's behaviors, the narrator acknowledges the sheer impossibility of deducing any kind of semantic or psychological content from what comes out of Friday's mouth. It is an indication of what kinds of assumptions, and pernicious and illogical beliefs, would be necessary to perceive this emission as representing Friday's mental states. It is as if there is no interior.

"The empirical slack in our own beliefs"

Logically, many of Coetzee's claims about logical disjunctions between language and mind hold up. Many of them are also broadly compatible, I think, with the assumption that has been most central to this book: that language and mind are fundamentally different kinds of things that follow different kinds of rules. Some of Coetzee's claims, however, raise difficulties that are not only logical and moral but also practical (particularly in light of *Foe*'s final pages). By his reasoning, *all* linguistic representation of minds and mental states comprises a category-mistake—whether comparability between language and mind is perceived or not. In other words, it's impossible to express thought through language without changing its character or forcing it to follow linguistic (rather than mental) rules. When this reasoning is coupled with the political consequences of speaking about and for other minds, it almost seems like a case for avoiding mental representation entirely. Is this what Coetzee is actually asking us to do—to forgo any attempts to express thought and instead talk about behavior exclusively?

In thinking about this question, I think we can find some illumination through W. V. O. Quine's concept of the "indeterminacy of translation," which also uses the example of a colonial encounter. Quine asks his readers to imagine two linguists performing "radical translation," which he defines as "the translation of the language of hitherto untouched people" (*Word and Object*, 28). As we'll see, this is a process very much comparable to the scenes of language instruction and interpretation that we encountered in *Foe* and *Waiting for the Barbarians*, where, as Quine phrases it, we encountered a "multiplicity of individual histories capable of issuing in identical behavior" (79). Here's how that happens: each linguist, Quine explains, begins this work by compiling a set of sentences where the referent of a given word is observed firsthand. As an example, when members of this untouched people see a rabbit, they point at it and say "gavagai." From this observed meaning, as well as others, the linguists deduce a set of hypotheses about the language's grammar and conventions. The trouble, Quine explains, is that the meanings assigned to "gavagai" necessarily rely on subjective judgment. One linguist might write down that "gavagai" means "rabbit"—but the other might write down that it means "animal" or "white."[19] Conceivably either one could be correct. The trouble is the cumulative effect of all the different subjective judgments each linguist makes, as well as the hypotheses each linguist bases on these judgments. By the end of the translation process, the differences between the linguists' accounts could be enormous. Or as Quine puts it, "manuals for translating one language into another can be set up in divergent ways, all compatible with the totality of speech dispositions, yet incompatible with one another" (27). Conceivably each linguist could create a manual that is true to experience, logically sound, and internally consistent. Yet insofar as these manuals have had to rely on a degree of subjective judgment, they could be completely unlike one another. And this is ultimately the point Quine wishes to make about language more generally, using the thought experiment to illustrate the "empirical slack in our own beliefs" (78). By virtue of their different conditioning histories, subjective experiences, and psychological dispositions, it's entirely possible that two people could speak what seems like the same language and yet fundamentally disagree about a word's or sentence's meaning. By Quine's reasoning, the problem of other minds, or of private worlds, isn't a problem of mind but of language. In that way, the indeterminacy of translation is a classic example of logical behaviorism—pointing out the nonmental origins of what appears to be a mental phenomenon.

What we see in *Waiting for the Barbarians* and *Foe*, of course, is what happens when this sort of behavioristic reasoning is undercooked or one-sided. Initially Coetzee's colonizing characters treat the minds of colonized subjects as if they were language-like—only to realize later on that their own minds are similarly constrained. I think Coetzee sees this realization as a valuable lesson for his characters, and readers, and so I doubt he'd ask us to eliminate mental representation entirely. But I don't think he would be as sanguine as Quine about tightening the "empirical slack in our own beliefs." Instead, he would draw our attention to the broader implications of such epistemological tightening—as well as the necessary differences, and uncomfortable similarities, between literary minds and actual ones. Our aim, we infer, cannot be to cross the gap between language and thought as if we were trying to fill in a map of unknown territory. Instead, we must recognize the logical and moral costs of crossing that gap—of recognizing the disjunctions between thought and language—and, at times, consider leaving it uncrossed.

Coda
Observations and/or Reflections

Over the course of *The Concept of Mind*, Ryle makes a number of claims about the value of literature for thinking about psychological language. One of the most surprising claims happens during his discussion of self-knowledge, which he thinks would pose fewer conceptual difficulties if we just excluded a particular word:

> Though it is not always convenient to avoid the practice, there is a considerable logical hazard in using the nouns "mind" and "minds" at all. The idiom makes it too easy to construct logically improper conjunctions, disjunctions, and cause-effect propositions such as "such and such took place not in my body but in my mind," "my mind made my hand write," "a person's mind and body interact with each other" and so on. Where logical candour is required of us we ought to follow the example set by novelists, biographers, and diarists, who speak only of persons doing and undergoing things. (150)

Ryle's points about the logical differences between "mind" and "body" are well-taken and are among this book's most important foundations. Nonetheless, his discussion here does present some problems, particularly for a critic talking about literature's relation to problems of mind. For someone in my position, the word "mind" is not a mere convenience. It's essential. While Ryle is right that the term is often misunderstood and misused, it still refers to a concept that's meaningful and that needs its own word. Ryle might not like what "mind" refers to or entails, but the term is useful and, when used thoughtfully, refers to phenomena and relations that other terms don't. Additionally, Ryle's account of "novelists, biographers, and diarists" is a peculiar one—recalling his accounts of theatrical performance that I discussed in chapter 3. Ryle's comments here are even more peculiar when we remember his devotion to the novels of Jane Austen. It's not impossible to find a novel, biography, or diary that avoids mental language and focuses on behavior entirely. But these books are in the minority. Moreover, you won't find Jane Austen's novels among them, which are famous for their representations of thinking and, as we see in this example from *Sense and Sensibility* (1811), thinking about thinking: "In her earnest meditations on the contents of the letter, on the depravity of that mind which could dictate it, and, probably, on the very different mind of a very different person, who had no other connection whatever with the affair than what her heart gave him with everything that passed, Elinor forgot the immediate distress of her sister" (175). Perhaps we could in fact rewrite this sentence without the word "mind" or its associated properties. But it's not clear how much of Austen's sentence would be left, or what, if anything, a reader ought to emulate about it.

This leads me to the even bigger problem with Ryle's comments here—a problem that very much cuts to the heart of my arguments in this book, despite my indebtedness to *The Concept of Mind*. Ryle tells us that we can learn from the "logical candour" of novelists, biographers, and diarists. But how logically candid are we being when we give into the mentalistic illusions of literary experience? When we group unlike concepts, like actual minds and literary minds, as if they were made of the same materials and followed the same rules? The fact that Ryle makes this error is evidence of how deeply mind-body category-mistakes are embedded into our assumptions and practices as readers of literature. In that way, it's also evidence for the value of reading behavioristically—of balancing our mentalistic perceptions of texts with our awareness of the logical and formal mechanisms that such mentalistic perceptions rely on.

Showing the value of such awareness, and the necessity of such conceptual work, was the primary goal of this book. But there was another goal too: giving readers a renewed ability to think about, and find significance in, their own experiences as readers. Granted, as I showed in chapter 1, psychological behaviorism played no small part in literary criticism's turn away from authorial and readerly psychology. But as literary criticism turns again to scientific explanations for the ways we read, and as the humanities continually reevaluate their relations to knowledge of the natural world, this ability to talk about our experiences as readers—to discuss what we perceive and what must or must not be true about those perceptions—could not be more important. And ultimately it is this ability that reading behavioristically both cultivates and relies on, as the perception of a literary mind is always an occasion to think about how language affects thought and why we read literature in the ways we do. Contrary to Ryle's advice, our aim shouldn't be to follow novels, biographies, or diaries as examples of using psychological concepts properly. Instead, we should aim to understand why we believe that novels, biographies, and diaries—along with poems and plays—can be examples of this at all.

Notes

Introduction. Literary Experience and the Concept of Mind

1. This position is consistent with property dualism. I defer to David Chalmers's definition of the concept in *The Conscious Mind*. Property dualism, he explains, is the belief that "conscious experience involves properties of an individual that are not entailed by the physical properties of that individual although they may depend lawfully on those properties. Consciousness is a *feature* of the world over and above the physical features of the world. This is not to say it's a separate 'substance.' . . . All we know is that there are properties of individuals in this world—the phenomenal properties—that are ontologically independent of physical properties" (125).

2. As will become clear, my use of the term "literary mind" is quite different from, and perhaps incompatible with, Mark Turner's use of the term in *The Literary Mind*. Whereas I am interested in the necessary differences between literary and actual minds, Turner's claim is that the ordinary operations of the actual mind are contingent on a kind of literariness. In that way, various literary forms might actually provide insight into the mechanisms of cognition. As he writes, "If we want to study the everyday mind, we can begin by turning to the literary mind exactly because the everyday mind is essentially literary" (7). Turner's argument is therefore not unrelated to that offered by George Lakoff and Mark Johnson in *Metaphors We Live By*.

3. See Banfield, *Unspeakable Sentences*, chaps. 1-3; Booth, *Rhetoric of Fiction*, chaps. 1, 2, 3, and 6; and Cohn, *Transparent Minds*, introduction, chap. 1, and epilogue.

4. My argument here will focus on the perceived reality of literary minds—not literary worlds. As I understand them, these are related problems; if both literary minds and fictional landscapes, for example, are analogous in the ways they feel *real*, then it's likely that both rely on category-mistakes. But I do not believe they are ultimately the same issue. A literary mind does not require the representation of fictional events or people; the perceptions of comparability between real minds and actual minds I describe in this book happen in novels and poems but could also

happen in letters or autobiography. In other words, literary minds *can* be fictional (i.e., refer to fictional people), but they don't have to be. For more on the perceived reality of fictional narratives, see Auyong, *When Fiction Feels Real*; Walton, *Mimesis as Make-Believe*; Goodman, *Languages of Art*, chap. 1.

5. This isn't to say that the perceived emergence of literary minds is logically comparable to the emergence of phenomenal experience from matter. Moreover, I am not suggesting that behaviorism can help solve the "hard problem" of consciousness. Instead, I think it can help us understand how literary texts manage to create the perception of mental properties where none could possibly exist. For more on the hard problem, see Chalmers, "Facing Up." For more on literature's relationship to the hard problem of consciousness, see Kramnick, *Paper Minds*, 1-16, 118-37.

6. For accounts of conditioning in twentieth-century literature, see Mao, *Fateful Beauty*, 177-215; Trask, *Cruising Modernism*, 74-107; Fielding, *Novel Theory*, 117-43; Selisker, *Human Programming*, 1-68.

7. For a more thorough history of early experimental psychology, see Danziger, *Constructing the Subject*; Danziger, "Origins of the Schema"; Boring, *History of Experimental Psychology*; Mandler, *History of Modern Experimental Psychology*. For a sense of early experimental psychology's place in literary and critical history, see Jay, "Modernism and the Specter of Psychologism"; Ryan, *Vanishing Subject*; Micale, *Mind of Modernism*.

8. See Harper, "First Psychological Laboratory."

9. See Pavlov, *Conditioned Reflexes*, 16-47, 395-411; Pavlov, *Lectures on Conditioned Reflexes*, 47-96; Todes, *Pavlov's Physiology Factory*, 217-52.

10. See Watson, "Place of the Conditioned Reflex."

11. See Hilgard and Marquis, *Conditioning and Learning*, 24.

12. Tolman, "Behaviorism and Purpose," 37n1.

13. See Thorndike, *Animal Intelligence*, 241-81.

14. Chomsky, *Rules and Representations*, 37.

15. From Skinner's memoir, *The Shaping of a Behaviorist* (1979): "I had been converted to the behavioristic position by Bertrand Russell." *An Outline of Philosophy*, he explained, was particularly important, as it included "a careful statement of several epistemological issues raised by behaviorism considerably more sophisticated than anything of Watson's" (10).

16. Ryle's relationship to behaviorism was complicated. His philosophical work is undoubtedly behavioristic. But Ryle didn't necessarily identify with behaviorism as a philosophical or psychological program, although he didn't reject it either. As he explained in *The Concept of Mind*, "The general trend in this book will undoubtedly, and harmlessly, be stigmatized as 'behaviourist'" (300).

17. Ryle's essay "Jane Austen and the Moralists" (1966) demonstrated this devotion and attempted to frame Austen as an Aristotelian moral philosopher (by way of Shaftsbury). The most famous story about Ryle's love for Austen, however, is likely

apocryphal. The earliest version I've found is from Anthony Lane's August 5, 1996, review of the films *Emma* and *Kingpin* for the *New Yorker*. But no version I've seen includes any attribution or documentation. Lane tells it as follows: "The philosopher Gilbert Ryle was once asked if he ever read novels. 'Oh yes,' he replied. 'All six of them, every year'" (79).

18. In *How to Do Things with Words* (1955), Austin suggested that performed utterances could "go wrong" in a way that was distinct from being true or false. When I bet on a horse after the race has ended, "the utterance is then, we may say, not indeed false but in general *unhappy*. And for this reason we call the doctrine of *the things that can be and go wrong* on the occasion of such utterances, the doctrine of the *Infelicities*" (14; italics in the original). Magidor's explanation of infelicity is more direct, though it isn't specific to category-mistakes either. "I use the term 'infelicitous' to mean something like 'seems odd or inappropriate,' without making any theoretical commitment as to the source of oddness or inappropriateness" (1n1).

19. The logical boundaries of this sentence-frame, however, are not limitless. "I have a now" would be an example of a gap-sign that produces absurdity—not because of the entailments of "I have" but rather the singular article "a."

20. For examples, see Strawson, "Categories"; Quine, *Word and Object*, chap. 7; Magidor, *Category Mistakes*; and Camp, "Generality Constraint."

21. I grant the possibility that casual readers might find sentence no. 8 more absurd than literary critics do. Every community has its own linguistic rules and conventions, even if it ostensibly speaks the same language as other communities. And these rules and conventions vary over time as well. Talking about what novels or poems or images "want" is an accepted part of critical discourse today. It is therefore ironic that there remains something of a prohibition against talking about what authors "intend." For more on this subject, see chap. 1.

22. This is a point that G. E. M. Anscombe makes in *Intention* (1957): "The primitive sign of wanting is *trying to get*; which of course can only be ascribed to creatures with sensation.... The ascription of sensible knowledge and of volution go together" (68). I address this issue more fully in chap. 1.

23. In my mind, Magidor's *Category Mistakes* supports this claim, citing literature as an example of why category-mistakes must be capable of possessing some degree of semantic meaning. "Metaphor, metonymy, and fictional discourse," she writes, "are three linguistic settings which often involve category-mistakes" (153). I would add, however, that metaphor, metonymy, and fictional discourse don't rely on category-mistakes in the same way. Metaphors and metonymies can themselves be examples of category-mistakes. A fictional narrative, however, isn't necessarily a category-mistake; a type-error is not the same thing as a falsehood. The fictional narrative could *contain* category-mistakes, however—possibly through metaphor or metonymy. Moreover, as I have been claiming, the category-mistake of conflating actual minds with literary minds is itself a *product* of reading rather than a condition of it.

24. For accounts of these different cognitive criticisms, see Kramnick, *Actions and Objects*; Silver, *Mind Is a Collection*; Richardson, *Neural Sublime*; Morgan, *Outward Mind*.

25. Jerry Fodor's explanation of token physicalism in psychology feels relevant here: "Even if (token) psychological events are (token) neurological events, it does not follow that the natural kind predicates of psychology are co-extensive with the natural kind predicates of any other discipline (including physics). That is, the assumption that every physical event does not guarantee that physics (or, *a fortiori*, any other discipline more general than psychology) can provide an appropriate vocabulary for psychology" ("Special Sciences," 105). In other words, even if we grant Scarry's claim that literature is composed of vegetable dye on plant pulp, this doesn't mean that the discourse of botany is meaningful for thinking about why we read in the ways that we do.

26. For more on novel reading and ToM, see Vermeule, *Why Do We Care*; Keen, *Empathy and the Novel*; and Palmer, *Fictional Minds*. See also Kramnick, *Paper Minds*, 101-18.

27. Today, "embodied," "embedded," "extended," and "enactive" are frequently grouped together under the heading of "4E cognition." Traditionally, cognitive scientists have assumed a fairly narrow definition of cognition, restricting research to processes based in the brain and cerebellum. 4E cognitive scientists, however, assert that this ignores the multiple bodily systems involved in such processes and amounts to a misunderstanding of the nature of cognition itself. 4E cognition therefore has meaningful similarities to phenomenology. For more on this, see Clark, *Supersizing the Mind*; Clark and Chalmers, "Extended Mind"; Noë, *Action in Perception*; Colombetti, *Feeling Body*. For more examples of 4E cognitive science being used by literary critics, see Kramnick, *Paper Minds*, 1-16; Bolens, *Style of Gestures*, 1-65; Van Hulle, *Modern Manuscripts*, 1-15, 243-47; Silver, *Mind Is a Collection*, 226-68; Moses, "Poetry and the Environmentally Extended Mind."

Chapter 1. Behaviorism and the Beginnings of Close Reading

1. See also Graff, *Poetic Statement and Critical Dogma*; Stewart, "Lyric Possession"; Altieri, "Fallacy of 'Fallacy.'"

2. Flatley, "How a Revolutionary Counter-mood Is Made," 505.

3. This isn't to suggest, however, that close reading was ever a unified set of techniques and assumptions about literary interpretation. While Richards's behavioristic influence was vast and pervasive, each new critic emphasized their own set of concerns—from literature's relationship to science (Brooks, Wimsatt), to canonicity (Brooks, Ransom), to questions about morality and theology (Tate, Ransom, Winters, Empson). And yet, even at the New Criticism's height, it was wrongly perceived as unified and consistent in its approaches. According to Mark Jancovich, Brooks and

Warren's *Understanding Poetry* (1938) was often considered to be the representative of a unified formalism (*Cultural Politics of the New Criticism*, 10). But in his essay "In Search of the New Criticism" (1984), Brooks expressed frustration at being the unwilling figurehead of the New Criticism and denied there was much conceptual unity among the New Critics. "As quasi-representative," Brooks wrote, "one has not only to answer for his own sins, but also to assume responsibility for the collective sins of a vague, undefined group" (41). For more on the history of the New Criticism and close reading, see Guillory, *Cultural Capital*, 134-76; Childs, *Birth of New Criticism*; Graff, *Professing Literature*, 121-84; Wellek, *History of Modern Criticism*; Krieger, *New Apologists for Poetry*, 123-66.

4. As Tolman noted, it was in fact C. D. Broad who first distinguished between *molar* and *molecular* behaviors. Broad's distinction, however, was a methodological one rather than a conceptual one. See Tolman, *Purposive Behavior*, 7n10.

5. In *I. A. Richards and the Rise of Cognitive Stylistics*, David West suggests that Richards's work before *Practical Criticism*—namely, *The Meaning of Meaning*, coauthored with C. K. Ogden—was very much indebted to behaviorism. In later chapters, however, West situates *Principles of Literary Criticism* in terms of Sherrington, and *Practical Criticism* in terms of Pavlov. See West, *I. A. Richards*, 55-78.

6. See also Goodblatt and Glicksohn, "From *Practical Criticism*."

7. For more on Richards and his legacy, see Krieger, *New Apologists for Poetry*, 57-139; Guillory, "Close Reading"; West, *I. A. Richards*, 79-126; Williams, *Culture and Society*, 245-54; and Hotopf, *Language, Thought, and Comprehension*, chaps. 1 and 2.

8. Donne, *Poems*. Currently housed at the British Library and made available online through the "Discovering Literature: Shakespeare & Renaissance" portal. See https://www.bl.uk/collection-items/first-edition-of-john-donres-poems-1633?mobile=on.

9. Hopkins, *Poems*, 51. See https://babel.hathitrust.org/cgi/pt?id=udel.31741113248746;view=1up;seq=71;size=125.

10. Richards is vague on these details. Also, after a century, the science is no longer on his side.

11. In "On Denoting" (1905), Russell grappled with the problem that "a phrase is denoting solely in virtue of its *form*" (479; italics in the original). In that way a sentence could appear to have a denoting function—"The present king of France is bald"—even though it is untrue or making a propositional claim about a fictional entity. In *Principles*, however, Richards seems to think this isn't a problem at all; it's simply a function of language and one necessary for other "human activities" (although he doesn't specify which activities he has in mind). See Russell, "On Denoting."

12. A number of modernist writers and critics developed similar schemes—all of which relied on versions of the category-mistake. In "Poetry and Grammar" (1935), Gertrude Stein offered the following account of *Tender Buttons* (1914): "I commenced

trying to do something in Tender Buttons about this thing. I went on and on trying to do this thing. I remember in writing An Acquaintance with Description looking at anything until something that was not the name of that thing but was in a way that actual thing would come to be written.... And so for me the problem of poetry was and it began with Tender Buttons to constantly realize the thing anything so that I could recreate that thing" (31). And in a passage from "Dante... Bruno... Vico... Joyce" (1929) that I will return to in the next chapter, Samuel Beckett described Joyce's "Anna Livia" as "not *about* something; *it is that something itself.*... When the sense is sleep, the words go to sleep. (See the end of *Anna Livia.*) When the sense is dancing, the words dance" (*Samuel Beckett: The Grove Centenary Edition*, 4:502-3).

13. For two noteworthy examples, see Starr, *Feeling Beauty*; and Armstrong, *How Literature Plays with the Brain*.

14. For additional, non-New Critical reactions against Richards, see Crane, *Critics and Criticism*, 38. See also Wellek, *History of Modern Criticism*.

15. I am not suggesting that the American New Criticism can be reduced to these figures. But it is true that *The Well Wrought Urn* and *The Verbal Icon* are often understood as representative New Critical works and as the foremost theorizations of close reading. As Frank Lentricchia writes, "The imposing history of W. K. Wimsatt and Cleanth Brooks—its historical acumen aside—has been taken since the time of its publication and even more so now as a final statement of the New-Critical poetic" (*After the New Criticism*, 3).

16. Guillory, *Cultural Capital*, 159.

17. Graff, *Poetic Statement and Critical Dogma*, 111.

18. I'm borrowing, cheekily, the language of Virginia Woolf's *To the Lighthouse* (1925): "Think of a kitchen table," Andrew tells Lily, "when you aren't there" (23). This, of course, is extrapolated from Russell's *Problems of Philosophy*. Russell's challenge was to understand the nature of the table in the absence of sense-data. The absence of sense-data, however, did not result in the laws of nature being suspended. In contrast, it is the very absence of readers and writers (i.e., perceiving subjects) that allows Brooks to imagine a completely free world of semantics. So while there is a thematical similarity between these situations, they are in fact nonanalogous.

19. In *The New Criticism*, Ransom offered a response to Brooks's earlier monograph *Modern Poetry and the Tradition* (1939). In so doing he anticipated some of the problems raised by Brooks's arguments about poetry and paradox. "My belief," Ransom wrote, "is that opposites can never be said to be resolved or reconciled merely because they have been got into the same poem, or got in to the same complex of affective experience to create there a kind of 'tension'; that if there is a resolution at all it must be a logical resolution; that when there is no resolution we have a poem without structural unity; and that this is precisely the intention of irony, which therefore is something very special, and ought to be occasional" (95).

20. Insofar as they are credited with coauthorship of *The Verbal Icon*, I refer to

Wimsatt and Beardsley in tandem throughout this chapter. My sense, however, is that Wimsatt was largely responsible for the more behavioristic and tendentious claims made about intention and affect. Beardsley's other books, including *Aesthetics: Problems in the Philosophy of Criticism* (1958), discuss these topics from a decidedly nonbehavioristic position. In *Aesthetics*, Beardsley's objections to what he identified as "intentionalism" were largely methodological and evidentiary. "What we learn about the nature of the object itself," he wrote, "is indirect evidence of what the artist intended it to be, and what we learn about intention is indirect evidence of what the object became" (20). If anything, Beardsley's later comments on intention seem to resonate with the ideas offered in Knapp and Michaels's "Against Theory." See also Beardsley, "Intentions and Interpretations."

21. See Jancovich, *Culture Politics of the New Criticism*; Moya, *Social Imperative*, 1–38; Spivak, "Close Reading"; Brown, "Cultural Studies and Close Reading"; Robbins, "Discipline and Parse"; Gallop, "Historiciziation of Literary Studies."

Chapter 2. Inner Sights

1. The relation of Beckett to Descartes is a contentious one. Recent archival work has revealed the eclecticism of Beckett's philosophical interests. Accordingly, a number of critics have suggested that Beckett's interest in, and indebtedness to, Descartes has been overemphasized. Instead, it is asserted that Beckett's exposure to Descartes happened primarily through post-Cartesian philosophers (such as Geulincx) and secondary sources such as Wilhelm Windelband's *A History of Philosophy*. For more on Beckett's relation to Descartes, see Feldman, *Beckett's Books*, chap. 3; Van Hulle and Nixon, *Samuel Beckett's Library*, chap. 7; and Tucker, *Samuel Beckett and Arnold Geulincx*.

2. Watson makes a similar point about memory: "Whence, after absence, the stimulus is presented once more, the responses involving the old manual habits appear along with the name (laryngeal habits) and the smiling, laughter (visceral habits), and the response is complete—'memory' is intact" (*Behaviorism*, 190).

3. While *Malone Dies* and *The Unnamable* also show Beckett attacking the *cogito*, I have focused on *Murphy* and *Molloy* here, as that's where behaviorism's critique of introspection is most meaningful.

4. For more on the development of Wundt's psychology, see Danziger, *Constructing the Subject*; Rieber and Robinson, *Wilhelm Wundt in History*.

5. In vol. 1 of *The Principles of Psychology* (1890), William James mounted an extensive critique of Wundt's methods—and lamented the necessity of introspection for studying psychological phenomena. The trouble with introspection, he explained, is twofold: First, it induces a sampling bias—because only certain mental states are accessible to introspection and others are not, those inaccessible states "drop out" of consideration. Second, it creates a false parallel between experimenter

and test subject as if both had equal access to (and knowledge of) the test subject's mental states. "The whole mind-stuff controversy would stop," he wrote, "if we could decide conclusively by introspection that what seem to us elementary feelings are really elementary and not compound" (191).

6. My translation. The original reads: "Ich lege Wert darauf zu konstatieren, dass in den Abstraktionstachen unmittlebare Bewusstseinsphenomene vorliegen.... Die Versuchspersonen glaubten tatsachlich die Eindrucke in der angegebenen Unbestimmtheit zu sehen" (67).

7. At other moments Wittgenstein asserted that certain kinds of self-knowledge were products of neither introspection nor self-observation. In his lecture "The Language of Sense Data and Private Experience" (1936), he offered pain as an example: "There would be no sense in saying 'I know I have a toothache because I am acting in a certain way.' There is a difference. But it does not mean that I know the toothache in myself by introspection, pointing in myself at something" (363).

8. It's worth remembering, perhaps, a point in Gilbert Ryle's essay "Categories" (1936). As I mentioned in the introduction, Ryle claimed that while propositions could be logically absurd, "nature" could not. To suggest that a person or object comprises a category-mistake would in fact be a category-mistake. See Ryle, "Categories," 189.

9. Ryle never states whether this folk psychology is inborn or learned. However, given Ryle's claim that many people learn the proper use of mental predicates from reading literature and seeing plays, we can reason that this folk psychology is likely acquired a posteriori.

10. Sellars's "Myth of the Given" doesn't lend itself to quick summaries (nor does Sellars's work more generally). But I'll do my best: In foundationalist epistemologies (e.g., logical positivism) it is assumed that empirical knowledge comes from direct contact with perceived objects. Empirical knowledge is therefore allowed to serve as a "given" for other types of knowledge. But Sellars argues that even empirical knowledge is epistemically dependent on other cognitive states. Therefore, it cannot function as a given. For Sellars's extended explanation, see *Empiricism and the Philosophy of Mind*, 15-79. For a helpful breakdown of Sellars's propositions, see deVries, "Wilfrid Sellars."

11. The source of the phrase "tracing paths for action" is unclear. Neither Watson nor Pavlov uses the phrase in their published writings.

12. For more on Beckett's relation to Schopenhauer, see Sheehan, *Modernism, Narrative and Humanism*, 150-78; Tonning, "'I am not reading philosophy': Beckett and Schopenhauer"; Büttner, "Schopenhauer's Recommendations to Beckett."

13. I have restricted myself here to Beckett's notes on behaviorism and introspection. Those interested in Beckett's relationship to psychoanalysis should consult the first six folios of TCD MS10971/7. In folios 1-5, Beckett discusses Karin Stephen's *Psychoanalysis and Medicine: The Wish to Fall Ill* (1933). In folio 6 he summarizes Freud's

lecture "The Anatomy of the Mental Personality," which was published in 1933 as part of the Hogarth Press's *New Introductory Lectures on Psychoanalysis*. For a full description of Beckett's reading notes, see Engelberts, Frost, and Maxwell, *"Notes Diverse Holo."* Only limited extracts from Beckett's notes, however, are published in this volume.

14. See Woodworth, "Imageless Thought."

15. I transcribed these notes in person at Trinity College's Berkeley Library on August 16, 2016. Trinity's manuscript record is available at https://manuscripts.catalogue.tcd.ie/CalmView/Record.aspx?src=CalmView.Catalog&id=IE+TCD+MSS+10962-10971.

16. For more on "Murphy's mind," as well as *Murphy*'s relation to philosophy of mind and psychology more broadly, see Begam, *Samuel Beckett and the End of Modernity*; Gontarski, *On Beckett*; Uhlmann, *Samuel Beckett and the Philosophical Image*; Van Hulle, "Extended Mind and Multiple Drafts"; Ackerley, introduction to *Demented Particulars*; Mooney, "Presocratic Scepticism"; Kemp, "Autonomy and Privacy."

17. For more on *Molloy* and different philosophical topics, see Begam, *Samuel Beckett and the End of Modernity*; Gontarski, *Revisioning Beckett*; Maude, *Beckett, Technology and the Body*. There are also those critics who, when analyzing *Molloy*, try to leave philosophy behind altogether. In *Beckett and Aesthetics* (2003), Daniel Albright reminds us that *Molloy* is first and foremost a literary object—and not merely an example of one theory or another. Are the voices of Molloy and Moran, he asks, "symptoms of paranoid hallucination in the mind of the character? Of Beckett himself? Could Dr. Freud cure the text? . . . Perhaps it is better to argue that these voices are generated by an aesthetic problem: the equivocation between the vocal and the written nature of language" (4).

Chapter 3. Mental Acts

1. When I use the phrase "mental actions," I am not suggesting that minds and bodies are made from different substances. Instead, as entailed by something like property dualism, there is a class of phenomena that are technically made of physical matter and yet, somehow, are more meaningfully discussed in terms of mental concepts and rules. I cannot stipulate how mental properties emerge from physical matter—except to appeal to Donald Davidson's claim in "Mental Events" (1970) that "mental characteristics are in some sense dependent, or supervenient, on physical characteristics" (*Essays on Actions and Events*, 214). At the same time, Davidson's essay "Agency" (1971) suggests that "action" itself is a physical concept. "We must conclude, perhaps with a shock of surprise, that our primitive actions, the ones we do not do by doing something else, mere movements of the body—these are all the actions there are. We never do more than move our bodies: the rest is up to nature" (*Essays on Actions and Events*, 59). There is therefore something of a logical mismatch between mental and physical "actions."

2. Cohn, "World of Harold Pinter," 55. For more on Pinter's relation to dramatic realism and the Angry Young Men, see Bernhard, "Beyond Realism"; Stulberg, "How (Not) to Write Broadcast Plays"; Grimes, *Harold Pinter's Politics*; Silverstein, *Harold Pinter*.

3. While behaviorism created a number of "boxes"—E. L. Thorndike's lever boxes, B. F. Skinner's boxes for operant conditioning (not to be confused with the "air crib" for humans)—the metaphorical "black box" originated elsewhere. Beginning in the 1940s and 1950s, physicists, electrical engineers, and cyberneticists began using the term "black box" to describe transformational circuits that were effectively inner workings out of view. It was then picked up as a metaphor within behaviorist psychology, although some—like Skinner himself—found it unhelpful. "The organism," he wrote in *About Behaviorism* (1974), "is, of course, not empty, and it cannot be adequately treated simply as a black box, but we must carefully distinguish between what is known about what is inside and what is merely inferred" (233).

4. For more on the psychologies of Beckett and Pinter, see Kennedy, *Six Dramatists*, chaps. 3 and 4; Begley, *Harold Pinter*, introduction and chap. 3.

5. In that way, these plays differ from "psychic" dramas such as Eugene O'Neill's *The Emperor Jones* (1920), where mental and physical events become indistinguishable by way of hallucination (see O'Neill, *Nine Plays*).

6. See James, *Principles of Psychology*, vol. 1, chap. 6.

7. One of the pillars of logical empiricism, Rudolf Carnap's "physicalist thesis" argued that all knowledge was, in theory, translatable into a fundamental language of physical description (*physikalischen sprache*). Like Carnap's thesis, Hempel's argument was technically an epistemological rather than metaphysical claim (although it's unclear how meaningful this distinction was for Carnap). See Carnap, *Logical Structure of the World*, 1–46; Carnap, "Psychology in Physical Language"; Richardson, *Carnap's Construction of the World*, 1–115. See also Quine, "Two Dogmas of Empiricism." For more on Neurath's behavioristic sociology, see Neurath, "Empirical Sociology."

8. I am not taking the position that lying or deception is the same as theatrical acting—only that they share certain logical and epistemological similarities. In contrast, see books 3 and 10 of Plato's *Republic*, where Plato accuses not only dramatic performance but also poets of being guilty of such deceit. As Plato explains, "Imitation is surely far from truth. . . . When anyone tells us that he has met some person who knows all the arts and everything else known to man—that there is nothing he does not know better than everybody else—we must tell him he is gullible and must have met a magician and been deceived. He was duped into thinking such a person omniscient because of his own inability to test and verify the difference between knowledge, ignorance, and imitation" (10.598d).

9. Insofar as epic theater aimed to provoke rational discussion in addition to aesthetic pleasure, the separation between rationality and emotion, and between mind

and body, was logically necessary. However, it would be a mistake to call this separation Cartesian or dualist, as these terms have valences that aren't part of Brecht's theory. As he wrote in "The Epic Theatre and Its Difficulties" (1927), "The essential part of the epic theatre is that it appeals less to the feelings than to the spectator's reason. Instead of sharing an experience the spectator must come to grips with things. At the same time it would be quite wrong to try and deny emotion to the theatre" (*Brecht on Theatre*, 23). See also Brecht, *Brecht on Theatre*, 33-99.

10. While Gobert is correct that the Cartesian passions bridged body and soul, the comment that "the material and immaterial are inextricable" doesn't fit well with the *Meditations*. In the sixth meditation, Descartes offers the extricability of the soul as proof of mind-body dualism: "I have a clear and distinct idea of myself in so far as I am simply a thinking, non-extended thing; and on the other hand I have a distinct idea of body, in so far as this is simply an extended, non-thinking thing. And accordingly, it is certain that I am really distinct from my body, and can exist without it" (115).

11. For a particularly informative and explicit example of this, see Balkin, "Monist Dramaturgy."

12. Rabaté is one of several contemporary critics who have found value in analyzing *Eleutheria*. Another is Daniel Albright, who in *Beckett and Aesthetics* (2003) asserted that "Beckett's relation to the long tradition of Western drama [can] be understood more easily in *Eleutheria* than in any of his subsequent plays" (48). Earlier critics, however, were less generous. In his touchstone work *Samuel Beckett* (1961), Hugh Kenner proclaimed that the play was a "misconceived dramatic enterprise" (140). Ruby Cohn wasn't much nicer. "Neither main plot nor subplot of *Eleutheria*," she wrote in *Samuel Beckett: The Comic Gamut* (1962), "are particularly well made" (140).

13. Quoted in Bair, *Samuel Beckett*, 403.

14. Beckett's original French is no help on this point: "Ceci explique aussi pourquoi il n'y a pas da'ction marginale au troisième acte, le côté Krap ètant tombe dans la fosse à la suite du virement de la scène" (4).

15. Albright presents a different interpretation of act 3—one that, in my mind, minimizes the effect of having the main and marginal actions performed simultaneously: "When the Krap household furniture is pushed to a corner of the stage, or off the stage into the pit, what sort of theatre is left? . . . Beckett arranged *Eleutheria* as a two-part parody: he first shows the incompetence of the realistic theatre, then the incompetence of the psychic theatre" (*Beckett and Aesthetics*, 40).

16. For more on the evolution of the *Krapp* manuscript, see Gontarski, "Crapp's First Tapes." See also the Samuel Beckett Digital Manuscript Project's genetic edition: https://www.beckettarchive.org/krapp/about/catalogue.

17. Alan Ackerman offers a different reading of *Krapp*'s catachrestic language, while also drawing on Gilbert Ryle. The "bony ghost," he writes, "parodies not only

the traditional Cartesian body-mind dualism but also the metaphysical language that enables it, drawing our attention, like Gilbert Ryle's *The Concept of Mind* (1949), to the mistake of looking for a 'Ghost in the Machine'" ("Prompter's Box," 421). My claim, of course, is that Beckett's accomplishment was in fact finding ways to put a ghost in the machine—to give mental concepts and actions otherwise impossible onstage. In my mind, *Krapp's Last Tape* doesn't parody mind-body dualism so much as make it work for the theater.

18. For more on these revisions, see Knowlson, "'Krapp's Last Tape.'"

19. Quoted in Knowlson, "'Krapp's Last Tape,'" 55.

20. In a 1961 interview with Harry Thompson, Pinter weighed in on the possibility of his work resembling Beckett's. "There is no question that Beckett is a writer whom I admire very much and have admired for a number of years. If Beckett's influence shows in my works that's all right with me. You don't work in a vacuum; you're bound to absorb and digest other writing; and I admire Beckett's work so much that something of its texture might appear in my own" ("Harold Pinter Replies," 8-9). For more on Beckett's relation to Pinter, see Diamond, *Pinter's Comic Play*, 89-109; Gordon, *Harold Pinter*, 1-48, 124-61; Taylor-Batty, *Theatre of Harold Pinter*, 1-48. See also Billington, *Life and Work of Harold Pinter*, 45-87.

21. "I had read *Murphy*, *Molloy*, and *Malone Dies* by 1955 but not *Godot*. I was acting in Ireland when *Godot* opened in London. My old friend Mick Goldstein saw the production and wrote to me about it" (Pinter, *Various Voices*, 17).

22. It was eventually returned to the library after Pinter's death.

23. Quoted in Billington, *Life and Work of Harold Pinter*, 43.

24. Billington, *Life and Work of Harold Pinter*, 366-67.

25. The philosopher John Cottingham identifies *The Homecoming* as presenting a caricature of Cartesian doubt (*Cartesian Reflections*, 276).

26. In *Empty Houses* (2011), David Kurnick makes a related point about the "Circe" section of James Joyce's *Ulysses* (1922). Joyce, Kurnick argues, "renders legible the content of interiority by lining the dialogue and narration with the properly 'offstage' information of the mind's content. The novel creates precisely the textualized 'closet drama' that *Exiles* was in the process of becoming via the more mundane process of theatrical failure: a fully discursivized space in which the contents of those recessed closets have been pushed into view" (179). My point about Pinter, however, is that these mental closets are never permitted to become the same kinds of actions as those performed onstage.

27. Pinter, *Collected Poems and Prose*, 32-33.

28. Pinter's poem "I Shall Tear Off My Terrible Cap" (1951) lends itself to a similar reading, although it predates *The Birthday Party* and "A View of the Party" by seven years. The misapplication of physical properties, etc., is less measured and artful than it would be several years later; here there are "onelegged dreams" and "walking brains," but there's nothing as grammatically awkward or logically absurd as "The

thought that Goldberg was . . . Never crossed Meg's words." Like so much of Pinter's early work, it invokes the horrors of psychiatric treatment—psychosurgery or ECT in particular.

> I in my straight jacket swung in the sun,
> In a hostile pause in a no man's time.
> The spring his green anchor had flung.
> Around me only the walking brains,
> And the plack of their onelegged dreams
> As I hung.
>
> I tell them this—
> Only the deaf can hear and the blind understand . . .
> I'll tear off my terrible cap. (*Collected Poems and Prose*, 9)

Chapter 4. The Form of Thought

1. As Coetzee acknowledges, Beckett was an important influence on his own writing and style: "Beckett meant a great deal to me in my own writing. . . . The essays I wrote on Beckett's style are not only academic exercises, in the colloquial sense of that word. They are also attempts to get closer to a secret, a secret of Beckett's that I wanted to make my own" (*Doubling the Point*, 25). For further discussions of Coetzee's relation to Beckett, see Hayes, *J. M. Coetzee and the Novel*, 33-71; Zimbler, *J. M. Coetzee and the Politics of Style*, 25-55; Tajiri, "Beckett, Coetzee, and Animals," 27-39; and Tajiri, "Beckett's Legacy." For a discussion of Coetzee's dissertation on Beckett, see Roach, "Hero and Bad Motherland"; Uhlmann, "Approaches to the (Beckett) Archives"; Rabaté, "Excuse My French"; Kellman, "J. M. Coetzee and Samuel Beckett."

2. In "Samuel Beckett and the Temptations of Style" (1973), Coetzee's position evolved somewhat, as he noted a degree of necessary resemblance between grammar and thought in Beckett's late fiction. As he wrote, there is a "deeper impulse toward stylization that is common to all of Beckett's later work. This occurs with the stylization of the impasse of reflexive consciousness, of the movement of the mind that we can call *A therefore Not-A* and that Beckett apothegmatizes in the phrase 'imagination dead imagine'" (*Doubling the Point*, 49). Insofar as *neither* thought nor language could express a logically coherent proposition, Coetzee understood them as having some necessary correlation.

3. Five years later, of course, Watson would write in *Behaviorism* (1924) that thinking was just "talking to ourselves" (237). But this was hardly an argument for correspondence between language and thinking, as Watson claimed that these were synonyms for the same phenomenon.

4. In "The Rhetoric of the Passive in English" (1980), Coetzee cites Isaac Newton's

A Treatise of the System of the World (ca. 1685) as a counterexample to the Sapir-Whorf hypothesis and as evidence of the ways grammatical operations can diverge from logical or psychological operations. Newton's arguments about causality fit easily into mathematical notation, Coetzee explains, as their sense of "time relations (left-to-right) and process (cause-results)" makes it hard for them to use the "subject-object sentence form" (167). In effect, Newton's physics couldn't overtake the "in-built metaphysics of his language." For an in-depth analysis of Coetzee's use of the passive voice, see Adams, "Acts without Agents."

5. This is but one point of grammatical interest in *Disgrace*, which juxtaposes David Lurie's discussions of the perfective tense—past actions that have ended—to his mistaken belief that the business of apartheid is very much settled. As Mark Sanders suggests, the very syntax of *Disgrace* "denies itself and its reader the capacity to say: these acts and events are over" ("Disgrace," 371).

6. For more on Coetzee's relations to colonialism and apartheid, see Attwell, *J. M. Coetzee and the Life of Writing*, 11-104, 211-33; Barnard, *Apartheid and Beyond*, 3-40; Attridge and Jolly, *Writing South Africa*; Durrant, *Postcolonial Narrative and the Work of Mourning*, chap. 1; Moody, *Art of Hunger*, chap. 4.

7. My claim, therefore, is that there is an important continuity between Coetzee's dissertation and his fiction. In a 1992 interview with David Attwell, however, Coetzee downplayed the possibility of such continuity: "Nothing one picks up from generative linguistics or from other forms of structuralism," he said, "helps one to put together a novel. What remained from those studies was probably no more than a very general residue: respect for other cultures, respect for ordinary speakers, for the unconscious knowledge we carry, each of us" (*Doubling the Point*, 25).

8. Many of these problems have parallels in Coetzee's representation of animals and animal minds. This is a topic that runs throughout his writings, including *Disgrace*, *Elizabeth Costello* (2003), *The Childhood of Jesus* (2013), *The Schooldays of Jesus* (2016), *The Death of Jesus* (2019), and *The Lives of Animals* (1999) (which then became a chapter in *Elizabeth Costello*). However, insofar as I've chosen to focus on the relations between mind and language specifically in this chapter, I do not discuss Coetzee's thoughts on animals. For more on that topic, see Hale, *Novel and the New Ethics*, chap. 4; Mulhall, *Wounded Animal*, chaps. 1-3; Leist and Singer, *J. M. Coetzee and Ethics*, chaps. 5-8; DeKoven, "Going to the Dogs in *Disgrace*"; Ciobanu, "Coetzee's Posthuman Ethics."

9. See Chomsky, *Syntactic Structures*, 34-84, 106-14.

10. For a more extended explanation of computationalism, see Putnam, "Psychological Predicates"; Block and Fodor, "What Psychological States Are Not"; Boden, *Mind as Machine*, chaps. 6 and 7.

11. Quoted in Ohmann, "Generative Grammars," 432.

12. Coetzee's analyses of *Murphy* and *More Pricks Than Kicks* are concerned primarily with the frequency of particular words and grammatical structures in these

texts. The calculation of frequency, however, is of little help in determining the psychological origins or significance of particular stylistic features: "A rule of thumb is beginning to emerge: the more conscious a verbal choice is likely to be, the less amenable to treatment en masse. It is a rule of thumb because we can only guess about which choices were consciously made by the author. The converse rule is that the less conscious the choice the more tenuous will be the interpretation we place on it. . . . As I pointed out in connection with Murphy (pp.26-30 above), syntactic features like the shortening of sentences and the dropping off of introductory clauses are signs of reported monologue, but they may simply be conventional signs, part of the repertoire of the post-Flaubertian writer and reader" ("English Fiction," 52-53).

13. Quoted in Coetzee, "English Fiction," 79.

14. For more on the relations among the colonization (particularly African colonization), interiority, and problems of mind, see Fanon, *Wretched of the Earth*, 170-234; Memmi, *Colonizer and the Colonized*; Linstrum, *Ruling Minds*, introduction, chaps. 1, 5, and 7; Keller, *Colonial Madness*; McCulloch, *Colonial Psychiatry and "The African Mind"*; Bhabha, "Remembering Fanon."

15. Uhlmann, "Process and Method."

16. Adams, "Acts without Agents."

17. Much as the Magistrate struggles to interpret the slips, these slips have also been an important point in Coetzee criticism. In *J. M. Coetzee: South Africa and the Politics of Writing* (1993), David Attwell suggests that these slips represent the "new, enigmatic status of the resources of historical knowledge" (77). However, in *J. M. Coetzee and the Ethics of Reading* (2004), Derek Attridge suggests that the slips are evidence of the novel's "problematizing the very idea of allegorical interpretation," wherein "they contribute to the novel a sense of realms of meaning inaccessible to the Magistrate's rational powers" (47). See also Ng, "Xinjiang's Indelible Footprint"; Neimneh, "Visceral Allegory of *Waiting for the Barbarians*."

18. For more on *Foe*'s representation of the relations between narration and colonialism, race, and sex, see also Begam, "Silence and Mut(e)ilation"; Rickel, "Speaking of Human Rights"; MacLeod, "'Do We of Necessity Become Puppets in a Story?'"

19. This "inscrutability of reference" is but one of the ways Quine sees different accounts of a language diverging. Quine also claimed that "holophrastic indeterminacy" —the unclear meanings produced by whole sentences rather than just individual words—was also a factor. For more on this, see Quine, "Indeterminacy of Translation Again"; Hylton, *Quine*, 197-230.

Works Cited

Achebe, Chinua. "An Image of Africa: Racism in Conrad's *Heart of Darkness*." *Massachusetts Review* 57, no. 1 (2016): 14-27. https://doi.org/10.1353/mar.2016.0003.

Ackerley, Chris, and Samuel Beckett. *Demented Particulars: The Annotated "Murphy."* Edinburgh: Edinburgh University Press, 2010.

Ackerman, Alan L. "The Prompter's Box: Birthdays and Beckett's Bony Ghost." *Modern Drama* 49, no. 4 (2006): 419-27. https://doi.org/10.1353/mdr.2007.0000.

Adams, Kelly. "Acts without Agents: The Language of Torture in J. M. Coetzee's *Waiting for the Barbarians*." *ariel: A Review of International English Literature* 46, no. 3 (2015): 165-77. https://doi.org/10.1353/ari.2015.0018.

Adorno, Theodor W., and Michael T. Jones. "Trying to Understand *Endgame*." *New German Critique*, no. 26 (1982): 119-50. https://doi.org/10.2307/488027.

Albright, Daniel. *Beckett and Aesthetics*. Cambridge: Cambridge University Press, 2003.

Altieri, Charles. "The Fallacy of 'Fallacy' and Its Implications for Contemporary Literary Theory." *Representations* 140, no. 1 (2017): 175-93. https://doi.org/10.1525/rep.2017.140.1.175.

Anscombe, G. E. M. *Intention*. Cambridge, MA: Harvard University Press (1957) 2000.

Armstrong, Paul B. *How Literature Plays with the Brain: The Neuroscience of Reading and Art*. Baltimore: Johns Hopkins University Press, 2013.

Artaud, Antonin. *The Theatre and Its Double*. Translated by Victor Corti. London: Calder (1938) 1970.

Attridge, Derek. *J. M. Coetzee and the Ethics of Reading: Literature in the Event*. Chicago: University of Chicago Press, 2004.

Attridge, Derek, and Rosemary Jane Jolly, eds. *Writing South Africa: Literature, Apartheid, and Democracy, 1970-1995*. Cambridge: Cambridge University Press, 2000.

Attwell, David. *J. M. Coetzee and the Life of Writing: Face-to-Face with Time*. Oxford: Oxford University Press, 2015.

———. *J. M. Coetzee: South Africa and the Politics of Writing*. Berkeley: University of California Press, 1993.

Austen, Jane. *Sense and Sensibility*. London: Penguin, 2003.
Austin, John L. *How to Do Things with Words*. Oxford: Oxford University Press (1955) 1980.
Auyoung, Elaine. *When Fiction Feels Real: Representation and the Reading Mind*. New York: Oxford University Press, 2018.
Bair, Deirdre. *Samuel Beckett: A Biography*. New York: Simon & Schuster, 2016.
Balkin, Sarah. "Monist Dramaturgy in Strindberg's *The Black Glove*." *Modern Drama* 60, no. 3 (2017): 251-77. https://doi.org/10.3138/md.0861r.
Banfield, Ann. *Unspeakable Sentences: Narration and Representation in the Language of Fiction*. London: Routledge & Kegan Paul (1982) 2015.
Barnard, Rita. *Apartheid and Beyond: South African Writers and the Politics of Place*. New York: Oxford University Press, 2012.
Beardsley, Monroe C. *Aesthetics: Problems in the Philosophy of Criticism*. New York: Harcourt, 1958.
———. "Intentions and Interpretations." In *The Aesthetic Point of View: Selected Essays*, edited by Michael J. Wreen and Donald M. Callen. Ithaca, NY: Cornell University Press, 1982.
Beatty, Paul. *The Sellout*. New York: Farrar, Straus & Giroux, 2016.
Beckett, Samuel. *Dream of Fair to Middling Women*. Edited by Eoin O'Brien and Edith Fournier. Dublin: Black Cat, 1992.
———. *Eleutheria*. Paris: Éditions de Minuit (1948) 1995.
———. *Eleuthéria: A Play in Three Acts*. Translated by Michael Brodsky. New York: Foxrock, 1995.
———. *Ends and Odds*. New York: Grove, 1981.
———. *Krapp's Last Tape, and Other Dramatic Pieces*. New York: Grove, 1960.
———. *Krapp's Last Tape: Samuel Beckett's Production Notebook*. Edited with an introduction and notes by James Knowlson. London: Faber, 1989.
———. *The Letters of Samuel Beckett*. Edited by George Craig, Martha Dow Fehsenfeld, Dan Gunn, and Lois More Overbeck. Cambridge: Cambridge University Press, 2011.
———. *Murphy*. New York: Grove (1936) 2011.
———. *Poems 1930-1989*. London: Calder, 2002.
———. "Psychology" notebook typescript, folios 7-18. Trinity College, Dublin (TCD10971/7).
———. *The Theatrical Notebooks of Samuel Beckett: Krapp's Last Tape*. Edited by James Knowlson. London: Faber, 1992.
———. *Three Novels*. New York: Grove Atlantic, 2009.
———. *Waiting for Godot: A Tragicomedy in Two Acts*. London: Faber, 1960.
———. *Watt*. New York: Grove (1953) 2009.
Beckett, Samuel, Paul Auster, and J. M. Coetzee. *Samuel Beckett: The Grove Centenary Edition*. 4 vols. New York: Grove, 2006.

Works Cited

Begam, Richard. *Samuel Beckett and the End of Modernity*. Stanford, CA: Stanford University Press, 1998.

———. "Silence and Mut(e)ilation: White Writing in J. M. Coetzee's *Foe*." *South Atlantic Quarterly* 93, no. 1 (1994): 111-29.

Begley, Varun. *Harold Pinter and the Twilight of Modernism*. Toronto: University of Toronto Press, 2005.

Bernhard, F. "Beyond Realism: The Plays of Harold Pinter." *Modern Drama* 8, no. 2 (1965): 185-91. https://doi.org/10.3138/md.8.2.185.

Best, Stephen, and Sharon Marcus. "Surface Reading: An Introduction." *Representations* 108, no. 1 (2009): 1-21. https://doi.org/10.1525/rep.2009.108.1.1.

Bhabha, Homi. "Remembering Fanon: Self, Psyche, and the Colonial Condition." In *Colonial Discourse and Post-colonial Theory*, edited by Patrick Williams and Laura Chrisman, 112-24. New York: Columbia University Press, 1994.

Biko, Steve. *I Write What I Like: A Selection of His Writings*. Edited by Aelred Stubbs. Chicago: University of Chicago Press, 2002.

Billington, Michael. *The Life and Work of Harold Pinter*. London: Faber, 2007.

Block, N. J., and J. A. Fodor. "What Psychological States Are Not." *Philosophical Review* 81, no. 2 (1972): 159-81. https://doi.org/10.2307/2183991.

Boden, Margaret. *Mind as Machine: A History of Cognitive Science*. 2 vols. Oxford: Oxford University Press, 2000.

Bolens, Guillemette. *The Style of Gestures: Embodiment and Cognition in Literary Narrative*. Foreword by Alain Berthoz. Baltimore: John Hopkins University Press, 2012.

Booth, Wayne C. *The Rhetoric of Fiction*. Chicago: University of Chicago Press, 1983.

Boring, Edwin G. *A History of Experimental Psychology*. New York: Appleton-Century, 1929.

Brecht, Bertolt. *Brecht on Theatre: The Development of an Aesthetic*. Edited and translated by John Willett. London: Methuen Drama, 1992.

Brooks, Cleanth. "In Search of the New Criticism." *American Scholar* 53, no. 1 (1984): 41-53.

———. *Modern Poetry and the Tradition*. Chapel Hill: University of North Carolina Press, 1939.

———. *The Well Wrought Urn: Studies in the Structure of Poetry*. New York: Harcourt, Brace, 1956.

Brooks, Cleanth, and Robert Penn Warren. *Understanding Poetry: An Anthology for College Students*. New York: Holt, 1938.

Brown, Angus Connell. "Cultural Studies and Close Reading." *PMLA* 132, no. 5 (2017): 1187-93. https://doi.org/10.1632/pmla.2017.132.5.1187.

Burgess, Anthony. *A Clockwork Orange*. New York: W. W. Norton (1962) 2019.

Büttner, Gottfried. "Schopenhauer's Recommendations to Beckett." *Samuel Beckett Today / Aujourd'hui* 11, no. 1 (2018): 114-22. https://doi.org/10.1163/18757405-01101016.

Camp, Elisabeth. "The Generality Constraint and Categorial Restrictions." *Philosophical Quarterly* 54, no. 215 (2004): 209-31. https://doi.org/10.1111/j.0031-8094.2004.00348.x.

Carnap, Rudolf. *The Logical Structure of the World and Pseudoproblems in Philosophy.* Chicago: Open Court (1928) 2003.

———. "Psychology in Physical Language." In *Logical Positivism*, edited by A. J. Ayer. Glencoe, IL: Free Press, 1959.

Cavell, Stanley. *Must We Mean What We Say? A Book of Essays.* New York: Scribner, 1969.

Chalmers, David John. *The Conscious Mind: In Search of a Theory of Conscious Experience.* New York: Oxford University Press, 1996.

———. "Facing Up to the Problem of Consciousness." *Journal of Consciousness Studies* 2, no. 3 (1995): 200-219.

Childs, Donald J. *The Birth of New Criticism: Conflict and Conciliation in the Early Work of William Empson, I. A. Richards, Robert Graves, and Laura Riding.* Montreal: McGill-Queen's University Press, 2014.

Chomsky, Noam. *Aspects of the Theory of Syntax.* Cambridge, MA: MIT Press (1965) 2015.

———. Review of *Verbal Behavior*, by B. F. Skinner. *Language* 35, no. 1 (1959): 26-58. https://doi.org/10.2307/411334.

———. *Rules and Representations.* New York: Columbia University Press, 1980.

———. *Syntactic Structures.* The Hague: Mouton, 1957.

Ciobanu, Calina. "Coetzee's Posthuman Ethics." *Modern Fiction Studies* 58, no. 4 (Winter 2012): 668-98.

Clark, A., and D. Chalmers. "The Extended Mind." *Analysis* 58, no. 1 (1998): 7-19. https://doi.org/10.1093/analys/58.1.7.

Clark, Andy. *Supersizing the Mind: Embodiment, Action, and Cognitive Extension.* Oxford: Oxford University Press, 2008.

Coetzee, J. M. *The Childhood of Jesus.* London: Vintage Books (2013) 2014.

———. *The Death of Jesus.* New York: Viking (2019) 2020.

———. *Disgrace.* New York: Penguin Books (1999) 2017.

———. *Doubling the Point: Essays and Interviews.* Edited by David Attwell. Cambridge, MA: Harvard University Press, 1992.

———. *Elizabeth Costello.* New York: Penguin Books (2003) 2004.

———. *Foe.* New York: Viking (1986) 1987.

———. *In the Heart of the Country.* New York: Penguin Books (1977) 1982.

———. *The Lives of Animals.* Edited and with an introduction by Amy Gutmann. Princeton, NJ: Princeton University Press, 1999.

———. *The Schooldays of Jesus.* London: Vintage (2016) 2017.

———. *Waiting for the Barbarians.* London: Secker & Warburg, 1980.

Works Cited

Coetzee, John Maxwell. "The English Fiction of Samuel Beckett: An Essay in Stylistic Analyses." PhD diss., University of Texas at Austin, 1969.
——. "The Rhetoric of the Passive in English." *Linguistics* 18, nos. 3-4 (1980). https://doi.org/10.1515/ling.1980.18.3-4.199.
Cohn, Dorrit. *Transparent Minds: Narrative Modes for Presenting Consciousness in Fiction*. Princeton, NJ: Princeton University Press, 1978.
Cohn, Ruby. *Samuel Beckett: The Comic Gamut*. New Brunswick, NJ: Rutgers University Press, 1962.
——. "The World of Harold Pinter." *Tulane Drama Review* 6, no. 3 (1962): 55-68. https://doi.org/10.2307/1124935.
Colombetti, Giovanna. *The Feeling Body: Affective Science Meets the Enactive Mind*. Cambridge, MA: MIT Press, 2013.
Connor, Steven. *Beckett, Modernism and the Material Imagination*. Cambridge: Cambridge University Press, 2014.
Cottingham, John. *Cartesian Reflections: Essays on Descartes's Philosophy*. Oxford: Oxford University Press, 2011.
Crane, Ronald S. *Critics and Criticism, Ancient and Modern*. Chicago: University of Chicago Press, 1952.
Dames, Nicholas. *The Physiology of the Novel: Reading, Neural Science, and the Form of Victorian Fiction*. Oxford: Oxford University Press, 2007.
Danziger, Kurt. *Constructing the Subject: Historical Origins of Psychological Research*. Cambridge: Cambridge University Press, 1990.
——. "Origins of the Schema of Stimulated Motion: Towards a Pre-history of Modern Psychology." *History of Science* 21, no. 2 (1983): 183-210. https://doi.org/10.1177/007327538302100204.
Davidson, Donald. *Essays on Actions and Events: Philosophical Essays Volume 1*. Oxford: Oxford University Press, 2001.
DeKoven, Marianne. "Going to the Dogs in *Disgrace*." *ELH* 76, no. 4 (Winter 2009): 847-75.
de Man, Paul. "Form and Intent in the New Criticism" (1971). In *Blindness and Insight: Essays in the Rhetoric of Contemporary Criticism*. Minneapolis: University of Minnesota Press, 1983.
Demastes, William W. *Staging Consciousness: Theater and the Materialization of Mind*. Ann Arbor: University of Michigan Press, 2002.
Descartes, René. *Descartes: Selected Philosophical Writings*. Translated by John Cottingham, Robert Stoothoff, and Dugald Murdoch. Cambridge: Cambridge University Press, 1992.
deVries, Willem. "Wilfrid Sellars." In *Stanford Encyclopedia of Philosophy*. Stanford University, May 10, 2020. https://plato.stanford.edu/entries/sellars/.
Diamond, Elin. *Pinter's Comic Play*. Lewisburg, PA: Bucknell University Press, 1985.

Donne, John. *Poems, by J. D. with Elegies on the Author's Death*. London: John Marriot; printed by M. F. [Miles Fletcher], 1633.
Durrant, Sam. *Postcolonial Narrative and the Work of Mourning: J. M. Coetzee, Wilson Harris, and Toni Morrison*. Albany: State University of New York Press, 2004.
Empson, William. *Seven Types of Ambiguity*. London: Chatto & Windus, 1930.
Engelberts, Matthijs, Everett Lloyd Frost, and Jane Maxwell. *"Notes Diverse Holo": Catalogues of Beckett's Reading Notes and Other Manuscripts at Trinity College Dublin, with Supporting Essays*. Amsterdam: Rodopi, 2006.
Esslin, Martin. *The Peopled Wound: The Work of Harold Pinter*. London: Methuen, 1970.
Fanon, Frantz. *Black Skin, White Masks*. Translated by Richard Philcox. New York: Grove (1952) 2008.
———. *The Wretched of the Earth*. Translated by Richard Philcox. New York: Grove (1961) 2005.
Faulkner, William. *Go Down, Moses*. New York: Vintage Books (1942) 2011.
Feldman, Matthew. *Beckett's Books: A Cultural History of the "Interwar Notes."* New York: Continuum, 2006.
Fielding, Heather. *Novel Theory and Technology in Modernist Britain*. Cambridge: Cambridge University Press, 2018.
Flatley, Jonathan. "How a Revolutionary Counter-mood Is Made." *New Literary History* 43, no. 3 (2012): 503-25. https://doi.org/10.1353/nlh.2012.0028.
Fodor, Jerry A. *The Language of Thought*. New York: Crowell, 1975.
———. "Special Sciences (or: The Disunity of Science as a Working Hypothesis)." *Synthese* 28, no. 2 (1974): 97-115. https://doi.org/10.1007/bf00485230.
Freeman, Donald C. *Linguistics and Literary Style*. New York: Holt, Rinehart & Winston, 1970.
Frow, John. *Character and Person*. Oxford: Oxford University Press, 2015.
Furlani, André. *Beckett after Wittgenstein*. Evanston, IL: Northwestern University Press, 2015.
Gallop, Jane. "The Historicization of Literary Studies and the Fate of Close Reading." *Profession* 2007, no. 1 (2007): 181-86. https://doi.org/10.1632/prof.2007.2007.1.181.
Garner, Stanton B. *Bodied Spaces: Phenomenology and Performance in Contemporary Drama*. Ithaca, NY: Cornell University Press, 1994.
Gibson, Andrew. *Beckett and Badiou: The Pathos of Intermittency*. Oxford: Oxford University Press, 2006.
Glicksohn, J., and C. Goodblatt. "Reclaiming I. A. Richards." *Poetics Today* 35, nos. 1-2 (2014): 173-89. https://doi.org/10.1215/03335372-2646872.
Gobert, R. Darren. *The Mind-Body Stage: Passion and Interaction in the Cartesian Theater*. Stanford, CA: Stanford University Press, 2013.
Goldman, Alvin I. *Simulating Minds: The Philosophy, Psychology, and Neuroscience of Mindreading*. Oxford: Oxford University Press, 2006.

Works Cited

Gontarski, S. E. "Crapp's First Tapes: Beckett's Manuscript Revisions of 'Krapp's Last Tape.'" *Journal of Modern Literature* 6, no. 1 (February 1977): 61-68.

———. *On Beckett: Essays and Criticism*. London: Anthem, 2014.

———. *Revisioning Beckett: Samuel Beckett's Decadent Turn*. Foreword by Anthony Uhlmann. New York: Bloomsbury Academic, 2018.

Goodblatt, Chanita, and Joseph Glickson. "From *Practical Criticism* to the Practice of Literary Criticism." *Poetics Today* 24, no. 2 (2003): 207-36. https://doi.org/10.1215/03335372-24-2-207.

Goodman, Nelson. *Languages of Art: An Approach to a Theory of Symbols*. Indianapolis: Hackett, 1976.

Gordon, Robert. *Harold Pinter: The Theatre of Power*. Ann Arbor: University of Michigan Press, 2013.

Graff, Gerald. *Poetic Statement and Critical Dogma*. Evanston, IL: Northwestern University Press, 1970.

———. *Professing Literature: An Institutional History*. Chicago: University of Chicago Press, 1987.

Grimes, Charles. *Harold Pinter's Politics: A Silence beyond Echo*. Madison, WI: Fairleigh Dickinson University Press, 2005.

Guillory, John. "Close Reading: Prologue and Epilogue." *ADE Bulletin* 149 (2010): 8-14. https://doi.org/10.1632/ade.149.8.

———. *Cultural Capital: The Problem of Literary Canon Formation*. Chicago: University of Chicago Press, 1993.

Hale, Dorothy. *The Novel and the New Ethics*. Stanford, CA: Stanford University Press, 2020.

Harper, Robert S. "The First Psychological Laboratory." *Isis* 41, no. 2 (1950): 158-61. https://doi.org/10.1086/349141.

Hayes, Patrick. *J. M. Coetzee and the Novel: Writing and Politics after Beckett*. Oxford: Oxford University Press, 2012.

Hempel, Carl. "The Logical Analysis of Psychology" (1935). In *Readings in the Philosophy of Psychology*, edited by Ned Block, translated by Wilfrid Sellars, 14-23. Cambridge, MA: Harvard University Press, 1980.

Herman, David. "Reminding Modernism." In *The Emergence of Mind: Representations of Consciousness in Narrative Discourse in English*. Lincoln: University of Nebraska Press, 2011.

Hilgard, Ernest Ropiequet, and Donald George Marquis. *Conditioning and Learning*. Revised by Gregory A. Kimble. New York: Appleton-Century-Crofts, 1961.

Hogan, Patrick Colm. *Beauty and Sublimity: A Cognitive Aesthetics of Literature and the Arts*. Cambridge: Cambridge University Press, 2016.

———. *Literature and Emotion*. London: Routledge, 2018.

———. *What Literature Teaches Us about Emotion*. Cambridge: Cambridge University Press, 2011.

Homan, Sidney. *Beckett's Theaters: Interpretations for Performance*. Lewisburg, PA: Bucknell University Press, 1984.

Hopkins, Gerard Manley. *Poems of Gerard Manley Hopkins Now First Published*. Edited with notes by Robert Bridges. London: H. Milford, 1918.

Hotopf, W. H. N. *Language, Thought and Comprehension: A Case Study of the Writings of I. A. Richards*. Bloomington: Indiana University Press, 1965.

Hull, Clark L. *Mathematico-Deductive Theory of Rote Learning: A Study in Scientific Methodology*. New Haven, CT: Yale University Press, 1940.

———. *Principles of Behavior: An Introduction to Behavior Theory*. New York: Appleton-Century-Crofts, 1943.

Hume, David. *A Treatise of Human Nature*. Reprinted from the original edition in three volumes and edited, with an analytical index, by L. A. Selby-Bigge. Oxford: Clarendon (1739) 1960.

Huxley, Aldous. *Brave New World*. New York: HarperCollins (1931) 2006.

Hylton, Peter. *Quine*. London: Routledge, 2007.

James, William. "Does Consciousness Exist?" In *The Writings of William James: A Comprehensive Edition*, edited by John J. McDermott. Chicago: University of Chicago Press, 1967.

———. *The Principles of Psychology in Two Volumes*. New York: Holt (1890) 1927.

Jancovich, Mark. *The Cultural Politics of the New Criticism*. Cambridge: Cambridge University Press, 1993.

Jay, Martin. "Modernism and the Specter of Psychologism." *Modernism/modernity* 3, no. 2 (1996): 93-111. https://doi.org/10.1353/mod.1996.0037.

Katz, Jerrold J. *The Philosophy of Language*. New York: Harper & Row, 1966.

Keen, Suzanne. *Empathy and the Novel*. Oxford: Oxford University Press, 2010.

Keller, Richard C. *Colonial Madness: Psychiatry in French North Africa*. Chicago: University of Chicago Press, 2007.

Kellman, Steven G. "J. M. Coetzee and Samuel Beckett: The Translingual Link." *Comparative Literature Studies* 33, no. 2 (1996): 161-72.

Kemp, Gary. "Autonomy and Privacy in Wittgenstein and Beckett." *Philosophy and Literature* 27, no. 1 (2003): 164-87. https://doi.org/10.1353/phl.2003.0027.

Kennedy, Andrew. *Six Dramatists in Search of a Language: Shaw, Eliot, Beckett, Pinter, Osborne, Arden*. Cambridge: Cambridge University Press, 1975.

Kenner, Hugh. *Samuel Beckett: A Critical Study*. Berkeley: University of California Press (1961) 1973.

Knapp, Steven, and Walter Benn Michaels. "Against Theory." *Critical Inquiry* 8, no. 4 (1982): 723-42. https://doi.org/10.1086/448178.

Knowlson, James. "'Krapp's Last Tape': The Evolution of a Play, 1958-75." *Journal of Beckett Studies* 1 (1976): 50-65.

Kramnick, Jonathan Brody. *Actions and Objects from Hobbes to Richardson*. Stanford, CA: Stanford University Press, 2010.

———. *Paper Minds: Literature and the Ecology of Consciousness*. Chicago: University of Chicago Press, 2018.

Krieger, Murray. *The New Apologists for Poetry*. Minneapolis: University of Minnesota Press, 1956.

Külpe, Oswald. *Outlines of Psychology, Based upon the Results of Experimental Investigation*. Translated from the German by Edward Bradford Titchener. London: Allen & Unwin (1893) 1921.

———. "Versuche über Abstraktion." *Bericht über den Kongress für experimentelle Psychologie in Giessen vom 19 bis 21 April 1904*. Leipzig: Verlag von Joahnnn Ambrosious Barth, 1904.

Kurnick, David. *Empty Houses: Theatrical Failure and the Novel*. Princeton, NJ: Princeton University Press, 2011.

Lakoff, George, and Mark Johnson. *Metaphors We Live By*. Chicago: University of Chicago Press, 1980.

Lane, Anthony. "The Dumbing of Emma." *New Yorker*, August 5, 1996.

Leist, Anton, and Peter Singer, eds. *J. M. Coetzee and Ethics: Philosophical Perspectives on Literature*. New York: Columbia University Press, 2010.

Lentricchia, Frank. *After the New Criticism*. Chicago: University of Chicago Press, 1980.

Lewis, Wyndham. *Snooty Baronet*. London: Cassell, 1932.

Leys, Ruth. "The Turn to Affect: A Critique." *Critical Inquiry* 37, no. 3 (2011): 434-72. https://doi.org/10.1086/659353.

Linstrum, Erik. *Ruling Minds: Psychology in the British Empire*. Cambridge, MA: Harvard University Press, 2016.

Locke, John. *An Essay Concerning Human Understanding*. Oxford: Clarendon (1689) 1979.

Love, Heather. "Close Reading and Thin Description." *Public Culture* 25, no. 3 (2013): 401-34. https://doi.org/10.1215/08992363-2144688.

Lynch, Deidre. *Loving Literature: A Cultural History*. Chicago: University of Chicago Press, 2015.

MacLeod, Lewis. "'Do We of Necessity Become Puppets in a Story?' or Narrating the World: On Speech, Silence, and Discourse in J. M. Coetzee's Foe." *MFS Modern Fiction Studies* 52, no. 1 (2006): 1-18.

Magidor, Ofra. *Category Mistakes*. Oxford: Oxford University Press, 2013.

Mandler, George. *A History of Modern Experimental Psychology: From James and Wundt to Cognitive Science*. Cambridge, MA: MIT Press, 2011.

Mao, Douglas. *Fateful Beauty: Aesthetic Environments, Juvenile Development, and Literature 1860-1960*. Princeton, NJ: Princeton University Press, 2008.

———. "The New Critics and the Text-Object." *ELH* 63, no. 1 (1996): 227-54. https://doi.org/10.1353/elh.1996.0007.

Massumi, Brian. *Parables for the Virtual: Movement, Affect, Sensation*. Durham, NC: Duke University Press, 2002.

Maude, Ulrika. *Beckett, Technology and the Body*. Cambridge: Cambridge University Press, 2011.

McCulloch, Jock. *Colonial Psychiatry and "The African Mind."* Cambridge: Cambridge University Press, 1995.

Memmi, Albert. *The Colonizer and the Colonized*. Translated by Howard Greenfield. Boston: Beacon, 1965.

Meyer, Max Friedrich. *Psychology of the Other-One*. Columbia, MO: Missouri Book, 1922.

Micale, Mark S., ed. *The Mind of Modernism: Medicine, Psychology, and the Cultural Arts in Europe and America, 1880–1940*. Stanford, CA: Stanford University Press, 2004.

Moody, Alys. *The Art of Hunger: Aesthetic Autonomy and the Afterlives of Modernism*. Oxford: Oxford University Press, 2018.

Mooney, Michael E. "Presocratic Scepticism: Samuel Beckett's Murphy Reconsidered." *ELH* 49, no. 1 (1982): 214–34. https://doi.org/10.2307/2872889.

Moore, G. E. "A Reply to My Critics" (1942). In *G. E. Moore: Selected Writings*, edited by Thomas Baldwin. London: Routledge, 2013.

Morgan, Benjamin. *The Outward Mind: Materialist Aesthetics in Victorian Science and Literature*. Chicago: University of Chicago Press, 2017.

Moses, Omri. "Poetry and the Environmentally Extended Mind." *New Literary History* 49, no. 3 (2018): 309–35. https://doi.org/10.1353/nlh.2018.0022.

Moya, Paula M. L. *The Social Imperative: Race, Close Reading, and Contemporary Literary Criticism*. Stanford, CA: Stanford University Press, 2016.

Mulhall, Stephen. *The Wounded Animal: J. M. Coetzee and the Difficulty of Reality in Literature and Philosophy*. Princeton, NJ: Princeton University Press, 2009.

Ndebele, Njabulo S. "The Rediscovery of the Ordinary: Some New Writings in South Africa" (1984). In *The Rediscovery of the Ordinary: Essays on South African Literature and Culture*. London: Picador, 2015.

Neimneh, Shadi. "The Visceral Allegory of *Waiting for the Barbarians*: A Postmodern Re-reading of J. M. Coetzee's Apartheid Novels." *Callaloo* 37, no. 3 (2014): 692–709.

Neurath, Otto. "Empirical Sociology" (1931). In *Otto Neurath: Empiricism and Sociology*, edited by Marie Neurath and Robert S. Cohen. Dordrecht: Reidel, 1973.

———. "Sociology in the Framework of Physicalism" (1931). In *Philosophical Papers, 1913–1946: With a Bibliography of Neurath in English*, edited by Robert S. Cohen, Marie Neurath, and Carolyn R. Fawcett. Dordrecht: Reidel, 1983.

Ng, Lynda. "Xinjiang's Indelible Footprint: Reading the New Imperialism in *English* and *Waiting for the Barbarians*." *Modern Fiction Studies* 64, no. 3 (Fall 2018): 512–36.

Noë, Alva. *Action in Perception*. Cambridge, MA: MIT Press, 2004.

Ogden, Charles Kay, Ivor Armstrong Richards, Bronislaw Malinowski, and F. G. Crookshank. *The Meaning of Meaning: A Study of the Influence of Language upon Thought and of the Science of Symbolism*. London: Kegan, Paul, Trench, & Trubner (1923) 1944.

Ohmann, Richard M. "Generative Grammars and the Concept of Literary Style." *Word* 20, no. 3 (1964): 423-39. https://doi.org/10.1080/00437956.1964.11659831.

———. *Shaw: The Style and the Man*. Middletown, CT: Wesleyan University Press, 1962.

O'Neill, Eugene. *Nine Plays*. New York: Modern Library, 1993.

Palmer, Alan. *Fictional Minds*. Lincoln: University of Nebraska Press, 2008.

Pavlov, Ivan Petrovich. *Conditioned Reflexes*. Translated by G. V. Anrep. Mineola, NY: Dover, 2003.

———. *Lectures on Conditioned Reflexes: Twenty-Five Years of Objective Study of the Higher Nervous Activity (Behavior) of Animals*. Translated and edited by W. Horsley Gantt and G. V. Fol'bort. New York: International, 1928.

———. *The Work of the Digestive Glands: A Facsimile of the First Russian Edition of 1897, Together with the First English Translation of 1902*. Translated by W. H. Thompson. Birmingham, AL: Classics of Medicine Library (1897) 1982.

Pillsbury, W. B. *The Essentials of Psychology*. New York: Macmillan, 1911.

Pinter, Harold. *The Birthday Party*. London: Methuen (1955) 1982.

———. *The Caretaker and the Dumb Waiter: Two Plays*. New York: Grove, 1965.

———. *Collected Poems and Prose*. London: Methuen, 1986.

———. *The Homecoming*. London: Methuen, 1965.

———. *The Hothouse*. London: Methuen (1958) 1982.

———. *Various Voices: Prose, Poetry, Politics*. New York: Grove, 1999.

Plato. *The Republic*. Translated by Richard W. Sterling and William C. Scott. New York: W. W. Norton, 1996.

Premack, David, and Guy Woodruff. "Does the Chimpanzee Have a Theory of Mind"? *Behavioral and Brain Sciences* 1, no. 4 (1978): 515-26.

Putnam, Hilary. "Psychological Predicates." In *Art, Mind, and Religion*, edited by W. H. Capitan and D. D. Merrill. Pittsburgh: University of Pittsburgh Press, 1967.

Quigley, Austin E. "*The Dumb Waiter*: Undermining the Tacit Dimension." *Modern Drama* 21, no. 1 (1978): 1-11. https://doi.org/10.3138/md.21.1.1.

———. *Pinter Problem*. Princeton, NJ: Princeton University, 1975.

Quine, W. V. O. "Indeterminacy of Translation Again." *Journal of Philosophy* 84, no. 1 (January 1987): 5-10.

———. "Mind and Verbal Dispositions." In *Mind and Language: Wolfson College Lectures 1974*, edited by Samuel D. Guttenplan, 83-96. Oxford: Clarendon, 1975.

———. "Two Dogmas of Empiricism." In *From a Logical Point of View: Nine Logico-Philosophical Essays*. Cambridge, MA: Harvard University Press, 1999.

———. *Word and Object*. Cambridge, MA: MIT Press, 1960.

Rabaté, Jean-Michel. "Excuse My French: Samuel Beckett's Style of No Style." *CR: The New Centennial Review* 16, no. 3 (2016): 133-50. https://doi.org/10.14321/crnewcentrevi.16.3.0133.

———. *Think, Pig! Beckett at the Limit of the Human*. New York: Fordham University Press, 2016.

Ransom, John Crowe. *The New Criticism*. Norfolk, CT: New Directions, 1941.

Richards, Ivor Armstrong. *Practical Criticism: A Study of Literary Judgment*. New York: Harcourt, Brace & World, 1966.

———. *Principles of Literary Criticism*. New York: Harcourt Brace (1924) 1961.

———. Review of *Behaviorism*, by John Broadus Watson. *New Criterion* 4, no. 2 (1926).

———. *Science and Poetry*. New York: Haskell (1926) 1974.

Richardson, Alan. *The Neural Sublime: Cognitive Theories and Romantic Texts*. Baltimore: Johns Hopkins University Press, 2010.

Richardson, Alan W. *Carnap's Construction of the World: The* Aufbau *and the Emergence of Logical Empiricism*. Cambridge: Cambridge University Press, 1998.

Rickel, Jennifer. "Speaking of Human Rights: Narrative Voice and the Paradox of the Unspeakable in J. M. Coetzee's *Foe* and *Disgrace*." *Journal of Narrative Theory* 43, no. 2 (2013): 160-85.

Rieber, Robert W., and David Robinson, eds. *Wilhelm Wundt in History: The Making of a Scientific Psychology*. New York: Kluwer, 2001.

Roach, Rebecca. "Hero and Bad Motherland: J. M. Coetzee's Computational Critique." *Contemporary Literature* 59, no. 1 (2018): 80-111. https://doi.org/10.3368/cl.59.1.80.

Robbins, Bruce. "Discipline and Parse: The Politics of Close Reading." *Los Angeles Review of Books*, May 14, 2017.

Russell, Bertrand. *The Analysis of Mind*. London: Macmillan (1921) 1961.

———. "Mathematical Logic as Based on the Theory of Types." *American Journal of Mathematics* 30, no. 3 (1908): 222-62. https://doi.org/10.2307/2369948.

———. "On Denoting." *Mind* 14, no. 4 (1905): 479-93. https://doi.org/10.1093/mind/xiv.4.479.

———. *An Outline of Philosophy*. New York: Signet (1927) 1960.

———. *The Principles of Mathematics*. Vol. 1. Cambridge: Cambridge University Press, 1903.

Russo, John Paul. *I. A. Richards: His Life and Work*. Baltimore: Johns Hopkins University Press, 1989.

Ryan, Judith. *The Vanishing Subject: Early Psychology and Literary Modernism*. Chicago: University of Chicago Press, 1991.

Ryle, Gilbert. "Categories" (1938). In *Collected Essays 1929-1968: Collected Papers Volume 2*. London: Routledge, 2016.

———. *The Concept of Mind: 60th Anniversary Edition*. With an introduction by Julia Tanney. London: Routledge (1949) 2009.

———. "Jane Austen and the Moralists" (1966). In *Critical Essays: Collected Papers*. London: Routledge, 2009.

Works Cited

Saltz, David Z. "Radical Mimesis: The 'Pinter Problem' Revisited." *Comparative Drama* 26, no. 3 (1992): 218-36. https://doi.org/10.1353/cdr.1992.0033.
Sanders, Mark. "Disgrace." *Interventions* 4, no. 3 (2002): 363-73. https://doi.org/10.1080/1369801022000013798.
Sartre, Jean-Paul. *Anti-Semite and Jew*. Translated by George Becker. New York: Schocken Books (1944) 1995.
Scarry, Elaine. *Dreaming by the Book*. Princeton, NJ: Princeton University Press, 1999.
Scolnicov, Hanna. *The Experimental Plays of Harold Pinter*. Newark: University of Delaware Press, 2012.
Selisker, Scott. *Human Programming: Brainwashing, Automatons, and American Unfreedom*. Minneapolis: University of Minnesota Press, 2016.
Sellars, Wilfrid. *Empiricism and the Philosophy of Mind*. With an introduction by Richard Rorty and a study guide by Robert Brandom. Cambridge, MA: Harvard University Press (1956) 1997.
Sheehan, Paul. *Modernism, Narrative and Humanism*. Cambridge: Cambridge University Press, 2002.
Silver, Sean. *The Mind Is a Collection: Case Studies in Eighteenth-Century Thought*. Philadelphia: University of Pennsylvania Press, 2015.
Silverstein, Marc. *Harold Pinter and the Language of Cultural Power*. Lewisburg, PA: Bucknell University Press, 1993.
Skillman, Nikki. *The Lyric in the Age of the Brain*. Cambridge, MA: Harvard University Press, 2016.
Skinner, B. F. *About Behaviorism*. New York: Vintage, 1974.
———. *The Behavior of Organisms*. New York: Appleton-Century, 1938.
———. *The Shaping of a Behaviorist: Part Two of an Autobiography*. New York: Knopf, 1979.
———. "'Superstition' in the Pigeon." *Journal of Experimental Psychology* 38, no. 2 (1948): 168-72. https://doi.org/10.1037/h0055873.
———. *Verbal Behavior*. New York: Appleton-Century, 1957.
———. *Walden Two*. Indianapolis: Hackett (1948) 2008.
Smith, Laurence D. *Behaviorism and Logical Positivism: A Reassessment of the Alliance*. Stanford, CA: Stanford University Press, 1986.
Spitzer, Leo. *Linguistics and Literary History: Essays in Stylistics*. Princeton, NJ: Princeton University Press, 1948.
Spivak, Gayatri Chakravorty. "Close Reading." *PMLA* 121, no. 5 (October 2006): 1608-17.
———. *A Critique of Postcolonial Reason: Toward a History of the Vanishing Present*. Cambridge, MA: Harvard University Press (1999) 2003.
Stanislavski, Constantin S. *An Actor Prepares*. Translated by Elizabeth Reynolds Hapgood. New York: Theatre Arts Books (1936) 1948.
Starr, G. Gabrielle. *Feeling Beauty: The Neuroscience of Aesthetic Experience*. Cambridge, MA: MIT Press, 2013.

Stein, Gertrude. "Poetry and Grammar" (1935). *American Poetry Review* 36, no. 1 (January 2007): 25-33.

Stewart, Susan. "Lyric Possession." *Critical Inquiry* 22, no. 1 (1995): 34-63. https://doi.org/10.1086/448781.

Strawson, P. F. "Categories." In *Ryle: A Collection of Critical Essays*, edited by Oscar P. Wood and George Pitcher. Garden City, NY: Doubleday, 1970.

Stulberg, Jacob. "How (Not) to Write Broadcast Plays: Pinter and the BBC." *Modern Drama* 58, no. 4 (2015): 502-23. https://doi.org/10.3138/md.0744.

Tajiri, Yoshiki. "Beckett, Coetzee, and Animals." In *Beckett and Animals*, edited by Mary Bryden. Cambridge: Cambridge University Press, 2013.

———. "Beckett's Legacy in the Work of J. M. Coetzee." *Samuel Beckett Today / Aujourd'hui* 19, no. 1 (2008): 361-70. https://doi.org/10.1163/18757405-019001029.

Tate, Allen. "The Present Function of Criticism" (1940). In *On the Limits of Poetry: Selected Essays, 1928-1948*. Freeport, NY: Books for Libraries Press, 1970.

Taylor-Batty, Mark. *The Theatre of Harold Pinter*. London: Bloomsbury, 2014.

Thompson, Harry. "Harold Pinter Replies." *New Theatre Magazine* 2 (January 1961): 8-10.

Thorndike, Edward L. *Animal Intelligence: Experimental Studies*. New York: Macmillan, 1911.

Todes, Daniel Philip. *Pavlov's Physiology Factory: Experiment, Interpretation, Laboratory Enterprise*. Baltimore: Johns Hopkins University Press, 2002.

Tolman, E. C. "Behaviorism and Purpose." *Journal of Philosophy* 22, no. 2 (1925): 36-41.

———. *Purposive Behavior in Animals and Men*. Berkeley: University of California Press (1932) 1949.

Tonning, Erik. "'I am not reading philosophy': Beckett and Schopenhauer." In *Beckett/Philosophy: A Collection*, edited by Matthew Feldman and Karim Mamdani. New York: Columbia University Press, 2018.

Trask, Michael Alfred. *Cruising Modernism: Class and Sexuality in American Literature and Social Thought*. Ithaca, NY: Cornell University Press, 2003.

Tucker, David. *Samuel Beckett and Arnold Geulincx: Tracing "a Literary Fantasia."* London: Bloomsbury, 2013.

Turner, Mark. *The Literary Mind: The Origin of Thought and Language*. Oxford: Oxford University Press, 1995.

Uhlmann, Anthony. "Approaches to the (Beckett) Archives: Popper, Coetzee, and Scientific Validity." *Journal of Beckett Studies* 26, no. 1 (2017): 103-17. https://doi.org/10.3366/jobs.2017.0190.

———. "Process and Method in *Waiting for the Barbarians*." *Texas Studies in Literature and Language* 58, no. 4 (2016): 435-50. https://doi.org/10.7560/tsll58406.

———. *Samuel Beckett and the Philosophical Image*. Cambridge: Cambridge University Press, 2006.

Van Hulle, Dirk. "The Extended Mind and Multiple Drafts: Beckett's Models of the Mind and the Postcognitivist Paradigm." *Samuel Beckett Today / Aujourd'hui* 24, no. 1 (2012): 277-90. https://doi.org/10.1163/18757405-024001019.

———. *Modern Manuscripts: The Extended Mind and Creative Undoing from Darwin to Beckett and Beyond*. London: Bloomsbury Academic, 2015.

Van Hulle, Dirk, and Mark Nixon. *Samuel Beckett's Library*. Cambridge: Cambridge University Press, 2017.

Varela, Francisco J., Eleanor Rosch, and Evan Thompson. *The Embodied Mind: Cognitive Science and Human Experience*. Cambridge, MA: MIT Press, 1992.

Vermeule, Blakey. *Why Do We Care about Literary Characters?* Baltimore: Johns Hopkins University Press, 2011.

Walton, Kendall L. *Mimesis as Make-Believe: On the Foundations of the Representational Arts*. Cambridge, MA: Harvard University Press, 1990.

Watson, John B. *Behavior: An Introduction to Comparative Psychology*. New York: H. Holt, 1914.

———. *Behaviorism*. London: Kegan Paul, 1924.

———. "The Place of the Conditioned-Reflex in Psychology." *Psychological Review* 23, no. 2 (1916): 89-116. https://doi.org/10.1037/h0070003.

———. "Psychology as the Behaviorist Views It." *Psychological Review* 20, no. 2 (1913): 158-77. https://doi.org/10.1037/h0074428.

———. *Psychology from the Standpoint of a Behaviorist*. Philadelphia: J. B. Lippincott, 1919.

Watson, John B., and Rosalie Rayner. "Conditioned Emotional Reactions." *Journal of Experimental Psychology* 3, no. 1 (1920): 1-14. https://doi.org/10.1037/h0069608.

Wellek, René. *A History of Modern Criticism: 1750-1950*. Vol. 6. New Haven, CT: Yale University Press, 1986.

West, David. *I. A. Richards and the Rise of Cognitive Stylistics*. London: Bloomsbury, 2013.

West, Rebecca. *The Strange Necessity: Essays by Rebecca West*. Garden City, NY: Doubleday, 1928.

Wicomb, Zoë. *Playing in the Light: A Novel*. New York: New Press (2006) 2008.

Williams, Raymond. *Culture and Society: 1780-1950*. New York: Columbia University Press 1983.

Wimsatt, W. K., and Monroe C. Beardsley. "Intention." In *Dictionary of World Literature*, edited by Joseph T. Shipley. New York: Philosophical Library, 1943.

———. *The Verbal Icon: Studies in the Meaning of Poetry*. Lexington: University Press of Kentucky (1954) 1962.

Wimsatt, W. K., and Cleanth Brooks. *Literary Criticism: A Short History*. New York: Knopf, 1957.

Wittgenstein, Ludwig. "The Language of Sense Data and Private Experience" (1936). In *Philosophical Occasions, 1912-1951*, edited by James C. Klagge and Alfred Nordmann. Indianapolis: Hackett, 1993.

———. *Philosophical Investigations*. Translated by G. E. M. Anscombe. Oxford: Wiley-Blackwell (1953) 2001.

Woodworth, Robert Sessions. *Contemporary Schools of Psychology*. London: Methuen, 1931.

———. "Imageless Thought." *Journal of Philosophy, Psychology and Scientific Methods* 3, no. 26 (1906): 701-7. https://doi.org/10.2307/2012049.

Woolf, Virginia. *Mrs. Dalloway*. New York: Harcourt (1925) 2005.

———. *To the Lighthouse*. New York: Harcourt (1925) 1981.

Wright, Richard. "How Bigger Was Born" (1940). In *Native Son*. New York: Harper Perennial, 2009.

———. *Native Son*. New York: Harper Perennial (1940) 2009.

Wundt, Wilhelm Max. *Outlines of Psychology*. Translated by C. H. Judd. Leipzig: Engelmann (1896) 1907.

———. *Principles of Physiological Psychology*. Translated by E. B. Titchener. London: Swan, Sonnenschein (1874) 1910.

Zimbler, Jarad. *J. M. Coetzee and the Politics of Style*. Cambridge: Cambridge University Press, 2014.

Zunshine, Lisa. *Why We Read Fiction: Theory of Mind and the Novel*. Columbus: Ohio State University Press, 2006.

Index

Achebe, Chinua, 154
actors/acting, 4, 30-31, 111-113, 137-138, 180n8
Adams, Kelly, 156, 183n4, 185n16
Adorno, Theodor, 103
affect, 27-28, 30, 34, 48, 52-56, 59-60, 64, 177n20
affective fallacy, 28, 35, 48, 59-60
"Affective Fallacy, The" (Wimsatt and Beardsley), 35, 48, 59-60
Anscombe, G. E. M., 35, 173n22
apartheid, 141-142, 155, 184n5, 185n6
Aristotle, 16-17
Artaud, Antonin, 112
Attridge, Derek, 160, 184n6, 185n17
audience, theatrical, 31, 104-106, 111, 115-123, 126, 133-137
Augustine, Saint, 62
Austen, Jane, 16, 168-169, 172n17
Austin, J. L., 18, 173n18
authorial intention, 3, 30, 32-36, 49, 54, 60-65, 177n20. *See also* "Intentional Fallacy, The"

Banfield, Ann, 3, 171n3
Beardsley, Monroe. *See* Wimsatt, W. K., and Beardsley, Monroe
Beatty, Paul, 6
Beckett, Samuel: behavioral observation in, 88-100; and behaviorism, 67-69, 76-83, 92-96, 99-100, 103-106, 177n3; and René Descartes, 24, 30, 66-69, 84, 96, 114, 177n1; dualism in works of, 83, 100-102, 114-125, 181n17; introspection in works of, 69, 83-93, 95, 97, 99-101, 114, 121-125; on James Joyce, 78-79, 175n12; memory in works of, 79-80, 92-94, 105, 108, 121-125; staging of the plays of, 105, 113, 115-119, 120-125, 181n15
Beckett, Samuel, works of: "Dante . . . Bruno . . . Vico . . . Joyce," 69, 76-80, 161, 175n17; *Dream of Fair to Middling Women*, 76, 81; *Eleutheria*, 31, 105, 113-120, 129, 181n12; *Endgame*, 103; *Krapp's Last Tape*, 31, 105, 113, 119-125, 129, 181n16, 181n17, 181n18; *Molloy*, 30, 66-69, 76, 92-102, 123, 125, 159, 177n3, 179n17; *Murphy*, 30, 66, 68-69, 76, 83-89, 100-103, 110, 113-114, 119, 123, 125, 159, 177n3, 179n16, 182n21; *Not I*, 138; "Our Examination Round His Factification for Incamination of Work in Progress," 76; *Proust*, 69, 79-81, 93; "Psychology" notebook transcripts, 69, 81-83, 85, 178n15; *Theatrical Notebooks*, 121-122, 124; *The Unnamable*, 129, 177n3; *Waiting for Godot*, 103-104, 112, 114; *Watt*, 71, 81, 85, 88, 94, 125, 152-153; *Whoroscope*, 68
behaviorism: consciousness, existence of, 7, 9-10, 38-41, 106-108; and dualism, 67, 106-111; history of, 7-15, 36-41, 69-76, 81-83, 106-111, 140-141, 143-149; and introspection, 36-38, 69, 72, 82-83, 95; and language, 11-13, 75, 143-149, 166-167; and literary criticism, 2-5, 29, 35-36, 41-44, 49-50, 54-55, 60, 63, 140-141, 169-170, 174n3, 175n5, 176n20; logical, 11, 13, 108-109, 167; negative connotations of, 5, 8, 77; and philosophy, 6, 9, 11-15, 40-41, 72-76, 108-111,

behaviorism (*cont.*)
  147-149, 172n15, 172n16; psychological, 7-11, 13, 36-40, 72, 82-83, 106-108, 143-145, 169; purposive, 9, 72; radical, 10, 143-145; Watsonian, 7-9, 11, 15, 35-41, 49, 60, 106-108
Best, Stephen, and Marcus, Sharon, 33
Biko, Steve, 155
Billington, Michael, 126, 182n20
Black Consciousness Movement, 155
Blin, Roger, 115
Brecht, Bertolt, 112, 180n9. *See also* epic theater
Brentano, Franz, 61, 70
Brooks, Cleanth: and intention, 32, 60-61, 65, 176n19; and paradox, 54-59, 176n19; on I. A. Richards, 35-36, 55-56; *The Well Wrought Urn*, 55-60, 65, 176n15; Wimsatt and Beardsley on, 59-60
Browning, Robert, 51-52, 56
Burgess, Anthony, 5

Carnap, Rudolf, 12-13, 108, 149, 180
catachresis, 53, 58, 123, 125, 132, 181n17
categories, 15-18, 173n20, 173n23, 178n8
category-mistakes: definition of, 15-18, 173n18, 173n19, 173n20, 173n21, 173n22, 173n23, 178n8; and intention, 34, 64; and literary and dramatic minds, 16, 21-29, 120-123, 131-132, 137, 166, 171n4; literary language as, 54-58, 79, 119, 175n12; mental representation as, 140, 156, 158, 166; mind-body category-mistake, 15-16, 21-29, 105, 109, 131-132, 140-141, 158, 169
Cavell, Stanley, 32-33, 35, 64
Chalmers, David, 4, 171n1, 172n5, 174n27
Chomsky, Noam: J. M. Coetzee on, 140, and literary criticism, 22, 31, 140, 142, 150-151; nativism of, 11, 31, 140-142, 144-149, 172n14, 184n9; review of *Verbal Behavior*, 11, 140, 145-146, 149, 162
close reading, 33, 35-37, 54-65, 174n3, 176n15, 177n21
clowns/clowning, 110-111, 137
Coetzee, J. M.: on animals, 184n8; and behaviorism, 140-142, 167; on Samuel Beckett, 140, 143, 152-153, 183n1-2, 184n12; and Chomskyan linguistics, 6, 142, 144, 150, 152; and colonialism, 21, 141-142, 156-160, 164-167, 184n6; mental representation as category-mistake in, 31, 140, 142-143, 152-153, 165-166; on the passive voice, 156, 183n4
Coetzee, J. M., works of: *Disgrace*, 141-142, 184n5, 184n8; *Foe*, 31, 142-143, 153-154, 160-167, 185n18; *In the Heart of the Country*, 141-142; *The English Fiction of Samuel Beckett*, 140-143, 149-150, 152-153, 156, 184n6, 184n12, 185n13; "The Rhetoric of the Passive in English," 156, 183n4; "Samuel Beckett and the Temptations of Style," 183n2; *Waiting for the Barbarians*, 142-143, 153-154, 156-161, 163, 166-167, 185n17
cogito, 30, 66-69, 91-92, 97-99, 125, 127, 177n3. *See also* Descartes, René
cognitive literary criticism, 15, 21-29, 54, 174n24
cognitive science, 4, 11, 21-29, 142, 174n27
Cohn, Ruby, 102, 171, 180n2, 181n12
Coleridge, Samuel Taylor, 22
colonialism, 6, 31, 141-143, 154-160, 164-167, 184n6, 185n18
Concept of Mind, The (Ryle): and behaviorism, 74-75, 172n16; and categories, 15-16; and René Descartes, 14-15; and dualism as category-mistake, 15, 19, 105, 109-111, 168-169, 181n17; and introspection, 74-75; knowing how versus knowing that, 105, 109-111, 135; and literature, 168-170; and theater, 110-111, 137-138
conditioning: classical, 7-10, 78-80; language acquisition as a result of, 145-146, 153, 162-163, 167; and literature, 5-6, 77-80, 172n6; operant, 5, 10-11, 144-146, 180n3; political connotations of, 5-6, 78
Conrad, Joseph, 154
consciousness: authorial 60, 139; behaviorist rejections of, 7, 9-10, 12, 36, 38, 40-41, 77, 82, 107-108, 143; as computational, 147, 184n10; hard problem of consciousness, 4, 172n5; nature of, 171n1, 172n5; as theater, 70, 93; theatrical depictions of, 113, 138

Davidson, Donald, 179n1
Defoe, Daniel, 160

Index

de Man, Paul, 33
Demastes, William, 112-113
Descartes, René: and Samuel Beckett, 24, 30, 66-69, 84, 96-99, 114, 177n1; and behaviorism, 106-107; *Discourse de la Méthode*, 66, 68; *Meditations on First Philosophy*, 68, 127, 169, 181n10; and Harold Pinter, 126-128; Ryle on, 14-15, 24, 74, 109-110; and theater, 113
Dickens, Charles, 16
Donne, John, 45-46, 48, 58, 61
dualism: and Samuel Beckett, 83, 100, 102, 114, 119, 125; behaviorist critique of, 67, 105-108; epistemological, 104-111, 113, 137; logical behaviorism and, 108-109; mind-body, 7, 15-16, 17, 19, 31, 66, 100, 104-109, 111-112, 114, 125, 181n10, 181n17; of mise-en-scéne, 105-106, 111, 114-125; and Harold Pinter, 104, 125, 133; property, 171n1, 179n1; Gilbert Ryle on, 17, 74, 105, 109, 111, 137; substance dualism, 107, 113; and theater, 112-113, 137, 181n10

electroconvulsive therapy (ECT), 125-126, 182n28
empiricism: and other minds, 104, 125, 134, 156, 167; introspection as empirical, 67, 74-75, 92-93, 96-100, 121-122; and language acquisition, 146, 162, 167; philosophy of, 30, 69-70, 149, 178n10, 180n7; and psychology, 7, 70-72
Empson, William, 54, 174n3
enactive cognition, 25-26, 174n27
epic theater, 112, 180n9. *See also* Brecht, Bertolt
etymon, 142, 150, 152. *See also* Spitzer, Leo
experimental psychology, 7-11, 36-38, 67, 70-71, 81-82, 172n7

Fanon, Frantz, 154-155, 164, 185n14
Faulkner, William, 151-152
Fechner, Gustav, 7, 70
Flatley, Jonathan, 34, 174n2
Fodor, Jerry, 40, 142, 147-148, 174n25, 184n10
formalism, 30, 36, 54-65, 174n3
Freeman, Donald, 22, 140, 150-151, 163

gap-sign, 18-20, 173n19. *See also* sentence-frame
Gestalt theory, 42, 50, 70, 81-82
Geulincx, Arnold, 66, 84, 114, 177n1
Graff, Gerald, 56, 174n1, 174n3, 176n17
grammar: deep grammatical structures, 31, 140, 146-148, 151, 162; and thought, 89, 131, 140-143, 149, 150-153, 183n2
Guillory, John, 55-56, 174n3, 175n7, 176n16

habit: and criticism, 43-44, 62; formation, 8-9, 177n2; perception as, 79-80; thought as, 2, 9, 40-41, 67, 103
Hempel, Carl, 2, 6, 12-13, 108-109, 180n7
Hogan, Patrick Colm, 26-27
Hopkins, Gerard Manley, 45, 47-48, 175n9
Hull, Clark, 9-10
Hume, David, 70, 93
Huxley, Aldous, 5

imageless thought, 81-82, 84, 179n14
indeterminacy of translation, 143, 166-167, 185n19. *See also* Quine, W. V. O.
intentional fallacy. *See* authorial intention; "Intentional Fallacy, The"
"Intentional Fallacy, The" (Wimsatt and Beardsley), 30, 32-33, 35-36, 49, 54, 60-64. *See also* authorial intention
interiority, 143, 153-160, 162, 164-165, 185n14
introspection: in Samuel Beckett, 30, 66, 69, 83-84, 86-89, 91, 92-93, 95, 97, 99-101, 119-125; and behaviorism, 36-38, 69, 72, 82-83, 95; critique of, 12, 38-39, 41-44, 67-69, 82, 107; as empirical, 67, 74-75, 92-93, 96-100, 121-122; as methodology, 7, 36-39, 41, 71-72, 82-83, 108, 177n5; philosophical accounts of, 70, 72-73, 75-76, 178n7
introspective psychology, 30, 44, 69, 81-84, 107

James, William, 7, 9, 42, 82, 107, 177n5
Joyce, James, 69, 76-80, 175n12, 182n26

Kant, Immanuel, 16-17, 50, 55
Katz, Jerrold, 142, 148-149
Keats, John, 61
Kenner, Hugh, 66, 83, 181n12

Knapp, Steven, and Michaels, Walter Benn, 32, 176n20
knowing how versus knowing that, 105, 109-111, 135. See also Ryle, Gilbert
Knowlson, James, 121, 124, 182n18, 19
Kramnick, Jonathan, 28, 172n5, 174n24, 174n25, 174n26, 174n27
Külpe, Oswald, 70-71, 81, 84-86

language acquisition, 11, 31, 142-148, 162-163
Lewis, Wyndham, 5
Leys, Ruth, 34
linguistics: 6, 31, 140-142, 150-151, 166-167, 184n7; Chomskyan, 6, 31, 140, 142, 150-151
literary experience, 19, 21-23, 27-28, 139, 169
literary minds: as category-mistake, 15, 27-29, 139, 169; and cognitive criticism, 21-27, 28, 171n4; as distinct from actual minds, 3-6, 19, 64-65, 99-100, 106, 164, 167, 171n4, 172n5, 173n23
Locke, John, 70
logical positivism, 12-13, 55, 178n10
logical types, 15-21, 35, 58, 131
Love, Heather, 33
Lynch, Deidre, 18, 22

Magidor, Ofra, 16, 173n18, 173n20, 173n23
Mao, Douglas, 58, 77, 172n6
Massumi, Brian, 34
memory: amnesia, 92-94; and behaviorism, 9, 41, 80, 108, 177n2; externalization of, 105, 121-125, 161; as mental phenomena, 75; voluntary and involuntary, 80, 93
mental action: nature of, 122-125, 129, 179n1; staging of, 102-105, 118-120, 132, 137. See also mental representation
mental illness, 82, 114, 126
mentalism: and behaviorism; 9, 11-13, 39, 67-69, 92, 109, 146; and introspection, 69, 89, 114; and psychology, 9, 38, 68, 86, 146
mental properties: attribution to literary texts, 1-4, 15, 19-29, 49, 51, 63-64, 100, 172n5; attribution to language, 161, 164; attribution to objects, 119, 124, 161, 164, 179n1

mental representation: as category-mistake, 31, 139; and theater, 101, 103, 137, 139; viability of, 142, 147, 165-167
metaphor, 49, 53, 58, 125, 133, 173n23, 180n3
Meyer, Max, 83, 88
mise-en-scène, 31, 103, 105, 113-119, 115, 119, 125-126, 128-129, 131, 137
modernism, 25-26, 90, 175n12
Moore, G. E., 42, 73, 96
Myth of Jones, 75, 95, 109. See also Sellars, Wilfrid

nativism, 11, 31, 140-142, 144-149, 172n14, 184n9. See also Chomsky, Noam
Ndebele, Njabulo S., 155
Neurath, Otto, 12-13, 108, 180n7
New Criticism: and affect, 35, 36, 48, 54, 56, 59; American, 50, 54-55, 63, 176n15; anti-historicism of, 35, 48, 55; and behaviorism, 26, 35-36, 41-44, 49-50, 54-55, 60, 62-63; and close reading, 33, 35-37, 54-65, 174n3, 176n15, 177n21; and intention, 32-33, 35-36, 49, 54, 60-63; and paradox, 54-59, 176n19; and scientism, 35, 54-56

occasionalism, 66, 83-84
Ogden, C. K., 41, 175n5
Ohmann, Richard, 22, 31, 140, 142, 150-152, 184n11
ontology: and categorization, 17, 36; of consciousness, 2, 36, 40-41, 43-44, 49; of dualism, 66, 102, 105-106, 112-113, 171n1; of literary minds, 22, 27, 100, 105-106, 128

paradox, 54-58, 63, 73, 96, 176n19
Pavlov, Ivan, 8, 10, 42, 50, 54, 78-79
performance: dualism and, 110-113, 137; theatrical, 4, 102-105, 111-113, 119, 137, 168; theory, 112-113
philosophy of mind, 2, 11-15, 40-41, 66-68, 72-76, 108-111, 147-149, 179n16
physicalism: of behaviorism, 12-13, 109, 180n7; of logical positivism, 13; and mental phenomena, 114; of theater, 30; token, 24, 40, 174n25
Pillsbury, Walter, 38

Index

Pinter, Harold: Samuel Beckett's influence on, 125, 127, 129, 182n20, 182n21; and behaviorism, 103, 104; and category-mistakes, 132; and dualism, 67, 106, 125, 127, 129, 133-135; language of, 127-128; and problems of mind, 125, 129; and psychology, 102-103, 180n4; and psychiatry, 125-126, 182n28; speech and thought in works of, 128-131, 131-132, 136-137; staging of works of, 31, 103, 105-106, 126, 128-130, 132-135, 137, 182n26

Pinter, Harold, works of: "A View of the Party," 131, 182; "I Shall Tear Off My Terrible Cap," 182n28; *The Birthday Party*, 31, 106, 126-133, 182n28; *The Caretaker*, 125-126; *The Dumb Waiter*, 31, 106, 126, 129, 132-136; *The Hothouse*, 125-126; *Various Voices*, 128-129, 182n21

Plato, 180n8

poverty of the stimulus, 11, 146. *See also* Chomsky, Noam

preparatory signals, 81, 84-85

problem of other minds: colonized subjects, inaccessibility of, 31, 142-143, 153-154, 157-158, 160-162, 166-167, 185n17; privileged access, 74, 76, 95; theory of mind (ToM), 13, 23-25, 76, 79, 110, 167, 174n26

Proust, Marcel, 69, 79-80, 93

psychiatry, 43-44, 82, 86-87, 125-126, 182n28, 185n14

psychoanalysis, 78, 178n13

psychological language, 30, 62, 69, 99-101, 108-109, 168

"Psychology as the Behaviorist Views It" (Watson), 1, 7-8, 38-39, 67, 72, 106-107

Quigley, Austin, 128, 134
Quine, W. V. O., 13, 29, 143, 166-167

Rabaté, Jean-Michel, 113, 181n12, 183n1
Ransom, John Crowe, 35, 54-55, 174n3, 176n19
Rayner, Rosalie, 6, 8. *See also* Watson, John Broadus
reader: experience of, 15, 23, 29, 44, 58, 60, 63, 78, 169; and intention, 32, 44; mind of, 23, 33-34, 51, 53, 56-58, 60, 62, 64
reductionism, 28, 30, 36, 54, 108

reinforcement, 7, 9, 11, 144-145
religion, 9, 14, 49, 82, 106-107
Richards, Ivor Armstrong (I. A.): and behaviorism, 29, 35, 41-44, 49, 60, 62-63, 175n5; and cognitive criticism, 22; critical experiments of, 44-45, 48-49; criticism of, 35, 54-56, 59-60; influence of, 35-36, 42, 59-63, 174n3, 175n7, 176n14; and poetic language, 50-53, 62, 62; *Practical Criticism*, 43-45, 49, 54, 60, 62, 175n5, 175n6; *Principles of Literary Criticism*, 22, 50, 52, 54, 175; and psychologism, 48-49; *Science and Poetry*, 51, 53-54; scientism of, 29-30, 36, 43, 50-55; on John Broadus Watson, 41, 43-44, 49, 60

Russell, Bertrand: and behaviorism, 12, 40-41, 172n15; and logical types, 16-17; and paradox, 57; and propositions, 176n18

Ryle, Gilbert: and Jane Austen, 16, 168-169, 172n17; and behaviorism, 2, 15, 74-75, 92, 172n16; and categories, 15-18; on René Descartes, 14-15, 24; "Categories," 17-18, 140, 178n8; dualism as category-mistake, 7, 14-15, 18-19, 29, 105, 109-111, 168-169, 181n17; and introspection, 74-75, 83; knowing how versus knowing that, 105, 109-111, 135; and literature, 168-170, 178n9; and sentence-frames, 18-21, 27; and theater, 110-111, 137-138. *See also The Concept of Mind*

Scarry, Elaine, 23-24, 174n25
Schopenhauer, Arthur, 66, 79-80, 178n12
self-knowledge. *See* introspection
Sellars, Wilfrid, 75-76, 83, 92, 95, 109, 178n10
sentence-frame, 18-20, 27, 173n19. *See also* gap-sign
Sherrington, Charles, 42, 50, 175n5
Sidney, Philip, 22
Skinner, B. F.: *About Behaviorism*, 7, 10, 12-13, 72, 81-82, 180n3; Noam Chomsky on, 11, 140, 145-146, 162; and introspection, 72, and language, 11, 140, 142-146, 149, 153, 162-163; operant conditioning, 5, 10-11, 144-146, 180n3; radical behaviorism of, 10; reputation of, 5, on Bertrand Russell, 12, 172n15; "'Superstition' in the Pigeon," 11, 145; *Verbal Behavior*, 11, 140, 143, 145-146; *Walden Two*, 5, 10

soul: and consciousness, 9, 22, 82, 107; and dualism, 14-15, 106-107, 112, 127, 181n10; and style, 148-150
South Africa, 141, 155, 184n6
Spitzer, Leo, 142, 150
Spivak, Gayatri Chakravorty, 160, 177n21
Stanislavski, Constantin, 112
Stanton, Garner, 112-113
Stein, Gertrude, 175n12
stimulus, 6, 8-11, 42, 44, 54, 69, 78-81, 84-85, 144-146, 177n2
syntax, 24, 141, 149-150, 153, 184n5

"talking to ourselves," thinking as, 2, 9, 67, 143, 183n3. *See also* Watson, John Broadus
Tate, Allen, 35, 54-55, 174n3
Tennyson, Alfred Lord, 60
theory of mind (ToM), 13, 23-25, 110, 174n26
Thorndike, Edward Lee, 7, 10, 36-38, 67, 144, 172, 180n3
Tolman, Edward Chase, 9, 40, 72, 172n12, 175n4
Turner, Mark, 171n2

Uhlmann, Anthony, 156, 179n16, 183n1, 185n15
unconscious, 12, 42-43, 150

Watson, John Broadus: behavior, nature of, 36-37, 39-40; and conditioning, 8, 77, 144-145; consciousness, rejection of, 2, 7, 9, 36, 38, 40-41, 72, 82, 108, 143; and dualism, 106-108; and experimental philosophy, 7, 70, 72; implicit behavior, 39, 67, 83; and introspection, 30, 38-39, 67, 69, 72, 83; and language, 141-143, 153, 163, 183n3; literary response to, 35, 41, 43-44, 49, 60; "Little Albert" experiment, 5-6, 8; and memory, 177n2; philosophical response to, 11-15, 35, 40, 172n15; "Psychology as the Behaviorist Views It," 1, 7-8, 38-39, 67, 72, 106-107; reputation of, 5
West, Rebecca, 77-78
Wicomb, Zoë, 155
Wimsatt, W. K., and Beardsley, Monroe: "The Affective Fallacy," 28, 35, 48, 59-60; on Cleanth Brooks, 60; differences between, 176n20; formalism of, 30, 36, 59-65; "The Intentional Fallacy," 30, 32-33, 35-36, 49, 60-64; and New Criticism, 54, 174n3, 176n15; on I. A. Richards, 35-36, 55, 60, 64
Wittgenstein, Ludwig, 1-2, 6, 12-14, 72-75, 109, 128, 178n7
Woodworth, Robert S., 81-83, 179n14
Woolf, Virginia, 15, 20-21, 24, 176n18
Wordsworth, William, 53, 56-57
Wright, Richard, 5-6
Wundt, William, 7-9, 37, 39, 41, 70-72, 81-82, 177n4, 177n5
Würzburg school, 42, 71-72, 81-82, 84

Zunshine, Lisa, 23-25

www.ingramcontent.com/pod-product-compliance
Lightning Source LLC
Chambersburg PA
CBHW030121240426
43673CB00041B/1354